The CASSELL

Dictionary of Regrettable Quotations

D1111811

The CASSELL
Dictionary of Regrettable Quotations

David Milsted

CASSELL

This book is for Ian, Alistair, Lewis and Rowan

First published in the UK 1999 by
Cassell
Wellington House
125 Strand
London WC2R 0BB

Reprinted 2000

Distributed in the United States
by Sterling Publishing Co. Inc.
587 Park Avenue South
New York, NY 10016-8810

British Library Cataloguing-in-Publication Data
A catalogue record for this book is available from the British Library.

ISBN 0-304-35213-6

Designed and typeset by Tim Higgins

Printed and bound in Great Britain by
MPG Books Ltd, Bodmin, Cornwall

Contents

Contents

Acknowledgements

J. Bradley, Glenn Chilton (University of Calgary), R. A. Collinssplatt, Mrs E. Cook, C. B. Cooper, Michael Cross, Manny Curtiss, Dr Bill Duffin, Geoff Edgington, Alan Edwards, Breda Egan, C. Frank Fischl, Professor Anthony Flew, Brian Franklin, Charles Fyffe, Naomi Goldblum, Rabia Harris, Professor John Hibbs, Bill High, Wing Commander T. F. G. Hudson, Maurice Jay, J. Jocelyn, Colin Jordan, N. G. van Kampen, (University of Utrecht), Joan F. Lafferty, Bernard Langley, Mrs Ursula E. K. Light, Andrew and Annette Lobb, C. Lynch, Roy Maxwell, Alex Milne, John N. G. Pisani, Roderick Ramage, Michael Rubinstein, Richard Smith, J. C. Stewart, Professor Garry J. Tee (University of Auckland), Mark Terrell, Francis Wheen, David Wilson, Christopher Yates.

Introduction

I say some things and, gosh, I wish I hadn't said them!

Hubert Horatio Humphrey – who expressed this wish shortly after greeting the news of an unsuccessful assassination attempt on President Ford with the observation that there were far too many guns in the hands of people who didn't know how to use them – joins the long roll-call of people who wish they could take back the regrettable things they've said or written.

This book celebrates the fact that they can't. It sets out to prove that the powerful and the expert can also be two-faced, stupid and wrong, and frequently manage to be all three at once. It is intended for the enjoyment of all those people who take an unnatural, twisted and uncharitable pleasure in this phenomenon.

Schadenfreude is a useful little German word, but it doesn't go quite far enough. It means 'taking pleasure in the misfortune of others' – which, when you think about it, is a rather cruel and reprehensible thing to do. What we need is a word that means 'taking pleasure in the misfortune of others when they have brought it on themselves and ought to have known better'. (Possibly there is such a word; the Germans are such thorough people.) It's one thing to laugh at someone who slips on a banana skin. It's another thing to laugh at someone who slips on a banana skin they have dropped themselves. And it is another thing altogether to laugh at someone who slips on a banana skin they have dropped themselves *while at the same time delivering a lecture*

on the danger of dropping banana skins. This is not just wrongness; it is wrongness established in superiority and delivered with
godlike certainty. It belongs to the Regrettable. It belongs – as
there is nowhere else for it to go – in this book.

The Cassell Dictionary of Regrettable Quotations, the product
of some five years' research, is the thinking person's bathroom
book; with over 1,500 entries it might oblige you to build another
bathroom, or even buy two copies. It has been compiled with the
assistance of many kind and helpful people, whom I gratefully
acknowledge. A special thank-you is due to Professor Garry Tee,
of the University of Auckland, who corrected some regrettable
errors in the book's earlier incarnation, and to my editor, Richard
Milbank, for enabling it to blossom in a world that, surely, has
never needed such a book so much.

I hope you have, in reading it, at least as much pleasure as
I have had writing it. If you have even half as much you'll be doing
pretty well.

DAVID MILSTED
Dorset, May 1999

Note to the reader

Within some of the themes the user will find clusters of two or more
quotations that need to be read together for their 'regrettability' to be
apparent. Such groups of quotations are isolated from other quotations
within the theme by means of tinted bars.

A

Advertising

The trade of advertising is now so near to perfection that it is not easy to propose any improvement.
The Idler, 1759.

The intrinsic nature of the vastly extended advertising of the new age will be influenced by the new growth of public intelligence ... Advertising will in the future become more and more intelligent in tone. It will seek to influence demand by argument instead of clamour ... Cheap attention-calling tricks will be wholly replaced, as they are already being replaced, by serious exposition.
T. Baron Russell, *A Hundred Years Hence*, 1905.

Peasants and priests and all sorts of practical and sensible people are coming back into power ... They will not be affected by advertisements, no more than the priests and peasants of the Middle Ages would have been affected by advertisements. Only a very soft-headed, sentimental and rather servile generation could possibly be affected by advertise-ments at all.
G. K. Chesterton, *What I Saw In America*, 1922.

The Thompson Anti-Bandit Gun is a powerful deterrent. It strikes terror into the heart of the most hardened and daring criminal. The moral effect of its known possession is an insurance of its own.
Advertisement in the *New York Times*, 31 January 1922, for what became known as the 'Chicago Typewriter', the weapon of choice of Al Capone.

The bomb's brilliant gleam reminds me of the brilliant shine GLEAM gives to floors. It's a science marvel!

Advertisement in the *Pittsburgh Press* during the week of the first H-bomb tests in February 1954.

LOOKS RIGHT! BUILT RIGHT! PRICES RIGHT!

The keynote slogan of what the agency Foote, Cone & Belding described as 'the greatest advertising campaign ever conceived', for the Ford Edsel car in 1957. Renowned for its ugliness – its radiator grille was unfavourably compared with a lavatory seat – it cost more than other cars in its class, and fewer than half of the 200,000 models sold proved fault-free. It was a disastrous flop.

See also CARS

You're never alone with a Strand.

Notably unsuccessful slogan, accompanying an image of a lonely man lighting up a Strand cigarette, in 1960. The public took this to mean that Strand cigarettes were for sad losers, and didn't buy them.

Fly By Aeroplane

A short-lived experiment in 'socialist advertising' in the USSR, c. 1960.

Pepsi Brings Your Ancestors Back From The Grave

The unfortunate literal translation of the slogan 'Come Alive with Pepsi', used in Hong Kong.

If you want well-being and hygiene – Vote Pulvapies!

An opportunistic campaign for Pulvapies Foot Deodorant timed to coincide with municipal elections in the town of Picoaza, Ecuador, in 1975. Voters elected the product mayor by writing its name on their ballot papers.

Have you tried Cod Pieces?

Bird's Eye woos the housewife in 1976.

Enjoy the charm of Grenada – unspoiled, peaceful and uncrowded.

Advertisement in *The Tatler*, November 1983, a week before US troops invaded the island.

BEAVER ESPAÑA

You get two weeks being drunk and disorderly.

SUMMER OF 69

It's not all sex, sex, sex, sex, sex, sex, sex, sex, sex, sex, sex, sex, sex, sex, sex, sex, sex, sex, sex, sex, sex, sex, sex, sex, sex, sex, sex, sex, sex, sex, sex,

sex, sex, sex, sex, sex, sex, sex, sex, sex, sex, sex, sex, sex, sex. There's a bit of sun and sea as well.

Advertisements for Club 18–30 holidays in 1995, withdrawn after 432 complaints were made to the Advertising Standards Authority.

It's a jungle out there.

The wording on a poster campaign showing a white woman looking nervously over her shoulder at a black man on a bus, one of a series issued by the Commission for Racial Equality in 1998 to draw attention to racism in public attitudes by advertising spoof products. The Advertising Standards Authority ruled that the campaign was itself racist, and ordered the CRE to submit all its future copy for prior approval – the first time such an order had ever been issued.

I could have paid off my debts a lot quicker, but I only did the things I actually believed in myself, like Cranberry Juice Lite.

Sarah Ferguson, Duchess of York, on preserving her integrity while pursuing a career in advertising, interviewed in the *Daily Telegraph*, 5 October 1998.

See also SMOKING

Afghanistan

I think the Soviets are likely to be wise enough to avoid getting bogged down in that kind of situation.

Harold Brown, US Secretary of State for Defence, on the likelihood of a Soviet invasion of Afghanistan: *US News and World Report*, 30 July 1979. At the end of December, the Soviet army invaded the country to topple the regime and replace it with a pro-Soviet government.

The attitude of all honest Afghans to Soviet troops is that of sincere hospitality and profound gratitude.

Tass, the official news agency of the USSR, April 1980. After nearly ten years of bitter war against their 'hosts', the last Soviet troops withdrew in February 1989.

AIDS

Everywhere I go I see increasing evidence of people swirling about in a human cesspit of their own making.

James Anderton, chief constable of Greater Manchester, 11 December 1986, on AIDS as 'the wages of sin'.

The most frightening fact about AIDS is that it can be spread by normal sex between men and women. This is still rare in Scotland.

Comforting words from a land where sheep outnumber people: the Scottish *Sunday Mail*, March 1987.

There will be one million AIDS cases in Britain by the end of 1991.

Report of the World Health Organization, July 1989. From 1984 to December 1998 there was a cumulative total of 15,500 reported AIDS cases in Britain.

Suppose HIV doesn't equal AIDS. Then we will have witnessed the biggest medical and scientific blunder this century.

March 1992: *The Sunday Times* gives a double-page spread to the 'lifestyle-only' theory of Professor Peter Duesberg of the University of California at Berkeley. While not all HIV cases lead to 'full-blown AIDS', no case of AIDS has ever been reported in which HIV was not first present.

You must not wear condoms. They do not stop disease. Anyone who tells you otherwise is a liar. They are designed to stop us from breeding.

Winnie Mandela broadcasts on Tobago Radio, June 1998.

See also POLITICIANS' GAFFES

Algeria

France will remain in Algeria. The bonds linking metropolitan France and Algeria are indissoluble.

Guy Mollet, Prime Minister of France, 9 February 1956. Algeria gained its independence in 1962.

The American Civil War

In Europe, it is generally believed that slavery has rendered the interests of one part of the Union contrary to those of another; but I have not found this to be the case. Slavery has not created interests in the South contrary to those of the North.

Alexis de Tocqueville, French political philosopher, *Democracy in America*, 1835.

The South has too much commonsense and good temper to break up the Union.

Abraham Lincoln, speaking as Republican candidate for the US presidency, 1860. A few months later the Southern states seceded to form the Confederacy.

Fort Sumter must not be surrendered, if there is force enough in the United States to hold it. That point is the head of the rebellion, and it is precisely there that a stand must be made. It must be reinforced at every hazard.

Editorial, *New York Times*, 13 April 1861.

The fall of Sumter was a substantial and crowning advantage, anticipated and provided for in the plans of the Administration.

Editorial, *New York Times*, 15 April 1861. Fort Sumter was a Union stronghold in Charlestown, South Carolina. After a three-day bombardment – the opening engagement of the Civil War – it was surrendered to Confederate forces.

Tennessee in no contingency will join the Gulf Confederacy.

Editorial, *New York Times*, 17 April 1861. Tennessee joined the Confederacy twenty days later.

No man of sense can for a moment doubt that the war will end in a month. The rebels, a mere band of ragamuffins, will fly on our approach like chaff before the wind. The Northern people are simply invincible.

Editorial, *Philadelphia Press*, 1861. The 'rebels' actually held out for four years.

President Lincoln desires the right to hold slaves to be fully recognized. The war is prosecuted for the Union, hence no question of slavery will arise.

Simon Cameron, US secretary of war: letter to General Benjamin Franklin Butler, military governor of New Orleans, 1862. On 1 January 1863 Lincoln issued the Emancipation Proclamation, declaring freedom for all slaves in areas 'in rebellion against the United States.'

My plans are perfect. May God have mercy on Lee, for I will have none.

General Joseph Hooker, on the eve of his crushing defeat by General Robert E. Lee at the Battle of Chancellorsville in May 1863.

The end is that Richmond is safe while Washington is menaced, and that Lee is master of the field. The conclusion must be plain that the great object of the Federals – the capture of Richmond – is absolutely unattainable.

The Times, 16 August 1864. Union forces captured Richmond on 3 April 1865; Lee surrendered to Grant at Appomattox six days later.

See also THE GETTYSBURG ADDRESS *and* LAST WORDS

The American War of Independence

Four or five frigates will do the business without any military force.

Lord North, British Prime Minister, on the rebellious American colonies, 1774.

Once vigorous measures appear to be the only means left of bringing the Americans to a due submission to the mother country, colonies will submit.

George III, letter, 15 February 1775. The mother country submitted in 1781.

A small action will set everything to rights.

Major John Pitcairn of the British army, 1775.

We cannot in this country conceive that there are men in England so infatuated as seriously to suspect the Congress, or people here, of a wish to erect ourselves into an independent state. If such an idea really obtains among those at the helm of affairs, one hour's residence in America would eradicate it. I never met one individual so inclined.

John Adams, delegate to the Continental Congress: letter to William Lee, an American in London, 4 October 1775. Adams helped to write the Declaration of Independence nine months later.

The power of the rebellion is pretty well broken ... If the fleet constantly blocked up the ports during the next summer the business might be concluded, almost without the intervention of an army.

Joseph Galloway, speaker of the Pennsylvania Assembly: letter to British Admiral Richard Howe, 21 January 1777.

Animals

Basilisk, a Serpent call'd a Cockatrice.
Bat, a small Bird resembling a Mouse.
Cockatrice, a Serpent call'd a Basilisk.
Dragon, a sort of Serpent.
Moth, a Fly which eats Clothes.
Rat, an Animal which infests Houses, &c.
Reptile, a creeping Thing, any thing that crawls upon its Belly.
Unicorn, a Beast said to be as big as a Horse, having one white Horn in the middle of its Forehead, about five handfuls long, found in the Province of Agoas in the Kingdom of Damotes in Ethiopia, said to be a timerous Beast, residing in the Woods, yet sometimes ventures into the Plains.
Whale, the greatest of Fishes.
Worm, a creeping Insect.

N. Bailey, *A Universal Etymological Dictionary*, 1724.

Bears ... produce a formless fœtus, giving birth to something like a bit of pulp, and this the mother-bear arranges into the proper legs and arms by licking it.

The Book of Beasts, 12th century.

When [the **beaver**] is pursued, knowing this to be on account of the virtue of its testicles for medicinal uses, not being able to flee any farther it stops and in order to be at peace with its pursuers bites off its testicles with its sharp teeth and leaves them to its enemies.

Leonardo da Vinci (1452–1519).

Bees are generated from decomposed veal.

St Isidore of Seville, 7th century.

Eels are not produced from sexual intercourse ... They originated in what are called the entrails of the earth, which are found spontaneously in mud and moist earth.

Aristotle, *Parts of Animals*, 4th century BC.

The **elephant**'s nature is such that if he tumbles down he cannot get up again. Hence it comes that he leans against a tree when he wants to go to sleep, for he has no joints in his knees.

The Book of Beasts, 12th century.

A diamond ... is yet made soft by the blood of a **goat**.

Sir Thomas Browne, *Pseudodoxia Epidemica*, 1646.

Floating islands are invariably **Krakens**.

Bishop Erik Pontoppidan, *A Natural History of Norway*, 1752–54.

The **Lamia** ... is thought to be the swiftest of all four-footed creatures ... and by its fraud it destroys men; for, when it sees a man, it lays upon its breast, and entices him to draw near ... It is said to be bred in Libya, and to have a face and breasts like a very beautiful woman.

A Description of Above Three Hundred Animals, 1795.

The corrupt and excrementous humours in man are corrupted into Lice.

Sir Thomas Browne, *Pseudodoxia Epidemica*, 1646.

The **lioness** giveth birth to cubs which remain three days without life. Then cometh the lion, breatheth upon them, and bringeth them to life.

William of Normandy, 13th century.

The **Manticora** ... a devourer, is bred among the Indians; having a triple row of teeth beneath and above ... face and ears like a man's; his tail like a Scorpion's, armed with a sting, and sharp pointed quills. His voice is like a small trumpet, or pipe.

A Description of Above Three Hundred Animals, 1795.

We have experienced also that the hairs of a horse's mane laid in the waters became **serpents**, and our friends have tried the same. No man denies but that serpents are easily engendered of man's flesh, especially of his marrow.

Giambattista Della Porta, *Natural Magic*, 1658.

I am not beating it. I am encouraging it with a stick.

Mary Chipperfield, of the Chipperfield circus family, on a video showing her beating a camel at her animal training centre, 5 February 1998.

Art

I hate bainting and boetry. Neither the one nor the other ever did any good.

Remark attributed to King George II as he viewed Hogarth's *The March to Finchley*.

It's a rummy business.

The entire text of a speech by J. M. W. Turner to the Royal Academy, 1850.

Abstract art? A product of the untalented, sold by the unprincipled to the utterly bewildered.

Al Capp, *National Observer*, 1963.

Cubism

The real meaning of this Cubist movement is nothing else than the total destruction of the art of painting.

Kenyon Cox, *Harper's Weekly*, 15 March 1913.

There is every evidence that New York has decided to give the Cubists, Futurists, and other freakists 'the laugh', a bad sign for these 'jokers of the brush'. In fact, some predict that New York's laugh will bury these new apostles of art in oblivion.

L. Merrick reviewing the Armory Show in *American Art News*, March 1913.

Fauvism

Certainly no man or woman of normal mental health would be attracted by the sadistic, obscene deformations of Cézanne, Modigliani, Matisse, Gauguin and the other Fauves.

John Hemming Fry, *The Revolt Against Beauty*, 1934.

Impressionism

This school has abolished two things: line, without which it is impossible to reproduce the form of a living being or an object; and colour, which gives form to the appearance of reality ... The practitioners fall into a senseless, mad, grotesque mess, fortunately without precedent in the history of art, for it is quite simply the negation of the most elementary rules of drawing and painting. A child's scrawls have a naïveté and a sincerity that make you smile, but the excesses of this school are nauseating or revolting.

Emile Cardon on the first Impressionist exhibition of 1874, in *La Presse*.

The new French School is simply putrescence and decomposition.

Dante Gabriel Rossetti, letter.

They provoke laughter and yet they are lamentable. They display the profoundest ignorance of drawing, of composition and colour. When children amuse themselves with a box of colour and a piece of paper, they do better.

La Chronique des Arts, 14 April 1877.

'Modern Art'

So-called modern or contemporary art in our modern beloved country contains all the isms of depravity, decadence and destruction. Cubism aims to destroy by designed disorder. Futurism aims to destroy by a machine myth. Dadaism aims to destroy by ridicule. Expressionism aims to destroy by aping the primitive and insane ... Abstractionism aims to destroy by the creation of brainstorms. Surrealism aims to destroy by the denial of reason ... Non-objectivity in so-called modern art was spawned as a simon-pure, Russian communist product ... Who has brought down this curse upon us; who has let into our homeland this horde of germ-carrying art vermin?

Representative George A. Dondero, of Michigan, addresses the US Congress on 19 August 1949.

Post-Impressionism

Works of idleness and impotent stupidity, a pornographic show ... The drawing is on the level of that of an untaught child of seven or eight years old, the sense of colour that of a tea-tray painter, the method that of a schoolboy who wipes his fingers on a slate after spitting on them.

Wilfrid Scawen Blunt, on the first British exhibition of the Post-Impressionists at the Grafton Gallery, 1910.

If the movement is spreading it should be treated like the rat-plague in Suffolk. The source of the infection ought to be destroyed ... Van Gogh is the typical matoid and degenerate of the modern sociologist. *Jeune Fille au Bleuet* and *Cornfield with Blackbirds* are the visualized ravings of an adult maniac. If that is art it must be ostracized, as the poets were banished from Plato's republic.

Robert Ross of the *Morning Post*, 1910.

The Renaissance

Gods without power, satyrs without rusticity, nymphs without innocence, men without humanity, gather into idiot groups upon the polluted canvas, and scenic affectations encumber the streets with preposterous marble. Lower and lower declines the level of abused intellect; the base school of landscape gradually usurps the place of the historical painting, which had sunk into prurient pedantry ...

John Ruskin, in *The Stones of Venice*, 1851–53.

The Royal Academy

The pride and self-respect which are the natural concomitants of genius will be more likely to keep a man out of the Academy than bring him into it.

The Times, 20 July 1830.

The reputation of the Academy has got to a point where election would be positively distressing to a serious painter.

Evening Standard, 22 February 1961.

Artists

Lawrence Alma-Tadema

The general effect was exactly like a microscopic view of a small detachment of black beetles, in search of a dead rat.

John Ruskin on *The Pyrrhic Dance*, 1869.

Paul Cézanne

M. Cézanne gives me the impression of being a sort of madman who paints in a fit of delirium tremens ... Why look for a dirty joke or a scandalous theme in the Olympia? In reality it is only one of the weird shapes generated by hashish.

'Marc de Montifaud', a female art critic, on *A Modern Olympia*, in *L'Artiste*.

Paul may have had the genius of a great painter, but he never had the persistence to become one.

Emile Zola, c. 1900.

What use have we now for Monsieur Cézanne? So much for the dealers who believed that one day they would make a clean-up with his works!

The art journal *La Lanterne*, 1905.

Edgar Degas

Tell him that in art there are certain qualities called drawing, colour, execution and control and he will laugh in your face.

Albert Wolff, art critic of *Le Figaro*, 1876.

Degas is nothing but a peeping Tom, behind the coulisses, and among the dressing-rooms of ballet dancers, noting only travesties of fallen debased womanhood, most disgusting and offensive.

The Churchman, 1886.

Degas is repulsive.

New York Times, 10 April 1886.

It is extraordinary that the pupil of Ingres ... should create such appalling creatures.

Wynford Dewhurst, *Impressionist Painting*, 1904.

Raoul Dufy

Dufy is merely a childish scene-painter, a scribbler of all sorts of nursery nonsense.

Sir Lionel Lindsay, *Addled Art*, 1946.

Paul Gauguin

A decorator tainted with insanity.

Kenyon Cox, *Harper's Weekly*, 15 March 1913.

William Holman Hunt

The face of this wild fantasy, though earnest and religious, is not that of a Saviour. It expresses such a strange mingling of disgust, fear, and imbecility, that we turn from it to relieve the sight. The manipulation, though morbidly delicate and laboured, is not so massive as the mute passion displayed in the general feeling and detail demands. Altogether this picture is a failure.

The Athenæum, 6 May 1854, on the most successful British religious painting ever created. Reproductions of *The Light of the World*, described by Frank Muir as 'perhaps the nearest thing the Church of England has had to an icon', sold by the hundred thousand after it was first displayed.

Edouard Manet

This is a young man's practical joke, a shameful open sore not worth exhibiting this way.

Louis Etienne, in *Le Jury et les Exposants*, on *Le Déjeuner sur l'herbe*, 1863.

Is this drawing? Is this painting? ... I see garments without feeling the anatomical structure that supports them and explains their movements. I see boneless fingers and heads without skulls. I see side-whiskers made of two strips of black cloth that could have been glued to the cheeks. What else do I see? The artist's lack of conviction and sincerity.

Jules Castagnary, in *Salons*, on *Le Déjeuner sur l'herbe*, 1863.

You scarcely knew if you were looking at a parcel of nude flesh or a bundle of laundry.

Jules Claretie, in *Le Figaro*, on *Venus et le Chat*, 23 June 1863.

Henri Matisse

Matisse is an unmitigated bore. Surely the vogue of those twisted and contorted human figures must be as short as it is artificial.

Harriet Monroe, *Chicago Tribune*, 23 February 1913.

John Everett Millais

In the foreground of the carpenter's shop is a hideous, wry-necked, blubbering, red-haired boy in a nightgown, who appears to have received a poke playing in an adjacent gutter, and to be holding it up for the contemplation of a kneeling woman, so horrible in her ugliness that (supposing it were possible for any human creature to exist for a moment with that dislocated throat) she would stand out from the rest of the company as a monster in the vilest cabaret in France or the lowest gin-shop in England.

Charles Dickens, on *Christ in the House of His Parents*, in *Household Words*, 1850.

Pablo Picasso

It's the work of a madman.

French art dealer Ambrose Vollard, on *Les Demoiselles d'Avignon*, 1907.

His work presents an unhealthy apology for the aesthetics of capitalism, provoking the resentment of ordinary people.

The Soviet critic V. Kemenev, c. 1935.

Camille Pissarro

No intelligence can accept such aberrations.

Albert Wolff reports on an exhibition at Durand-Ruel's gallery for *Le Figaro*, 1876.

Rembrandt van Rijn

Rembrandt is not to be compared in the painting of character with our extraordinarily gifted English artist, Mr Rippingille.

John Hunt, art critic and scholar (1775–1848).

Pierre-Auguste Renoir

He has no talent at all, that boy. Tell him please to give up painting.

Edouard Manet, 1864.

Just try to explain to Monsieur Renoir that the torso of a woman is not a mass of decomposing flesh, its green and violet spots indicating the state of complete putrefaction of a corpse.

Albert Wolff, *Le Figaro*, 1865.

Of the work of M. Renoir it is hard to speak with gravity. A glance at some of the canvases which bear his name will explain more fully than any words of mine the difficulty one might experience in taking such work seriously.

Philip Burne-Jones, in *The Nineteenth Century Magazine*, March 1905.

Titian

Why should Titian and the Venetians be named in a discourse on art? Such idiots are not artists.

William Blake annotates a copy of Sir Joshua Reynolds' *Discourses* in 1807.

There, against the wall, without obstructing rag or leaf, you may look your fill upon the foulest, the vilest, the most obscene picture the world possesses – Titian's *Venus* ... There are pictures of nude women which suggest no impure thought – I am well aware of that. I am not railing at such. What I am trying to emphasize is that Titian's *Venus* is very far from being one of that sort. Without any question it was painted for a bagnio and it was probably refused because it was a trifle too strong.

Mark Twain – sometime writer of pornographic stories – in *A Tramp Abroad*, 1880, finds offence in 'the attitude of one of her arms and a hand'.

Henri de Toulouse-Lautrec

Buy Maurins! Lautrec is merely a painter of a period.

Edgar Degas advises art investor Henry Laurent in 1893. Laurent duly bought hundreds of paintings by the now-forgotten Maurins.

James McNeill Whistler

I never saw anything so impudent on the walls of any exhibition, in any country … a daub … absolute rubbish … it had no pretence to be called painting.

John Ruskin, on *Symphony in Red and Green*, 1872.

See also HOAXES

Autobiography

I shall never write a formal memoir (I have never been my own subject, a sign of truly sickening narcissism).

Gore Vidal, preface to *Armageddon: Essays 1983–1987*. In 1996 he published the autobiographical *Palimpsest: A Memoir*.

B

The Beatles

I want to manage those four boys. It wouldn't take me more than two half days a week.

Brian Epstein makes a note in his diary for 9 November 1961, after visiting the Cavern Club.

We don't like their sound. Groups of guitars are on the way out.

A commissioning executive at Decca Records sends a memo in 1962.

We don't think they'll do anything in this market.

Alan Livingston, head of Capitol Records, turns them down in advance of their first US tour in 1964.

The Beatles are not merely awful, I would consider it sacrilegious to say anything less than that they are godawful. They are so unbelievably horrible, so appallingly unmusical, so dogmatically insensitive to the magic of the art, that they qualify as crowned heads of anti-music, even as the imposter popes went down in history as 'anti-popes'.

The US political and social commentator William F. Buckley, *On the Right*, 1964.

The Beatles? They're a passing phase, symptoms of the uncertainty of the times and the confusion about us.

The evangelist Billy Graham, 1965.

If he had said, 'Bomb the White House tomorrow', there would have been 10,000 people who would have done it. It was in the best interests of the United States to have my dad killed. Definitely.

Sean Lennon, son of John Lennon, on his father's murder in 1980; the *New Yorker*, 14 April 1998.

Birds

Barnacle, a Soland Goose; a Fowl in the Bass, an Island on the Coasts of Scotland, supposed by some to grow on the Trees, or by others, to be bred out of rotten Planks of Ships, &c.

N. Bailey, *A Universal Etymological English Dictionary*, 1724.

The Swallow does not migrate in winter, but hibernates each autumn in ponds and streams.

The ornithologist Daines Barrington (1727–1800) – whose theories on birdsong, published in 1773, nevertheless remain valid.

That birds can be taught to talk better than other animals is explained by the fact that their mouths are Nordic in structure.

Nazi ornithology: Professor Hermann Gauch, *The New Foundation for Research into Social Race Problems*, 1933.

The Boer Wars

You need not worry your head about the Boers fighting. I undertake to lead my regiment through South Africa from one end to the other, armed only with pickhandles.

Colonel Tucker of the 80th Regiment of Foot gives early warning of a succession of British defeats in the first Boer War (1880–81).

It appears certain that, after one serious defeat, they would be too deficient in discipline and organization to make any further real stand.

Military Notes on the Dutch Republics, War Office Intelligence Department, 1899.

The Boers are not like the Sudanese, who stood up to a fair fight. They are always running away on their little ponies.

General Kitchener bemoans the Boers' unsporting habit of not standing still to get shot in the second Boer War (1899–1902).

Get up, you lumps, and behave like Englishmen.

Anonymous British officer, addressing Australian troops of the Victoria Rifles during the second Boer War.

Books and Writers

Jane Austen

We are willing to return the manuscript for the same sum as we paid for it.

A publisher's rejection of *Northanger Abbey*, published elsewhere in 1803.

Richard Bach

Jonathan Livingston Seagull will never make it as a paperback.

James Galton of the Popular Library; it was published in paperback by Avon Books and sold over 10 million copies.

Honoré de Balzac

Little imagination is shown in invention, in the creating of character or plot, or in the definition of passion ... M. de Balzac's place in French literature will be neither considerable nor high.

Balzac's reputation survived the judgment of Eugène Poitou in *Revue des Deux Mondes*, December 1856.

Charles Baudelaire

In a hundred years the histories of French literature will only mention it as a curio.

Emile Zola on *Les Fleurs du Mal*, published in 1857, which exerted a powerful influence on 20th-century poetry and is now regarded as its author's masterpiece.

Samuel Beckett

The suggestion that something larger is being said about the human predicament won't hold water, any more than Beckett's incontinent heroes can.

The Spectator reviews the trilogy *Molloy*, *Malone Dies*, and *The Unnameable* in 1959. The suspicion that Beckett's work did indeed have something to say led to the award of the Nobel Prize for Literature ten years later.

Emily Brontë

All the faults of *Jane Eyre* are magnified a thousandfold, and the only consolation which we have in reflecting upon it is that it will never be generally read.

James Lorimer of the *North British Review* on *Wuthering Heights*, 1849.

Truman Capote

A failure of the imagination.

Norman Mailer, in 1965, condemns *In Cold Blood* as a piece of extended journalism passing itself off as a novel. Mailer published his own failure of the imagination, *The Executioner's Song*, in 1979.

Lewis Carroll

We fancy any real child might be more puzzled than enchanted by this stiff, overwrought story.

Alice's Adventures in Wonderland reviewed in *Children's Books*, 1865.

Samuel Taylor Coleridge

What great work has he written? We put this question to his disciples;
for we cannot name one considerable poem of his that is likely to remain
upon the thresh-floor of fame ... We fear we shall seem, to our children,
to have been pygmies, indeed, in intellect, since such a man as Coleridge
would appear great to us!

London Weekly Review, June 1828.

Joseph Conrad

It would be useless to pretend that these works can be very widely read.

The *Manchester Guardian* reviews *Youth* and *Heart of Darkness* on 10 December
1902.

Len Deighton

Not only does it tend to bog down in the middle, but the author tends to
stay too long with non-essentials. He seems to have little idea of pace, and
is enchanted with his words, his tough style, and that puts me off.

A publisher's rejection of *The Ipcress File* in 1963.

Charles Dickens

He has never played any part in any movement more significant than that
of a fly upon a wheel.

The *Saturday Review* swats the novelist in January 1857.

We do not believe in the permanence of his reputation. Fifty years hence,
most of his allusions will be harder to understand than the allusions
in *The Dunciad*, and our children will wonder what their ancestors
could have meant by putting Mr Dickens at the head of the novelists of
the day.

Second swat: the *Saturday Review*, May 1858.

Emily Dickinson

An eccentric, dreamy, half-educated recluse in an out-of-the-way
New England village (or anywhere else) cannot with impunity set at
defiance the laws of gravitation and grammar. Oblivion lingers in
the immediate neighbourhood.

Thomas Bailey Aldrich, the *Atlantic Monthly*, January 1892.

John Donne

Dr Donne's verses are like the Peace of God; they pass all understanding.

King James I, c. 1610.

Arthur Conan Doyle

Neither long enough for a serial nor short enough for a single story.

The 'packaging theory' of publishing: a rejection, in 1887, for *A Study in Scarlet*.

T. S. Eliot

If Mr Eliot had been pleased to write in demotic English, *The Waste Land* might not have been, as it is to all but anthropologists and literati, so much waste-paper.

The *Manchester Guardian*, 1917.

William Faulkner

You're the only damn fool in New York who would publish it.

Alfred Harcourt, of Harcourt, Brace, to editor Harrison Smith, on *The Sound and the Fury*, 1929.

The final blow-up of what was once a remarkable, if minor, talent.

Clifton Fulman of the *New Yorker*, on *Absalom, Absalom*, 31 October 1936. Faulkner won the Nobel Prize for Literature in 1949.

Gustave Flaubert

You have buried your novel underneath a heap of details which are well done but utterly superfluous.

A publisher's reaction to *Madame Bovary*, 1856.

Monsieur Flaubert is not a writer.

Review of *Madame Bovary* in *Le Figaro*, 1857.

Frederick Forsyth

No reader interest.

W. H. Allen & Co. reject *The Day of the Jackal* in April 1970.

The Diary of Anne Frank

The girl doesn't, it seems to me, have a special perception or feeling which would lift that book above the 'curiosity' level.

A publisher's rejection, in 1952, of what was to become the best-known testament of the Holocaust.

William Golding

It does not seem to us that you have been wholly successful in working out an admittedly promising idea.

A publisher's rejection of *The Lord of the Flies* in 1954.

Kenneth Grahame

As a contribution to natural history the work is negligible.

The Times Literary Supplement doesn't quite get the point of *The Wind in the Willows* in 1908.

Günter Grass

It can never be translated.

A British publisher declines to take on *The Tin Drum* in 1962.

Radclyffe Hall

I would rather put a phial of prussic acid into the hands of a healthy boy or girl than the book in question.

James Douglas on a fate worse than death – reading the lesbian novel *The Well of Loneliness*, 1928.

Joseph Heller

I haven't really the foggiest idea what the man is trying to say ... Apparently the author intends it to be funny – possibly even satire – but it is really not funny on any intellectual level. He has two devices, both bad, which he works constantly ... This, you may imagine, constitutes a continual and unmitigated bore.

A publisher's rejection, in 1961, of *Catch-22*.

Thor Heyerdahl

This is a long, solemn, tedious Pacific voyage best suited, I would think, to some kind of drastic abridgement in a journal like the *National Geographic*. It's definitely not for us.

William Styron of McGraw-Hill, on *The Kon-Tiki Expedition*, 1947. After Rand McNally published the book in 1952 it topped the bestseller list for over a year.

John Irving

The story is only mildly interesting, and it does nothing new with language or with form. Thanks for showing it to us, though.

This rejection, by the *Paris Review* in 1979, was of a short story, *The Pension Grillparzer*, which forms part of the novel *The World According to Garp*. In the novel, Garp has the story rejected by a magazine; just for fun, Irving sent it out to various magazines under his own name. Irving incorporated this rejection in his novel, as 'it was so much better than the rejection I had written'.

Henry James

It is becoming painfully evident that Mr James has written himself out as far as the international novel is concerned, and probably as far as any novel-writing is concerned.

William Morton Payne, *The Dial*, December 1884. Despite this gloomy prognosis, Mr James somehow struggled on to write *The Bostonians, The Turn of the Screw, What Maisie Knew, The Wings of the Dove, The Ambassadors*, and *The Golden Bowl*.

James Joyce

I finished *Ulysses* and I think it is a mis-fire. The book is diffuse. It is brackish. It is pretentious. It is underbred, not only in the obvious sense, but in the literary sense. A first-rate writer, I mean, respects writing too much to be tricky.

A multifariously regrettable quotation: Virginia Woolf's diary entry for 6 September 1922.

The telephone directory is, because of its rigorous selection and repression, a work of art compared to the wastepaper basket. And *Ulysses* is a wastepaper basket.

Gerald Gould, *The English Novel of Today*, 1924.

My God, what a clumsy *olla putrida* James Joyce is! Nothing but old fags and cabbage-stumps of quotations from the Bible and the rest, stewed in the juice of deliberate, journalistic dirty-mindedness.

D. H. Lawrence on *Ulysses*, 1928.

John Keats

The Phrenzy of the 'Poems' was bad enough in its way; but it did not alarm us half so seriously as the calm, settled, imperturbable drivelling idiocy of 'Endymion' ... Mr Hunt is a small poet, but he is a clever man. Mr Keats is a still-smaller poet, and he is only a boy of pretty abilities, which he has done everything in his power to spoil ... We venture to make one small prophecy, that his bookseller will not a second time venture £50 upon anything that he can write. It is a better and wiser thing to be a starved apothecary than a starved poet; so back to the shop, Mr John, back to 'plaisters, pills, and ointment-boxes,' etc. But for Heaven's sake, young Sangrando, be a little more sparing of extenuatives and soporifics in your practice than you have been with your poetry.

Attributed to John Lockhart and John Wilson, *Blackwood's Magazine*, August 1818.

Here are Johnny Keats' p—ss a bed poetry, and three novels by God knows whom. No more Keats, I entreat: flay him alive; if some of you don't, I must skin him myself: there is no bearing the drivelling idiotism of the Mankin.

Lord Byron, letter to John Murray, 12 October 1820.

A Mr John Keats, a young man who left a decent calling for the melancholy trade of Cockney-poetry, has lately died of a consumption, after having written two or three little books of verses, much neglected by the public ... The New School, however, will have it that he was slaughtered by a criticism of the Quarterly Review – 'O flesh, how art thou fishified!' – We are not now to defend a publication so well able to defend itself. But the fact is that the Quarterly Review finding before it a work at once silly and presumptuous, full of the servile slang that Cockaigne dictates to its servitors, and the vulgar indecorums which that Grub Street Empire rejoiceth to applaud, told the truth of the volume, and recommended a change of manners and masters to the scribbler. Keats wrote on; but he wrote indecently, probably in the indulgence of his social propensities.

Blackwood's Magazine, 1821.

Fricassée of dead dog.

Thomas Carlyle (1795–1881) on the *Collected Works*.

Rudyard Kipling

I'm sorry, Mr Kipling, but you just don't know how to use the English language.

The editor of the *San Francisco Examiner*, having published one short story, decides it was an error of judgment, 1889.

Richard Freiherr von Krafft-Ebbing

This book should convey solace by being put to the most ignominious use to which paper can be applied.

The *British Medical Journal* reviews *Psycopathia Sexualis*, 1876.

Judith Krantz

'Scruples' is a ridiculous title. Nobody will know what it means. We've got to get Crown to change it.

Howard Kaminsky, president of Warner Books, 25 June 1981, after Warner bought the paperback rights in advance of hardback publication. Crown scrupled.

D. H. Lawrence

Mr Lawrence has a diseased mind. He is obsessed by sex ... We have no doubt he will be ostracized by all except the most degenerate coteries in the literary world.

John Bull on *Lady Chatterley's Lover*, 20 October 1928.

Unfortunately, one is obliged to wade through many pages of extraneous material in order to discover and savour sidelights on the management of a Midland estate, and in this reviewer's opinion the book cannot take the place of J. R. Miller's *Practical Gamekeeper*.

Field and Stream, in the 1940s, searches for the good bits in *Lady Chatterley's Lover*.

John Le Carré

You're welcome to Le Carré – he hasn't got any future.

An anonymous publisher plays pass-the-parcel with *The Spy Who Came in from the Cold*, 1963.

Norman Mailer

In my opinion it is barely publishable.

A nice double-entendre: a publisher's rejection of *The Naked Lunch* in 1948.

Thomas Mann

The novel *Buddenbrooks* is nothing but two thick tomes in which the author describes the worthless story of worthless people in worthless chatter.

Eduard Engel, 1901.

Herman Melville

Sad stuff, dull and dreary, or ridiculous. Mr Melville's Quakers are the wretchedest dolts and drivellers, and his Mad Captain is a monstrous bore.

The *Southern Quarterly Review* on *Moby Dick*, 1851.

We regret to say that our united opinion is entirely against the book as we do not think it would be at all suitable for the Juvenile Market in this country. It is very long, rather old-fashioned, and in our opinion not deserving of the reputation which it seems to enjoy.

British publisher's rejection of *Moby Dick*, 1851.

John Milton

If length be not considered a merit, *Paradise Lost* has no other.

Edmund Waller, 1680.

His fame is gone out like a candle in a snuff and his memory will always stink.

William Winstanley, *Lives of the Most Famous English Poets*, 1687.

Our language sank under him.

Joseph Addison, quoted by Samuel Johnson in his *Lives of the Poets*, 1779–81.

Vladimir Nabokov

It should be, and probably has been, told to a psychiatrist … It is over-whelmingly nauseating, even to an enlightened Freudian … It is a totally perverse performance all round … I am most disturbed at the thought that the writer has asked that this be published. I can see no possible cause that could be served by its publication now. I recommend that it be buried under a stone for a thousand years.

The truly enlightened Freudian might think this told us less about the author than the publisher who rejected *Lolita*, in 1955.

George Orwell

I am highly critical of many aspects of internal and external Soviet policy; but I could not possibly publish a general attack of this kind.

Victor Gollancz rejects *Animal Farm* in 1944.

It would be less offensive if the predominant caste in the fable were not pigs.

Jonathan Cape rejects *Animal Farm* in 1944.

It is impossible to sell animal stories in the USA.

The Dial Press, New York, rejects *Animal Farm* in 1945.

Nineteen Eighty-Four is a failure.

Laurence Brander, *George Orwell*, 1954.

Alexander Pope

Who is this Pope I hear so much about? I cannot discover what is his merit. Why will not my subjects write in prose?

King George II.

Marcel Proust

My dear fellow, I may be dead from the neck up, but rack my brains as I may I can't see why a chap should need thirty pages to describe how he turns over in bed before going to sleep.

Marc Humbolt of the publishers Ollendorf rejects *Swann's Way* on 12 February 1912; Proust published it at his own expense the following year.

Percy Bysshe Shelley

The school to which he belonged, or rather which he established, can never become popular.

Philadelphia Monthly Magazine, 15 July 1828.

Shel Silverstein

It falls between two stools – it ain't a kid's book and it ain't an adult one. I'm sorry but I don't think you're going to find a publisher for it.

William Cole of Simon & Schuster, 1963, on *The Giving Tree*, which was published the following year by Harper & Row and sold over 2 million copies, making its author America's best-selling children's writer.

Laurence Sterne

Nothing odd will do long. *Tristram Shandy* did not last.

Samuel Johnson, quoted by Boswell. *The Life and Opinions of Tristram Shandy*, first published between 1759 and 1767, is still in print.

James Tiptree Jr

It has been suggested that Tiptree is female, a theory I find absurd, for there is to me something ineluctably masculine about Tiptree's writing. I don't think the novels of Jane Austen could have been written by a man nor the stories of Ernest Hemingway by a woman, and in the same way I believe the author of the James Tiptree stories is male.

Robert Silverburg, in his introduction to James Tiptree Jr's *Warm Worlds and Otherwise*, 1975. Two years later, Tiptree was revealed as Alice Sheldon, a 61-year-old spinster.

Mark Twain

A hundred years from now it is very likely that 'The Jumping Frog' alone will be remembered.

Harry Thurston Peck, editor of *The Bookman*, January 1901. His prediction seems unlikely to be fulfilled.

H. G. Wells

It is not interesting enough for the general reader and not thorough enough for the scientific reader.

Publisher's rejection of *The Time Machine*, 1895.

I think the verdict would be: 'Oh don't read that horrid book.'

Or: 'Oh don't listen to that stupid publisher.' Rejection of *The War of the Worlds*, 1898.

Walt Whitman

Walt Whitman is as unacquainted with art as a hog is with mathematics.

The *London Critic*, 1855, on a little-known ability of hogs.

William Wordsworth

This will never do. The case of Mr Wordsworth is manifestly hopeless; and we give him up as altogether incurable and beyond the power of criticism.

Lucky old Wordsworth. Francis Jeffrey, the *Edinburgh Review*, November 1814.

Emile Zola

His instinctive inclination to depict demented persons, criminals, prostitutes, and semi-maniacs ... his symbolism, his pessimism, his coprolalia, and his predilection for slang, sufficiently characterize M. Zola as a high-class degenerate. That he is a sexual psychopath is betrayed on every page of his novels.

Max Nordau (1849–1923), *Degeneration*.

The British Empire

The furtherance of the English Empire for the bringing of the whole uncivilized world under British rule, for the recovery of the United States, for the making of the Anglo-Saxon race but one empire – what a dream! But yet it is probable.

Last will and testament of Cecil Rhodes, founder of Rhodesia, 1902.

The cessation of any Colony or Protectorate – save as the result of a crushing defeat in war – is simply unthinkable and would never be accepted by the nation.

Lord Lugard of Abinger, former governor of Hong Kong and Nigeria, speaking in 1938. India gained independence, without the need for crushing defeats, nine years later.

Are you sure you want to go through with this?

HRH Prince Philip, to Jomo Kenyatta, the new Prime Minister of Kenya, during the independence ceremony of 1963. The remark was picked up by microphones and broadcast to the crowd.

Broadcasting Boobs

At the present moment the whole Fleet is lit up. When I say 'lit up' I mean lit up by fairy lamps. It's fantastic. It isn't a Fleet at all ... it's Fairyland. The whole Fleet is in Fairyland. Now if you'll follow me through ... If you don't mind ... (*Incomprehensible*) The next few moments, you'll find the Fleet doing odd things. (*Prolonged silence*) I'm sorry, I was telling some people to shut up talking – Oh, it's gone! It's gone. There's no Fleet. It's ... it's disappeared. No magician who ever could have waved his wand could have waved it with more acumen than he has now at this present moment. The Fleet's gone. It's disappeared. I was talking to you in the middle of this damn (*cough*) in the middle of this Fleet and what's happened is the Fleet's gone and disappeared and gone ... (*Cut to studio announcer*).

Lieutenant-Commander Tommy Woodroffe, who had taken precautions against the cold air, commentates for BBC radio on the 1937 Spithead Naval Review and, crucially, misses the moment the lights were turned off.

If there's a goal now I'll eat my hat.

Tommy Woodroffe again, at the 1938 FA Cup Final. There was, and he did.

I guess that'll hold the little bastards.

Donald Carney – 'Uncle Don' – the Children's Programme presenter on Station WOR, mistakenly thinks his microphone has been turned off; 1930s.

Princess Margaret, wearing an off-the-hat face.

Max Robertson, setting the scene for BBC radio listeners at the wedding of Princess Anne and Captain Mark Phillips, 1972.

The art of the quill has been practised since Caxton – and probably before.

David Frost, TV interview, 1977.

My fellow Americans, I have signed legislation to outlaw Russia for ever. We begin bombing in five minutes.

President Ronald Reagan tests a radio microphone in 1981. He was on air.

Beware people who want to make you a millionaire! ... The promotion details say, 'We will place your money in a bank in Escrow in Spain.' Well, we've searched a gazetteer and we can't find the town of Escrow anywhere.

You and Yours, BBC Radio 4, 20 October 1995. 'Escrow' is a type of bank account.

So, what exactly does 100% taxation mean?

Nicky Campbell interviews an economic expert on BBC Radio 5 Live, October 1998. He received the obvious answer.

See also DOUBLE-ENTENDRES

Business and Finance

The public will never accept artificial silks. Lister's will stay with the real thing.

The directors of Lister's Bradford Mill decline an offer to purchase the right to manufacture Rayon, invented by Hilaire de Chardonnet in 1884. He sold the patent to Courtaulds instead.

I sling my ideas out to my staff and I say, 'Make them work!' I look for things where the trading systems are fuddy-duddy, archaic, then I move in.

John Bloom, the head of Rolls Razor Ltd., purveyor of cut-price washing machines (and, in theory, much else), quoted in the spring of 1964. In August the firm went bust, owing £4 million, having supplied thousands of faulty washing machines (and not much else).

Few exercises exhilarate the financial world more than speculating what the Pennsylvania–New York Central Transportation Company will be doing in ten years if the great plans now being laid for the system come to fruition.

Fortune Magazine hails the merger of the two great US rail companies in 1965. In 1970 the merged Penn–Central went bust with debts of $4,600,000,000.

In the long term I feel confident that with the increasing acceptance of tufted carpets we must go from strength to strength.

Cyril Lord, head of the eponymous floor covering manufacturer, August 1966. Two years later – having built a factory that didn't make vinyl flooring and another that didn't make artificial astrakhan, but did make a sort of artificial turf that turned blue and slimy on exposure to the weather – his firm went bust.

On the evidence available, there appears to be no immediate danger of insolvency.

Conclusion of a Board of Trade enquiry into the affairs of the cut-price Fire, Auto and Marine Insurance Co., January 1967. It went bust a week later, leaving several hundred thousand people, mostly car-owners, uninsured and uncompensated.

But of course, it was all fun.

Emile Savundra, presiding genius of the Fire, Auto and Marine Insurance Co., appearing on David Frost's TV show, outlines his business philosophy in February 1967. He was later convicted of fraud, fined £50,000, and jailed for eight years.

You'd have to have a death wish to kill *Life* magazine.

James R. Shepley, President of Time Inc., January 1970. Mr Shepley became tired of *Life* in December 1972, and closed it down.

Jim Slater has now earned himself a position of paramount respectability in the City for his novel and wide-ranging techniques.

The Times recommends Slater Walker Securities Ltd. in 1969.

I want to become the world's greatest international financier in the next ten years.

Jim Slater, 1972.

Slater Walker is now safe from calamity.

Patrick Hutber, writing in the *Sunday Telegraph* shortly before the total collapse of Slater Walker Securities Ltd. in 1975.

Stocks are on the bargain counter.

Joseph Granville, publisher of *The Granville Market Letter*, April 1973. The Dow Jones index, then at 950, began a 20-month decline to a low point of 578 in December 1974.

This is a sucker's rally.

Joseph Granville, in *The Granville Market Letter*, August 1982, predicts that the Dow Jones index will fall to a range of 450–600 by the end of 1983. At the end of December 1983 it stood at 1259.

It could no more lose money than I could have a baby.

Mayor Jean Drapeau of Montreal looks forward to hosting the 1976 Olympic Games on 29 January 1973. The Montreal Olympic Games lost around $1 billion, but the mayor failed to make medical history.

I could become the Colonel Sanders of beer.

The brother of US President Jimmy Carter launches 'Billy's Beer' in 1977, despite his mother's objection that it gave her diarrhoea. Billy Carter's Falls City Brewing Co. went bust in 1978.

The Con Ed system is in the best shape for fifteen years, and there's no problem about the summer.

Charles Franklin Luce, chairman of Consolidated Edison Inc., New York's electricity supplier, 10 July 1977. Three days later a massive Con Ed failure blacked out metropolitan New York for over 24 hours.

Another brilliant, strategic move that should put Braniff in splendid shape for the 80s.

Salomon Brothers' airline analyst Julius Saldutis hails the acumen of Braniff Airlines chairman Harding Lawrence in *Business Week*, 19 March 1979. The 80s saw Braniff go bust.

I'm flying high and couldn't be more confident about the future.

Laker Airways boss Freddy Laker, three days before the collapse of his company in 1982.

I love Britain ... Ethics and morals count in Britain like nowhere else in the world.

Mohammed Fayed, self-confessed briber of MPs, on his reasons for wishing to acquire Harrods, 1985. A Board of Trade inquiry established that he had mis-represented the origins of his wealth.

I don't hold myself responsible because I have not had anything to do with the affairs of BCCI for the past three years.

Agha Hassan Abedi, founder and – for sixteen years – head of the Bank of Credit and Commerce International; a statement issued on 15 July 1991, a few days after BCCI collapsed under the weight of nineteen years of criminality and fraudulent trading.

It's easy to say with hindsight that we were wrong to put all our eggs in one basket.

Donald MacLeod, Director of Finance for Comhairle nan Eilan (the Western Isles Council) which lost £23 million in the collapse of BCCI – including £1.3 million deposited just fifteen minutes before the Bank of England closed it down.

Last summer I suggested that British Aerospace would be in no particular hurry to sell Rover as it was released from its undertaking given to the government when it bought the car maker five years earlier. Today, after getting a glimpse of how well Rover performed in 1993, it still holds true.

Michael Smith, business editor of the *Observer*, 30 January 1994. British Aerospace sold Rover to BMW the following day.

I don't believe the *Observer* will be sold in the foreseeable future.

Tom Bower, official biographer of *Observer* owner Roland 'Tiny' Rowland, writing one month prior to the newspaper's sale to the trustees of the *Guardian* in 1994.

I shouldn't mind being a junior hospital doctor. It might be quite relaxing to do their job.

Sir Ian Vallance, Chairman of BT (formerly British Telecom) responds to critics of his £663,000 basic annual salary in February 1995.

Don't panic! Derivatives are here to help. Send for your RISK-FREE trial issue now!

Advertisement for *Derivatives Quarterly*, a magazine exploring the mysteries of financial derivatives trading, a form of spread-betting on the movement of the markets, in February 1995. In the same month, Nick Leeson, a derivatives trader with Baring's Bank, gambled and lost so much money that Baring's ('the Queen's banker') closed down.

Economists may sometimes seem about as useful as a chocolate teapot, but as this year's Nobel prize for economics shows, it isn't always so. On October 4th, the $1m prize was awarded to two Americans, Robert Merton of Harvard University and Myron Scholes of Stanford University ... Their work on how to price financial options ... turned risk management from a guessing game into a science.

The Economist, 17 October 1997, hails the award of the Nobel prize to the founders of Long-Term Capital Management Inc., the pioneer and the biggest of the 'hedge funds', a sort of souped-up derivates scheme into which investors worldwide, both private and corporate, poured tens of billions of dollars in the happy conviction that, whatever happened to the markets, they couldn't lose. The 'science of risk management' came unstuck in the autumn of 1998, following the recession in Japan, the crises in the Pacific Rim, and the collapse of the Russian economy. International banks wrote off debts of $3.5 billion to rescue LTCM from bankruptcy in order to avoid a worldwide banking collapse and a recession in the USA and Europe.

Like the *Titanic*, Long-Term Capital Management was supposed to be unsinkable ... At the very least, Wall Street's finest were blinded by the reputations of LTCM's founders...

Very true. *The Economist*, 3 October 1998.

See also CARS, COMPUTERS, THE ECONOMY, THE GREAT DEPRESSION, ROBERT MAXWELL, POLITICIANS' PROMISES *and* THE WALL STREET CRASH

C

Canals

Panama

To seek or make known any better route than the one from Porto Bello to Panama is forbidden under the penalty of death.

King Philip II of Spain issues an edict in the 1550s.

I have crossed both at the site of the Panama Railroad and at three other points more to the south. From all I could see, combined with all I have read on the subject, I cannot entertain the slightest hope that a ship canal will ever be found possible across any part of it.

Surveyor John C. Trautwine reports in the *Journal of the Franklin Institute*, May 1854.

The Panama Canal is actually a thing of the past, and Nature in her works will soon obliterate all traces of French energy and money expended on the Isthmus.

Scientific American rejoices in the bankruptcy of the Compagnie Universelle Interoceanique in January 1891. The US government then bought out the French interest for $40 million, bankrolled an uprising in Panama (which was then a province of Columbia), built the canal, and opened it to shipping in 1914.

Suez

A most futile attempt and totally impossible to be carried out.

Chancellor of the Exchequer Benjamin Disraeli, speaking in the House of Commons in 1858. As Prime Minister in 1875 he bought Britain a half share in the completed project.

I have a very strong opinion that such a canal will not and cannot be made ... and that steam navigation by land will and ought to be the means of transit through Egypt.

Novelist Anthony Trollope, who had seen government service in Egypt, in *The West Indies and the Spanish Main*, 1859.

No one will ever collect a farthing in tolls from this impossible canal.

The *Globe*, 30 November 1869 – thirteen days after the first voyage through the Suez Canal.

Cars

Prehistory

If a man were to propose to convey us regularly to Edinburgh in seven days, and bring us back in seven more, should we not vote him to Bedlam?

Sir Henry Herbert MP amuses the House of Commons in 1671.

Regular travel at such a prodigious speed must surely result in death from an apoplexy.

A local doctor writes to the *Bath Argus* in the late 1780s, after John Palmer's mail coach service cut the journey time between London and Bath from three days to seventeen hours.

Internal Combustion

The discovery with which we are dealing involves forces of a nature too dangerous to fit into any of our usual concepts.

The *US Congressional Record* of 1875, on an enquiry into 'the so-called internal combustion engine'.

The ordinary 'horseless carriage' is at present a luxury for the wealthy; and although its price will probably fall in the future, it will never, of course, come into as common use as the bicycle.

The *Literary Digest*, 14 October 1899.

The actual building of roads devoted to motor cars is not for the near future, in spite of many rumours to that effect.

Harper's Weekly, 2 August 1902.

Nothing has come along that can beat the horse and buggy.

In 1903, US businessman Chauncey Depew advises his nephew not to invest $5,000 in the Ford Motor Company.

The horse is here to stay, but the automobile is only a novelty – a fad.

The president of the Michigan Savings Bank advises Horace Rackham, also in 1903. Some years later, Rackham sold his $5,000 shareholding in Ford for $12,500,000.

That the automobile has practically reached the limit of its development is suggested by the fact that during the past year no improvements of a radical nature have been introduced.

Scientific American, 2 January 1909.

In 15 years, more electricity will be sold for electric vehicles than for light.

Thomas Edison, talking up the market for his patented nickel-cadmium battery in 1910.

The motor-car will never usurp the place of the horse.

The Economist, 1911.

In less than twenty-five years the motor car will be obsolete, because the aeroplane will run along the ground as well as fly over it.

Sir Philip Gibbs, in *The Day After Tomorrow: What is Going to Happen to the World* (1928), conjures up a vision of multi-storey airports.

I am not one of those people who believe that speed per se is really going to make for dangerous driving on our roads today … I do not believe the retention of the speed limit will really have any effect in helping to reduce the number of accidents.

Lord Erskine, supporting the government Bill to abolish the speed limit, 1930. It was reintroduced four years later, after a huge rise in accidents.

If cars continue to be made at the same rate as now and with increasing cheapness, there will soon be no pedestrians left.

Leslie Hore-Belisha MP, the minister of transport who introduced driving tests and zebra crossings, 1935.

Next year's cars should be rolling out of Detroit with plastic bodies.

L. M. Bloomingdale, *The Future of Plastics*, in the *Yale Scientific Magazine*, Spring 1941.

A study of the engine indicated that the unit was, in certain details, most inefficient … It is very doubtful whether it was even capable of giving reliable service had it produced a performance commensurate with its size. Looking at the general picture, we do not consider that the design represents any special brilliance … and it is suggested that it is not to be

regarded as an example of first-class modern design to be copied by
British Industry.

Report of the Humber Motor Co. on the German 'People's Car', later known as
the Volkswagen Beetle, 1946. British car manufacturers had been invited to the
Wolfsburg factory at the end of World War II, with a view to taking over production
of the car, free of charge. They declined.

British designers have nothing to learn from this brand of design.

Ernest Beech, British president of Ford, on the VW Beetle, 1946.

The Volkswagen does not meet the fundamental technical requirements
of a motor car.

Sir William Rootes, 1946. Over 20 million Volkswagen Beetles were sold in the
following four decades.

It is doubtful if German production would be such as to challenge our
strong position in most markets outside Europe.

Conclusion of a Board of Trade report into the West German motor industry, 1950.

The deluxe open-road car will probably be 20 feet long, and powered by
a gas turbine engine, little brother of the jet engine.

Prediction for 1965 from Leo Cherne of the Research Institute of America in 1955.

The Edsel is here to stay.

Henry Ford II on the car that bore his son's name, 7 December 1957. Despite a
relaunch with a new design, better engineering, and a $20 million advertising budget,
the car flopped again; it was scrapped in November 1958. Ford Inc. lost $350
million on the project, and one thousand dealers, some of whom had paid $100,000
for their Edsel franchises, went out of business.

See also ADVERTISING

Though import sales could hit 425,000 in 1959, they may never go that
high again.

Business Week, 17 January 1958, sees no reason for US car manufacturers to
fear imports.

With over 50 foreign cars already on sale here, the Japanese auto industry
isn't likely to carve out a big slice of the US market for itself.

Business Week, 2 August 1968. By the end of the 1980s, imports accounted for
28.5% of US car sales.

The Wankel will eventually dwarf such major post-war technological developments as xerography, the Polaroid camera and colour television.

General Motors announce a move away from the piston engine in 1969.

The reciprocating engine is as dead as a dodo.

Sports Illustrated hails the ascendancy of the Wankel rotary engine, 1969.

The World has changed. So has Mazda.

Advertisement for Mazda cars, last champions of the gas-guzzling Wankel rotary engine, killed off by the oil crisis: 1976.

The company is not bust. We are merely in a cyclical decline.

Lord Stokes, chairman of British Leyland, 1974. The following year, the British government was obliged to spend taxpayers' money to keep his company in business. British Leyland (also known as Leyland Cars and BL) eventually became Rover Cars and was bought by British Aerospace, who sold it to BMW.

Cartooning

I rather doubt if 'cartooning' (as it is called here) is really your line. Neither drawings or ideas measure up to the standard required here, I'm afraid.

A rejection letter from Russell Brockbank, cartoon editor of *Punch*, to Mel Calman, 18 September 1956. In 1969 Calman became the 'pocket cartoonist' at *The Times*.

Celebrity

It is possible that the five girl typists from Surbiton will, when the history of these confused times is written, become as famous as the six martyrs of Tolpuddle.

The *Daily Mirror*, 1968, on five typists who volunteered to work 30 minutes' overtime without pay to aid the 'I'm Backing Britain' campaign during the latest economic crisis. The *Mirror*'s offer of 'I'm Backing Britain' T-shirts backfired when they turned out to be labelled 'Made in Portugal'. The campaign itself did not last much longer.

I call it the Mark Spitz Game Plan. My objective is to make an institutional tie-up for Mark very soon with two of the big blue-chip companies. It might be a GM or a Bristol-Myers, or somebody of that calibre. Then I'm planning to work out two TV specials in which Mark will star during the 1972–73 season. After that we're going heavily into the merchandising area worldwide ... We feel that Mark Spitz will have a major motion picture career.

Hollywood agent Norman Brokaw, 1972, on his new signing. Mark Spitz won five gold medals for swimming at the Munich Olympics and then, after trying Mr Brokaw's Game Plan for a while, became a dentist.

We all know that people with very meagre talents can become household names by appearing on television.

Noel Edmonds (*Daily Telegraph*, July 1994) never spoke a truer word.

Charles and Diana

Last night Britain sighed with sadness for Di – and sent her a massive wave of sympathy as she faced incredible strain. Friends and MPs lashed the 'shabby and intrusive' treatment she was receiving.

Daily Star, 5 June 1992.

Royal Marriage in Torment – Special Report: Pages 2, 3, 4 & 5.

Daily Star, 5 June 1992.

The Royals: A Family at War.

Evening Standard, page 1 headline, 5 June 1992.

Suicidal Despair, Loveless Marriage.

Evening Standard, pages 2–3 headline, 5 June 1992.

Is It Time To Leave The Royals Alone?

Evening Standard, editorial headline, 5 June 1992.

It is painful to dwell on the melancholy state of the marriage of the heir to the throne.

The *Daily Mail*, editorial, 6 June 1992.

Diana: The Unhappiness Behind the Smile. Turn to Pages 17, 18 and 19.

The *Daily Mail*, page 1, 6 June 1992.

The Sunday Times and the *Sun* which together have invested more than £500,000 in Andrew Morton's book suggest the Princess has somehow co-operated in the publication. Well, they would, wouldn't they? The

Mirror today publishes the Princess's complete rebuttal of that claim in the most clear and precise terms.

The *Daily Mirror*, 8 June 1992.

Diana last night warmly embraced the former flatmate who contributed to the controversial book about her marriage ... Diana clearly told the world: 'I approve of everything she has done.'

The *Daily Mirror*, 11 June 1992.

I now know why Prince Charles spent his time talking to vegetables – because he knew he would get more sense out of them than the fruit he married.

Andrew Morton, the *Sun*, 14 August 1997. After the death of Diana, Princess of Wales, on 31 August, he brought out a new edition of his book *Diana: Her True Story*, in order to 'honour her memory'.

She has for many years criticized Prince Charles for being a distant, un-demonstrative father. In the long run he's been the more responsible parent and certainly inflicted less damage, anguish and hurt.

Lynda Lee-Potter, *Daily Mail*, 27 August 1997.

Throughout their childhood she gave her sons endless loving cuddles ... She adored her children.

Lynda Lee-Potter, *Daily Mail*, 1 September 1997, after Diana's death.

A woman who, if her IQ were five points lower, would have to be watered daily.

'Mrs Blair's Diary', the *Observer*, 31 August 1997, the day of Diana's death.

China

The great fact was clear: the Generalissimo had justified those who had long held that his government was firmly embedded in popular support, and that given peace it could establish an effective administration in China ... Never in modern times had the great nation of 450,000,000 people been so close to an era of peace.

Time, 3 September 1945, celebrates the dawn of an era under the Nationalist leader, Chiang Kai-shek. After three years of vicious and debilitating civil war, Mao Tse-tung declared the People's Republic of China on 1 October 1949.

I do not have any doubts that we will recover the mainland, that the Communists will be crushed and that the Republic of China ... will be re-established.

Generalissimo Chiang Kai-shek, after the Nationalists' retreat to the island of Formosa (now Taiwan), 1 March 1950.

After Chiang Kai-shek has landed and maintained himself for three months on the mainland, the Communist menace to Asia will be finished and the whole of Asia will turn anti-Communist.

Henry R. Luce, publisher of *Time, Life* and *Fortune*: memo to John Billings, managing editor of *Life*, 22 December 1952.

See also THE KOREAN WAR

We are firmly convinced that no force whatsoever can disrupt the great unity between the Chinese and Soviet peoples.

Chou En-lai, Prime Minister of the People's Republic of China, ushers in a decade of military stand-off between China and the USSR in Outer Mongolia; 1965.

There was no tragedy in Tiananmen: there was no bloodbath. There is no change in China's policy. The open door remains open.

Li Peng, Prime Minister of the People's Republic of China, after the crushing by tanks and troops of the student pro-democracy movement in Tiananmen Square, Beijing; June 1987.

The CIA

Chile

The CIA had nothing to do with the coup, to the best of my knowledge and belief, and I only put in that qualification in case some madman appears down there who, without instruction, talked to somebody. I have absolutely no reason to suppose it.

Henry Kissinger, US Secretary of State-designate, in confirmation hearings, 17 September 1973. The government of President Salvador Allende, elected in 1970, had recently been overthrown in a military coup led by General Augusto Pinochet.

Either explicitly or implicitly, the US Government has been charged with involvement or complicity in the coup. This is absolutely false. As official spokesmen of the US Government have stated repeatedly, we were not involved in the coup in any way.

Jack B. Kubisch, US assistant Secretary of State for inter-American affairs, statement in Congress, 20 September 1973.

In 1974, CIA Director William Colby testified in Congress that the CIA had spent over $8 million to 'destabilize' President Allende's government between 1970 and 1973, and that the 'madman' who directed and authorized the operation was none other than Henry Kissinger himself.

See also DICTATORS

Cuba

It is generally believed that the Cuban Army has been successfully penetrated by opposition groups and that it will not fight in the event of a showdown.

CIA Internal Information Report, No. CS-3/470,587, March 1961.

I stood right here at Ike's desk and told him I was certain our Guatemalan operation would succeed, and, Mr President, the prospects for this plan are even better than they were for that one.

Allen Dulles, director of the CIA, briefs President John F. Kennedy in April 1961 on the CIA's plan for a covert invasion of Cuba at the Bay of Pigs.

There will not be, under any conditions, any intervention in Cuba by the United States armed forces. This government will do everything it possibly can ... to make sure that there are no Americans involved in any action inside Cuba.

President John F. Kennedy, press conference, 12 April 1961.

In the early hours of 15 April, eight United States B-26 bombers, painted in the colours of the Cuban air force and with Cuban exile pilots, took off from a CIA airbase in Nicaragua to bomb air bases in Cuba.

The State Department is unaware of any invasion.

Joseph W. Reap, spokesman for the US State Department, 17 April 1961.

All we know about Cuba is what we read on the wire services.

Pierre Salinger, White House press secretary, 17 April 1961.

The American people are entitled to know whether we are intervening in Cuba or intend to do so in the future. The answer to that question is no.

Dean Rusk, US Secretary of State, press conference, 17 April 1961.

On the night of 16–17 April 1961 a force of 1,500 CIA-trained Cuban exiles was escorted to the Cuban coast by US Navy destroyers, and landed at the Bay of Pigs. Cuban forces won a total victory on 20 April; four US Air Force pilots were among the invaders' casualties.

See also DICTATORS

Guatemala

The department has no evidence that this is anything other than a revolt of Guatemalans against the government.

Statement by the US State Department, 18 June 1954, following reports that an 'Army of Liberation' had invaded from Honduras to overthrow the left-wing Guatemalan government of President Jacobo Arbenz Guzmán.

The situation does not involve aggression but is a revolt of Guatemalans against Guatemalans.

Henry Cabot Lodge, US ambassador to the United Nations, June 1954.
   The successful coup against President Guzmán was organized and funded by the CIA, which bombed Guatemala City with its own air force of Thunderbolts. It was carried out to assist the operations of US banana growers in the region, and gave rise to the expression 'banana republic'.

See also CUBA *within this entry*

Indonesia

We are not intervening in the internal affairs of this country.

John Foster Dulles, US Secretary of State, responds to allegations that the CIA is supporting a rebellion against the government of President Sukarno of Indonesia, March 1958.

Our policy is one of careful neutrality and proper deportment all the way through so as not to be taking sides where it is none of our business.

President Dwight D. Eisenhower denies charges of US involvement in Indonesia's affairs, 30 April 1958.

It is unfortunate that high officials of the Indonesian Government have given circulation to the false report that the United States Government was sanctioning aid to Indonesia's rebels ... The United States is not ready to step in and overthrow a constituted government. Those are the hard facts.

New York Times, editorial, 9 May 1958.
   On 18 May, Indonesian anti-aircraft fire shot down a B-26 bomber and its CIA-recruited US Air Force pilot, Allen Lawrence Pope.

The U-2 Incident

The instrumentation carried by the U-2 permits obtaining precise information about clear-air turbulence, convective clouds, wind shear, the jet stream and such widespread weather patterns as typhoons.

Statement issued by the National Aeronautic and Space Administration (NASA), 5 May 1960, following the announcement by Soviet Prime Minister Nikita Khrushchev that the USSR had shot down an American U-2 spy plane over its territory. NASA described the pilot, Gary Powers, as 'a civilian employee of the Lockheed Corporation' and claimed the plane was a 'flying weather laboratory'.

There was no, absolutely no – NO – attempt to violate Soviet airspace, and never has been.

Lincoln White, spokesman for the US State Department, 6 May 1960.

Premier Khrushchev personally ordered the rocket destruction of an unarmed US aircraft which had drifted into Soviet airspace, probably because its pilot became unconscious when his oxygen equipment failed. Khrushchev has revealed himself and his beastly character to the hilt; he is a pig in human form.

New York Daily Mirror, editorial, 7 May 1960.

On 7 May, Khrushchev revealed that Powers had been captured alive and had confessed that he had been on a CIA spying mission over the USSR. The US government, which had assumed that Powers had followed his orders to destroy the plane (and himself) in the event of an attack, then confirmed that such missions had regularly been flown over the USSR since 1956.

See also THE IRAN-CONTRA SCANDAL

William Jefferson Clinton

There is no question that an admission of making false statements to government officials and interfering with the FBI is an impeachable offence … I think it is plain that the President should resign and spare the country the agony of impeachment and removal proceedings.

As a young Democrat politician, reported in the *Arkansas Democrat*, 6 August 1974.

I tried it once, but I didn't inhale.

US presidential candidate Bill Clinton, 1992, responding to charges that he had smoked cannabis while a Fullbright student at Oxford University.

I answered this question before.

US presidential candidate Bill Clinton, interviewed on *60 Minutes* in 1992, deals with questions about an alleged extra-marital affair with night-club singer Gennifer Flowers by referring to previous answers he hadn't given.

I have nothing else to say. We, we did, if, the, I, I, the stories are just as they have been said. They're outrageous and they're not so.

US President Bill Clinton, December 1993, on allegations that his proven extra-marital affair with night-club singer Gennifer Flowers had gone on many years longer than he'd admitted to.

I have never had sexual relations with Monica Lewinsky. I've never had an affair with her.

US President Bill Clinton, deposition of 17 January 1998, on allegations of sex with a White House intern.

There is no improper relationship ... There is not a sexual relationship, an improper sexual relationship or any other kind of improper relationship.

US President Bill Clinton, interviewed by Jim Lehrer on PBS, 21 January 1998.

It is not an improper relationship, and I know what the word means ... The relationship was not sexual.

US President Bill Clinton, interviewed on *Roll Call*, 21 January 1998.

I want to say one thing to the American people. I want you to listen to me. I'm going to say this again. I did not have sexual relations with that woman, Miss Lewinsky.

US President Bill Clinton, speaking to the media, 25 January 1998.

I don't think this will evaporate, but I anticipate it will slowly dissipate over time, reaching insubstantiality.

Hillary Clinton, on the Monica Lewinsky scandal, quoted in the *Washington Post*, 12 February 1998.

It depends upon what the meaning of the word 'is' means. If 'is' means is, and never has been, that's one thing. If it means, there is none, that was a completely true statement.

US President Bill Clinton, in a transcript of his evidence to the Grand Jury released on 21 September 1998, on the meaning of 'There is no improper relationship.'

See also PORNOGRAPHY

The Coal Board

British Coal will still be around 100 years from now.

Advertisement for National Coal Board Technical Services in *Business Administration*, 1973. British Coal (formerly the National Coal Board) was privatized and split up in the 1990s.

See also POLITICIANS' PROMISES

The Cold War

The Crimea Conference ... spells the end of the system of unilateral action, the exclusive alliances, the spheres of influence, the balances of power, and all the other expedients that have been tried for centuries – and have always failed.

US President Franklin D. Roosevelt, after meeting with Churchill and Stalin at Yalta, 1 March 1945.

Never in the past has there been any place on the globe where the vital interests of American and Russian people have clashed or even been antagonistic, and there is no reason to suppose there should be now or in the future ever such a place.

Dean Acheson, US under-Secretary of State, 1945.

Communism

Marx's audacious attempt to destroy the bases of contemporary society with the aid of what seemed to be the cardinal principles of political economy has utterly failed.

The St Petersburg journal *Grazhdanin*, 13 March 1883.

The Socialist ideas he tried to propagate failed to make a lasting impression.

The *Daily Alta California*, 18 March 1883.

England is at last ripe for revolution.

Leon Trotsky, 1925.

Every year humanity takes a step towards Communism. Maybe not you, but at all events your grandson will surely be a Communist.

Soviet leader Nikita Khrushchev, to Sir William Hayter, British ambassador to Moscow, June 1956.

I personally believe Dulles to be a Communist agent.

Robert H. Welch Jr., retired US industrialist and founder of the John Birch Society, commenting in 1963 on John Foster Dulles, President Eisenhower's Secretary of State (1953–59) – generally regarded as the hardline architect of US Cold War policy.

Based on an accumulation of detailed evidence so extensive and so palpable that it seems to put this conviction beyond any reasonable doubt ... [he is] ... a dedicated, conscious agent of the Communist conspiracy.

Robert H. Welch Jr., on President Eisenhower, 1963.

See also CONSPIRACY THEORIES, McCARTHYISM, THE RUSSIAN REVOLUTION *and* THE USSR

Computers

This extraordinary monument of theoretical genius accordingly remains, and doubtless will forever remain, a theoretical possibility.

A biographer's assessment, in 1884, of Charles Babbage's 'Analytical Engine', the forerunner of all modern computers, designed in the 1830s. Babbage (1791–1871) also designed a 'Difference Engine', the prototype for all calculating machines.

I think there is a world market for about five computers.

Remark attributed to Thomas J. Watson, chairman of IBM, 1943.

Where a calculator on the ENIAC is equipped with 18,000 vacuum tubes and weighs 30 tons, computers in the future may have only 1,000 vacuum tubes and perhaps only weigh 1H tons.

Popular Mechanics, March 1949.

I have travelled the length and breadth of this country, and have talked with the best people in business administration. I can assure you on the highest authority that data processing is a fad and won't last out the year.

The business books editor of Prentice Hall publishers responds to Karl V. Karlstrom, a junior editor who had recommended a manuscript on the new science of data processing, 1957.

What the hell is it good for?

Robert Lloyd, of IBM's Advanced Computing Systems Division, on the microprocessor, 1968.

Your paper ... is too speculative and involves no new physics.

In 1969, the *Physical Review* rejects a paper by Leo Esaki and Raphael Tsu on 'superconducting superlattices' – the essential components of personal computers, compact discs, and satellite television.

There is no reason for anyone to have a computer in their home.

Ken Olson, president of Digital Equipment Corporation, 1977.

With Windows 95, all the things you do now will be easier and faster, and what you've always wanted to do is now possible.

Introducing Microsoft Windows 95, 1995.

Conception

And if, in the act of copulation, the woman look earnestly on the man, and fix her mind on him, the child will resemble its father. Nay, if a woman, even in unlawful copulation, fix her mind upon her husband, the child will resemble him even if he did not beget it.

Aristotle, *The Masterpiece*, 4th century BC.

The act of coition being over, let the woman repose herself upon her right side, with her head lying low and her body declining, that by sleeping in that posture, the cani, on the right side of the matrix, may prove the place of conception; for therein is the greatest generative heat, which is the chief procuring cause of male children, and rarely fails the expectations of those that experience it.

Aristotle, *The Masterpiece*, 4th century BC.

If it is a male, the right breast swells first, the right eye is brighter than the left, the face is high-coloured, because the colour is such as the blood is, and the male is conceived of the purer blood and of more perfect seed than the female.

Aristotle, *The Masterpiece*, 4th century BC.

If they wish to have a male child let the man take the womb and vulva of a hare and have it dried and pulverized; blend it with wine and let him drink it. Let the woman do the same with the testicles of a hare and let her be with her husband at the end of her menstrual period and she will conceive a male.

A powerful argument for daughters: Trotula, professor of medicine at the University of Salerno, *The Diseases of Women*, c. 1059.

Semen descends principally from the liver.

Vincent of Beauvais, *Speculum Naturalæ*, 1244–54.

A great portion of semen cometh from the brain.

Ambrose Paré, *De hominis generatione*, 1573.

Twins and triplets undoubtedly originate in second and third copulations, immediately following the first, each drawing and then impregnating an egg. The fact that twins are born as soon as possible after each other supports this view.

Professor Oswald Squire Fowler, *Sexual Science*, 1870.

He believes that in coition the sperm is injected from one testicle only, the right one producing a boy, the left one a girl. If a boy is to be generated, Sixt says, the husband must lie to the right of his wife and put the right knee over first, thus producing tension, which draws up the right testicle into place. 'If,' Sixt says, 'the left testicle should somehow be drawn up towards the abdomen, it may be pushed down quite easily, during coition, and the right one pushed up to be sure of attaining the desired end.'

Professor Oswald Squire Fowler, *Sexual Science*, 1870.

Do a pregnant mother's experiences affect the offspring? Indeed they do. The eminent Dr Napheys reports the case of a pregnant lady who saw some grapes, longed intently for them, and constantly thought of them. During her period of gestation she was attacked and much alarmed by a turkey-cock. In due time she gave birth to a child having a large cluster of globular tumours growing from the tongue and exactly resembling our common grapes. And on the child's chest there grew a red excrescence exactly resembling a turkey's wattles.

Professor Oswald Squire Fowler, *Sexual Science*, 1870.

Confessions

I have the ability to think like a thief.

Allen Klein explains why he would make a good manager for the Beatles (minus Paul McCartney) in 1972. Seven years later he was jailed for tax evasion.

I have looked on a lot of women with lust. I've committed adultery in my heart many times. God recognizes I will do this and forgives me.

US President Jimmy Carter, interviewed in *Playboy*, November 1976.

Of course I was economical with the *actualité*.

Alan Clark, former defence and trade minister, in evidence at the trial of three directors of an engineering firm charged with the illegal supply of arms to Iraq, November 1992; in fact they had done so with the full knowledge and cooperation of Mr Clark and the government. The trial collapsed after Clark's evidence was heard.

I get a bit confused when morality is invoked.

Sir Stephen Egerton, assistant under-secretary (Middle East) at the Foreign Office, in evidence to the Scott Inquiry into the arms-for-Iraq scandal, 1993.

Conspiracy Theories

Indeed, it may well be that men of goodwill like Woodrow Wilson, Jimmy Carter and George Bush ... are in reality unknowingly and unwittingly carrying out the mission and mouthing the phrases of a tightly-knit cabal whose goal is nothing less than a new order for the human race under the domination of Lucifer and his followers ... Rest assured, there is a behind-the-scenes Establishment in this nation, as in every other. It has enormous power. It has controlled the economic and foreign policy objectives of the United States for the past seventy years.

Pat Robertson, former US Republican presidential candidate and head of the Christian Coalition, formulates an all-purpose conspiracy theory for the new Millennium: *The New World Order*, 1991.

The great story here ... is this vast right-wing conspiracy that has been conspiring against my husband since the day he announced for president.

Hillary Clinton, on NBC's *Today* show, dismisses reports of an affair between her husband and a White House intern called Monica Lewinsky, 27 January 1998.

Information has exposed Monica Lewinsky as a spy assigned by the former Soviet Union.

The *Guangdong Writer*, a Chinese news magazine, September 1998.

Contraception

The woman ought, in the moment during coitus when the man ejaculates his sperm, to hold her breath, draw her body back a little so that the semen cannot penetrate to the Os Uteri, then immediately get up and sit down with bent knees and, in this position, provoke sneezes.

Soranus, *Gynæcology*, AD 138.

No woman should be kept on the Pill for 20 years until, in fact, a sufficient number have been kept on the Pill for 20 years.

Sir Allen Sterling Parks, 1970.

Cricket

There's been a heavy fall of rain here at Trent Bridge but fortunately it didn't touch the ground.

Commentator Brian Johnston, BBC *Test Match Special*.

It is extremely cold here. The England fielders are keeping their hands in their pockets between balls.

Commentator Christopher Martin-Jenkins, BBC *Test Match Special*.

You've come over at a very appropriate time; Ray Illingworth has just relieved himself at the pavilion end.

Brian Johnston welcomes listeners to Grace Road, Leicester, c. 1973.

If the West Indies are on top, they're magnificent. If they are down, they grovel. I intend to make them grovel.

England captain Tony Greig looks forward to facing the West Indies in 1976. England lost the series 3–0.

I am, of course, a great Willey supporter.

BBC radio commentator Trevor Bailey voices his admiration of Northamptonshire batsman Peter Willey.

Deryck Murray has batted well. He is the nigger in the woodpile as far as the English are concerned.

Brian Johnston again, during an England v West Indies test match, 1980.

Cricket legitimizes the demarcation by men of yet another time and space where they can be free of women and united with other men.

Joan Smith, *New Statesman*, c. 1980.

With the retirement of 'Dickie' Bird, something sad will have gone out of English cricket.

Prime Minister John Major, BBC2, 1996.

See also DOUBLE-ENTENDRES *and* SPORT

Crime and Criminals

Criminal brains are at a minimum of development in the anterior and superior parts, in the parts that make us what we are and place us above the animals and make us men. Criminal brains are placed by their nature entirely outside the human species.

The anthropologist François Voisin, *De l'idiotie chez les enfants*, 1843.

The average size of criminals' heads is probably about the same as that of ordinary people's heads; but both small and large heads are found in greater proportion, the medium-sized heads being deficient ... Attention has also been called to the prevalence of the prehensile foot among criminals.

Havelock Ellis, *The Criminal*, 1890.

The Eyes of the Habitual Criminal are usually small and uneasy; in

the homicide cold ... in the sexual offender, generally light, and project-
ing in their orbits.

August Drahms, chaplain of San Quentin prison, *The Criminal: His Personality
and Environment, a Scientific Study*, 1900.

The Mafia, one of the most picturesquely villainous secret societies the
world has ever known, exists no more. After holding absolute sway over
Sicily for centuries, murdering, blackmailing, terrorizing ... it has met
its fate at the hands of the Fascist government.

Arnaldo Cortesi, Rome correspondent of the *New York Times*, 'The Mafia is
Dead, a New Sicily is Born', 4 March 1928. The Mafia was revived, as a means of
opposing fascism, by occupying US forces during World War II.

Crime will be virtually abolished by transferring to the preventive process
of school and education the problems of conduct which police, courts,
and prisons now seek to remedy when it is too late.

The US National Education Association's contribution to *What Shall We Be Like
in 1950?* in the *Literary Digest*, 10 January 1931.

Crime will be considered a disease after 1985 and will cease to exist
by AD 2000.

John Langdon-Davies, *A Short History of the Future*, 1936.

I haven't committed a crime. What I did was fail to comply with
the law.

David Dinkins, Mayor of New York, fends off allegations of tax evasion,
1993.

Louise Woodward ... is innocent. Support our campaign for Louise's
release.

The *Mirror*, 1 November 1997.

LOUISE WOODWARD IS A LYING MONSTER
The *Mirror*, 29 May 1998.

The Crimean War

Follow the enemy and try to prevent the enemy carrying away the guns.

On 25 October 1854 Lord Raglan, on a hilltop, refers to one lot of enemy guns
in one position; Lord Lucan, down in the valley, can only see another lot of guns in
a different position. The result: the Charge, and loss, of the Light Brigade.

Cults

Knowing of your congregation's deep involvement in the major social and constitutional issues of our country is a great inspiration to me.

Walter Mondale, Democratic vice president of the USA, sends a thank-you message to the Rev. Jim Jones, who had sent in a campaign contribution, in 1976. Jones used it to help persuade the government of Guyana to allow him to set up a religious commune there. In November 1978, facing a Congressional investigation, Jones ordered the murder of Congressman Leo Ryan and five of his assistants, then told his 1,000 followers to commit suicide by drinking Kool-Aid laced with cyanide: 913 adults and children obeyed. Jones shot himself.

Czechoslovakia

How horrible, fantastic, incredible it is that we should be digging trenches and trying on gas-masks here because of a quarrel in a far-away country between people of whom we know nothing.

Neville Chamberlain, Prime Minister of Great Britain, on Hitler's territorial ambitions in Czechoslovakia: BBC radio broadcast, 27 September 1938.

See also WORLD WAR II

I was asked at the airport whether our sovereignty was jeopardized and I am saying frankly that it is not.

Alexander Dubček, first secretary of the Communist Party of Czechoslovakia, speaks to the press in August 1968 on the threat of Soviet invasion. A few days later he was flown to Moscow for 'consultations', and arrived in handcuffs and chains.

The Soviet Army was invited to protect the sovereignty of the People's Republic of Czechoslovakia.

Leonid Brezhnev, general secretary of the Communist Party of the USSR, on the invasion of Czechoslovakia in August 1968, after which the following joke circulated in Prague: Q: 'What are 60,000 Soviet troops doing in Czechoslovakia?' A: 'Looking for the people who invited them.'

See also THE HUNGARIAN UPRISING

D

Democracy

If there is any conclusion in politics, on which we can securely rely, both from history, and from the laws which govern human action, it is this, THAT UNIVERSAL SUFFRAGE AND FREEDOM NEVER WERE AND NEVER CAN BE CO-EXISTENT.

John Augustine-Smith, professor of moral and political philosophy and president of the College of William and Mary, 1817.

I say that for men who are charged with the high and important duty of choosing the best man to represent the country in Parliament to go sneaking to the ballot-box, and, poking in a piece of paper, looking round to see that no-one could read it, is a course which is unconstitutional and unworthy of the character of straightforward and honest Englishmen.

Lord Palmerston, former Foreign Secretary and future Prime Minister, speech, 1852.

The education fitting a man to decide on the important interests and mighty questions involved in the government of a great nation can never be acquired by those who, because they are earning their bread by daily toil, can never possess the leisure for study or for thought.

The Earl of Harrowby, 1852.

I doubt very much whether a democracy is a government that would suit this country.

Benjamin Disraeli, 1865.

Democracy cannot survive another world war.

David Lloyd George, British Prime Minister during World War I, interviewed in the *News Chronicle*, 1936.

Democracy will be dead by 1950.

John Langdon-Davies, *A Short History of the Future*, 1936.

Democracy is finished in England.

Joseph P. Kennedy, US ambassador to the United Kingdom, interviewed in the *Boston Globe*, November 1940.

I intend to open the country up to democracy, and anyone who is against this I will jail, I will crush.

President João Figueredo of Brazil, inauguration speech, 1979.

Dictators

Field Marshal Idi Amin

GOOD LUCK TO PRESIDENT AMIN ...
GOOD RIDDANCE TO OBOTE
General Amin, a beefy, softly-spoken man of the Madi tribe, sets an example of self-restraint. First reports seem to suggest ... a military government which, with any luck, may turn out to be of like nature and ambitions to those which have successfully brought law and order and relatively clean administration to Ghana and Nigeria.

Daily Telegraph, editorial, January 1971.

THE CHAMP WHO ROSE FROM THE RANKS TO SEIZE POWER
Military men are trained to act. Not for them the posturing of the Obotes or the Kaundas who prefer the glory of the international platform rather than the dull but necessary task of running a smooth administration. Amin looks capable of that task.

Daily Express, editorial, January 1971.

A thoroughly nice man ... as gentle as a lamb.

Daily Mirror, editorial, January 1971.

Without doubt a benevolent, honest, dedicated and hardworking man.

Financial Times, editorial, 1972.

One feels Uganda cannot afford General Amin's warmhearted generosity.

The Times, editorial, 1972.

In view of the success of my economic revolution in Uganda, I offer myself to be appointed Head of the Commonwealth.

Message to Her Majesty Queen Elizabeth II, 1975.

As conqueror of the British Empire I am prepared to die in defence of the motherland, Uganda.

Broadcast shortly before fleeing to Libya as Tanzanian troops invaded in support of Ugandan opposition forces, April 1979.

During his eight years of dictatorship, Amin robbed and expelled Uganda's Asian population, bankrupted its economy, and murdered some 300,000 of its citizens.

See also PRISONS

Fidel Castro

Señor Castro has been accused of Communist sympathies, but this means very little since all opponents of the regime are automatically called Communists. In fact he is further to the right than General Batista.

The Economist, 26 April 1958, on Cuba's future Marxist dictator.

I give Castro a year. No longer.

Cuba's deposed dictator, Fulgencio Batista, on the prospects of his successor, 1959. In 1998 Fidel Castro celebrated 40 years in office with a visit from Pope John Paul II.

See also THE CIA

Eastern Europe

I was only giving these men their say. I should not be taken as agreeing with them.

Robert Maxwell, owner of the Pergamon Press, refutes allegations that various biographies of Eastern European dictators, written and published by him, were nothing more than propaganda pieces designed to ingratiate him with their subjects and enable his companies to trade in their countries, 1986.

The following extracts are from biographies written, in the form of question-and-answer sessions, by Robert Maxwell and published by Pergamon Press:

Dear Mr President, how do you explain the fact that you have been holding the highest political state post in your country for such a long time?

Todor Zhivkov: Statesman and Builder of New Bulgaria, 1982.

I wish you good health and power to continue your constant, tireless activity for the good of your country.

Ceausescu: builder of Modern Rumania and International Statesman, 1983.

Hungary had no alternative but to call for the military help of the Soviet Union to prevent a civil war.

János Kádár: Selected Speeches and Interviews, 1985.

All three dictators were removed from power by their own people in the uprisings of 1989. Ceausescu and his wife were tried and shot.

See also ROBERT MAXWELL

Adolf Hitler

The story of Hitler's struggle cannot be read without admiration for the courage, the perseverance, and the vital force which enabled him to challenge, defy, conciliate, and overcome all the authorities and resistance in his path.

Winston Churchill reviews *Mein Kampf* in *Great Contemporaries*, 1937.

My uncle is a peaceful man. He thinks war is not worth the candle.

The dictator's nephew, Willie Hitler, 1937.

I do not consider Hitler to be as bad as he is depicted. He is showing an ability that is amazing and he seems to be gaining his victories without much bloodshed.

Mohandas (Mahatma) Gandhi, remark to Rajkumari Amrit, May 1940.

Thank God, I've always avoided persecuting my enemies.

Adolf Hitler, 1941.

No-one would go to Hitler's funeral if he was alive today.

Labour MP Ron Brown, 1989.

See also NAZI GERMANY, POLITICIANS' PROMISES *and* WORLD WAR II

Ferdinand Marcos

We love your adherence to democratic principles – and to the democratic process.

US vice-president George Bush salutes, in 1983, the President of the Philippines, whose democratic actions included the rigging of elections and the assassination of Benigno Aquino, the opposition leader whose widow, Corazón, became president after Marcos was overthrown in 1986.

Mobutu Sese Seko

If you want to steal, steal a little cleverly, in a nice way. If you steal so much as to become rich overnight, you will be caught.

The dictator of Zaire, speech on corruption, 1976. He stole an estimated $5 billion from his country's treasury.

See also ZAIRE

Benito Mussolini

I could not help being charmed, as so many other people have been, by Signor Mussolini's gentle and simple bearing and by his calm detached poise in spite of so many burdens and dangers.

Winston Churchill, writing in *The Times*, 21 January 1927.

There can be no doubt as to the verdict of future generations on his achievement. He is the greatest figure of our age. Mussolini will dominate the 20th century as Napoleon dominated the early nineteenth.

The *Daily Mail* of 28 March 1928 publishes the thoughts of its proprietor, Lord Rothermere, who later was to describe Hitler as 'a perfect gentleman'.

Ignorant and prejudiced people talk of Italian affairs as if that nation were subject to some tyranny which it would willingly throw off. With that rather morbid commiseration for fanatical minorities which is the rule with certain imperfectly informed sections of British public opinion, this country long ago shut its eyes to the magnificent work that the Fascist régime was doing. I have several times heard Mussolini himself express his gratitude to the *Daily Mail* as having been the first British newspaper to put his aims fairly before the world.

Ward Price, the *Daily Mail*, 1932.

Park Chung Hee

We have no political prisoners – only Communists and others involved in conspiracies against the country.

President Park Chung Hee of South Korea displays his credentials in 1974.

General Augusto Pinochet

I was only an aspirant dictator, not a real one. History teaches you that dictators never end up well.

The former dictator of Chile, interviewed in the *New Yorker* on 16 October 1998. Shortly afterwards, on a visit to London, he was arrested on an extradition warrant from Spain to face charges of hostage-taking, torture, and murder.

THE MAN WHO WILL SEND PINOCHET HOME

Jack Straw would no more extradite General Pinochet to Spain than he would lie about his age – 52 – in order to be the oldest swinger on a Club 18–30 holiday ... There will barely have been a doubt in his mind that, one way or another, the old dictator would have to be sent home ... Even if Salvadore Allende had been Jack Straw's brother-in-law, the over-arching symbolism of a government that takes symbolism very seriously would still conspire to send Pinochet home.

Siôn Simon, associate editor of the *Spectator*, writing in the *Independent on Sunday*, 6 December 1998. On 9 December the British Home Secretary, Jack Straw, announced that General Pinochet was to remain in Britain to face extradition hearings.

Joseph Stalin

Gaiety is the outstanding feature of the Soviet Union.

Stalin's comment after watching a display of folk-dancing by collectivized farm workers to mark his birthday in 1935.

There is something else in him besides this revolutionary Bolshevist thing. ... I think that something [has] entered into his nature of the way in which a Christian gentleman should behave.

US President Franklin D. Roosevelt briefs his Cabinet on Stalin after the Yalta Conference, 1945, citing the dictator's early training for the priesthood.

This great man of the Soviet peoples struck me as a wise, kindly old man. His eyes reflect peace and kindness; that is why the peoples he is leading are so attached to him.

The president of the Yugoslav Smallholders' Party after a meeting in 1948.

Disease: Cause and Cure

All diseases of Christians are to be ascribed to demons.

St Augustine, AD 354–430.

You know, Tolstoy, like myself, wasn't taken in by superstitions like science and medicine.

George Bernard Shaw (quoted in *Facts and Fallacies*, by Chris Morgan and David Langford, 1981).

Anæsthesia

The abolishment of pain in surgery is a chimera. It is absurd to go on seeking it ... Knife and pain are two words in surgery that must forever be associated in the consciousness of the patient. To this compulsory combination we shall have to adjust ourselves.

Dr Alfred Velpeau, professor at the Paris Faculty of Medicine, 1839.

Bacteria

Pasteur's theory of germs is a ridiculous fiction. How do you think that these germs in the air can be numerous enough to develop into all these organic infusions? If that were true, they would be numerous enough to form a thick fog, as dense as iron.

Physiologist Professor Pierre Pochet, 1872.

The simplest way to kill most microbes is to throw them into an open street or river and let the sun shine on them, which explains that when great cities have recklessly thrown all their sewage into the open river the water has sometimes been cleaner twenty miles below the city than thirty miles above it ... In the first frenzy of microbe killing, surgical instruments were dipped in carbolic oil. Microbes are so fond of carbolic oil that they thrive in it.

George Bernard Shaw, preface to *The Doctor's Dilemma*, 1911.

A genuine kiss generates so much heat it destroys germs.

Dr S. L. Katzoff, San Francisco Institute of Human Relations, April 1940.

Blindness

It's a scientific fact that if you shave your moustache, you weaken your eyes.

William 'Alfalfa Bill' Murray, governor of Oklahoma, quoted in 1932.

Cancer

No illness is more simple to cure than cancer (this also applies to mental diseases and heart trouble) through a return to the most elementary natural eating and drinking: Diet No. 7.

George Ohsawa, in *Zen Macrobiotics* (1965) recommends whole-grain cereal and minimal liquids.

The Common Cold

He said, 'Macaulay, who writes the account of St Kilda, set out with a prejudice against prejudices, and wanted to be a smart modern thinker; and yet he affirms for a truth, that when a ship arrives there, all the inhabitants are seized with a cold ...

'The late Reverend Mr Christian, of Docking – after ruminating a little, "The cause," (says he) "is a natural one. The situation of St Kilda renders

a North-West Wind indispensably necessary before a stranger can land.
The wind, not the stranger, causes an epidemic cold."'

Dr. Samuel Johnson, recorded by James Boswell, spring 1768. *A Voyage to
St Kilda* was in fact written by Martin Martin.

Epilepsy

The sound of a flute will cure epilepsy, and a sciatic gout.

Theophrastus, c. 370–285 BC.

For epilepsy in adults I recommend spirit of human brain or a powder,
to be compounded only in May, June and July, from the livers of live
green frogs.

Professor Johnann Hartmann, University of Marburg, *Praxis Chymiatrica*,
1633.

Gout

A young man does not take the gout until he indulges in coition.

Hippocrates, c. 469–377 BC.

Headaches

If an ounce of elephant bone is drunk with ten ounces of wild mountain
mint from something which a leper first touched, it does the most for a
headache.

St Albertus Magnus, c. 1250.

Hygiene

Damp baths are to be eschewed except by the rich … And this in
summer only, for in winter I would advise them to abstain from ordinary
baths entirely.

Francis Raspard, physician of Bruges, *A Great and Perpetual Almanack*, 1551.

It may be that it does contain a few good principles, but its scrupulous
application has presented such difficulties that it would be necessary,
in Paris for instance, to place in quarantine the personnel of a hospital
during the great part of a year, and that, moreover, to obtain results that
remain entirely problematical.

Dr Charles Dubois, Paris obstetrician: a memorandum to the French Academy,
23 September 1858, on 'Semmelweis's Procedure' – the recommendation by the
Hungarian obstetrician, Dr Ignaz Simmelweis, that medical staff should wash their
hands between handling dead bodies and examining women who had recently
given birth. Although this resulted in a fall in the death rate at the Viennese
Lying-In Hospital, from 11% to 1%, Semmelweis lost his job.

Lice

If the excrement of an elephant should be smeared on skin in which lice appear and left until it dries upon the skin, the lice will not remain on it but will depart immediately.

St Albertus Magnus, c. 1250.

Malaria

Malaria has been licked.

World Health Organization press release, May 1973. Later the same day, WHO deputy general secretary Dr Tom Lambo was admitted to hospital suffering from malaria. The disease has since made a notable comeback.

Pædiatrics

One half of the children born die before their eighth year. This is Nature's law; why try to contradict it?

Jean-Jacques Rousseau – an admirer of the noble and short-lived savage – in the child-rearing manual *Emile, ou l'éducation*, 1762.

Smallpox

If we are afflicted with smallpox, it is because we had a carnival last winter, feasting the flesh, which has offended the Lord.

Anonymous Roman Catholic priest, Montreal, 1885.

Cowpox ... fails to exercise any specific power against Small Pox.

Edgar Crookshank, professor of comparative pathology and bacteriology, King's College, London: *History and Pathology of Vaccination*, 1889.

It was fancifully represented as an amulet or charm against smallpox, by the idle gossip of incredulous persons who listened only to the jingle of names.

Medical historian Charles Creighton, *Jenner and Vaccination*, 1889.

The medical broadcasters and writers of leading articles still keep repeating like parrots that vaccination abolished smallpox, though vaccinia is now killing more children than smallpox.

George Bernard Shaw, *Everybody's Political What's What*, 1944.

   Thanks, ultimately, to Jenner's cowpox vaccine, smallpox has now been abolished by a worldwide programme of vaccination. The entire planetary population of the smallpox virus is now contained in one laboratory.

Surgery

There cannot always be fresh fields of conquest by the knife; there must be portions of the human frame that will ever remain sacred from its intrusions, at least in the surgeon's hands. That we have already, if not quite, reached these final limits, there can be little question. The abdomen, the chest, and the brain will be forever shut from the intrusion of the wise and humane surgeon.

Sir John Eric Erichsen, later to become the Royal Surgeon: 1837.

Tar-Water

It is not only good in fevers, diseases of the lungs, cancer, scrofula, throat diseases, apoplexies, chronic diseases of all kinds, but also as a general drink for infants.

Bishop Berkeley, *Further Thoughts on Tar-Water*, 1752.

Venereal Disease

Every man who has sexual relations with two women at the same time risks syphilis, even if the two women are faithful to him, for all libertine behaviour spontaneously ignites this disease.

Alexandre Weill, *The Laws and Mysteries of Love*, 1891.

Whisky

If a body could just find out the exact proper proportion and quantity that ought to be drunk every day, and keep to that, I verily trow that he might live forever ... and that doctors and kirkyards would go out of fashion.

James Hogg, c. 1820.

Wounds

If the wound is large, the weapon with which the patient has been wounded should be anointed daily; otherwise, every two to three days. The weapon should be kept in pure linen and in a warm place but not too hot, nor squalid, lest the patient should suffer harm.

Daniel Beckher, *Medicus Microcosmus*, 1622.

See also AIDS, CONCEPTION, CONTRACEPTION, DRUGS, MASTURBATION, MENSTRUATION, SEX *and* SMOKING

Double-entendres

How long is the Minister prepared to hold up the skirts of the Wrens for the convenience of His Majesty's sailors?

Conservative MP Dame Irene Ward, on delays in supplying uniforms for the Women's Royal Naval Service, 1940.

I belong to the fag-end of Victorian liberalism.

Novelist E. M. Forster, not known in his lifetime as a homosexual, BBC Home Service broadcast, 1946.

We are going to play a hiding and finding game! Now, are your balls high up or low down? Close your eyes a minute, and dance around, and look for them. Are they high up? Or are they low down? If you have found your balls, toss them over your shoulder and play with them!

Music and Movement, BBC Home Service for Schools, c. 1957.

The Man Who Is Gunning For Kennedy

Daily Express caption to a picture of President Kennedy's Republican adversary, Barry Goldwater, on 22 November 1963, the day Kennedy was assassinated.

There's Neil Harvey at leg slip, with his legs wide apart waiting for a tickle.

Brian Johnston, BBC cricket commentator, 1950s.

Glenn Turner looks a bit shaky and unsteady, but I think he's going to bat on – one ball left.

Brian Johnston, BBC cricket commentator, 1970s, after Turner had been painfully struck in the 'box area'.

The bowler's Holding, the batsman's Willey.

Brian Johnston describes the scene as West Indian fast bowler Michael Holding bowls to England's Peter Willey, 1976.

Wherever I go in this country, people know there is a problem.

Billie Snedden, leader of the Australian Liberal Party, campaigning during the general election of 1974.

Every Prime Minister should have a Willie.

Margaret Thatcher on her deputy, William Whitelaw, after he was elevated to the House of Lords, 1983.

What the Welsh Assembly needs now to capture the public imagination is, of course, for Ron Davies to get caught with his trousers down.

The *Western Mail*, 26 September 1998, on the Welsh secretary and Labour candidate for leader of the Welsh Assembly. On 26 October he resigned, following a mysterious and unfortunate encounter on Clapham Common.

See also BROADCASTING BOOBS, CRICKET *and*
POLITICIANS' GAFFES

Drugs

Among the remedies which it has pleased Almighty God to give to man to relieve his sufferings, none is so universal and so efficacious as opium.

Thomas Sydenham on his tincture of opium, 1670.

Exhilaration and lasting euphoria, which in no way differs from the euphoria of the healthy person ... You perceive an increase in self-control and possess more vitality and capacity for work. In other words, you are simply more normal, and it is soon hard to believe that you are under the influence of any drug.

Sigmund Freud on cocaine, *Uber Coca*, 1884.

Cocaine can take the place of food, make the coward brave, the silent eloquent, free the victims of alcohol and opium habit from their bondage, and, as an anæsthetic, render the sufferer insensitive to pain.

Magazine advertisement, USA, 1885.

It possesses many advantages over morphine ... It is not hypnotic and there is no danger of acquiring the habit.

James R. L. Daly analyses heroin in the *Boston Medical and Surgical Journal*, 1900.

The form that is usually grown in gardens, *C. sativa gigantea*, is an ornamental foliaged plant, and in rich soils will grow 6–10 ft. It is useful for making a quick-growing summer screen, or in groups of three to five plants in a large border or shrubbery. Raise from seed sown in any good garden soil in April. Its foliage is attractive.

Odhams New Illustrated Gardening Encyclopædia, c. 1930, entry under 'Cannabis'.

E

The Earth

It is once and for all clear that the earth is in the middle of the universe and all weights move towards it.

Ptolemy, 2nd century AD.

Is there anyone anywhere so foolish as to think there are Antipodeans – men who stand with their feet opposite to ours, men with their legs in the air and their heads hanging down? Can there be a place on earth where things are upside down, where the trees grow downwards, and the rain, hail and snow fall upward? The mad idea that the earth is round is the cause of this imbecile legend.

Lactantius Firminianus, tutor to Constantine the Great, *De opificio dei*, AD 304.

People give ear to an upstart astrologer who strove to show that the earth revolves, not the heavens or the firmament, the sun and the moon. Whoever wishes to appear clever must devise some new system, which of all systems is of course the very best. This fool wishes to reverse the entire science of astronomy.

Martin Luther on Copernicus, 1543.

Animals, which move, have limbs and muscles; the earth has no limbs and muscles, hence it does not move.

Scipio Chiaramonti, professor of philosophy and mathematics at the University of Pisa, 1633. According to this reasoning, the earth is a cauliflower.

I, Galileo, being in my seventieth year, being a prisoner on my knees, and before your Eminences, having before my eyes the Holy Gospel, which

I touch with my hands, abjure, curse and detest the error and the heresy of the movement of the earth.

The statement Galileo Galilei was obliged to swear to in order to be released from prison in 1634. In 1994 Pope John Paul II offered him a posthumous apology and admitted the Roman Catholic Church had got it wrong. In the same year, a poll suggested that 40% of British people thought the sun revolves around the earth.

The world was created on 22nd October, 4004 BC at 6 o'clock in the evening.

James Ussher, Archbishop of Armagh, *Annals of the World*, 1650–54.

Heaven and earth, centre and circumference, were created together, in the same instant, and clouds full of water ... This work took place and Man was created by the Trinity on the twenty-third of October, 4004 BC, at nine o'clock in the morning.

Dr John Lightfoot, vice-chancellor of Cambridge University, adjusts Archbishop Ussher's calculation in 1659.

Many hypotheses of geotectonics have caused considerable damage to geotectonics, giving non-specialists the impression that this is a field in which the most superficially conceived fantasy reigns. The clearest example is Wegener's theory of continental drift ... fantastic and nothing to do with science.

Soviet academician Vladimir Vladimirovich Belorussov, 1954.

Something will certainly remain after the theory of plate tectonics goes. Let us keep our minds open and look for alternatives. I am sure that in the near future we shall need them.

Vladimir Vladimirovich Belorussov, 1979.

Wegener's theory of continental drift, vilified by geologists when first put forward in the 1920s, gave rise to the science of plate tectonics in the 1960s and is now universally accepted.

The Economy

Germany
During the past two years it has been asserted with increasing frequency and vehemence that if, somehow, the German economy could be freed

from materials and manpower regulations, price controls and other bureaucratic paraphernalia, then recovery would be expedited ... Yet there has never been the slightest possibility of getting German recovery by this wholesale repeal, and it is quite possible that its reiteration has delayed German recovery.

Professor J. K. Galbraith, *The German Economy*, 1948. The 'bonfire of controls' begun shortly afterwards by German finance minister Ludwig Erhard led directly to the postwar German 'economic miracle'.

Japan

WHY DISASTER THEORISTS ARE WRONG
The spiralling stock market and property prices of the late Eighties were going to end in tears ... but even this has not happened, as the Bank of Japan and the Ministry of Finance have gently deflated the 'bubble economy' to bring people back to their senses.

Terry McCarthy, 'View From Tokyo', the *Independent*, 15 February 1992.

TEARS FLOW OVER NIKKEI'S MISERY
The Tokyo stock exchange soap opera is going into a new weepie phase ... By Friday morning, with the Nikkei at 18,286, well below the supposed psychological support level of 20,000, it was handkerchief time all round.

Terry McCarthy, 'View From Tokyo', the *Independent*, 14 April 1992.

Russia

Whatever happens to the politics, there will be strong economic growth based on private enterprise. Russia's economy, which is now the size of California's, will grow faster over the next 20 years than that of most OECD countries ... Foreigners will reap good returns ... Those who move fast will gain a special advantage from being first – and from the current undervaluation of Russian assets ...

Professor Richard Layard, of the London School of Economics, *The Coming Russian Boom*, 1997.

In the late summer of 1998 the Russian economy fell apart, trading in the rouble and government debt repayment were suspended, and the entire capitalization of the Moscow stock market fell to less than that of Marks & Spencer. Economic activity in the cities was taken over by gangsters, and the countryside reverted to a barter system.

United Kingdom

The 1970s, barring any major set-to between the major powers, show a steady increase in our national prosperity.

UK multinational chairman Leonard Macham, *The Times*, 30 December 1969.

Despite the lack of superpower confrontation, the 1970s in the UK saw an oil crisis, prolonged miners' and power workers' strikes, a three-day week, a banking scandal, inflation running up to 28% per annum, and the necessity for an emergency loan from the IMF. The decade closed with the 'Winter of Discontent'.

ECONOMIC RECOVERY BEGINS TO BLOSSOM

Each week, we will note the economic news, and assign it Green Shoots points. A sighting of a blossom, such as a surge in gross national product, would merit five points, but a withering of the bud, such as a collapse in retail sales, would merit minus five.

The Sunday Times, 26 April 1992 (front page).

Recently there have been as many brown as green shoots, with few signs of sustained growth. We are therefore suspending the index until new signs of growth appear.

The Sunday Times, 5 July 1992 (back page).

Like his predecessor, John Major is not for turning. Once he has negoti-ated a deal or made a promise, he stands by it ... Last night ... he said that even if other countries devalue or revalue their currency in the European exchange rate mechanism, Britain will not join in. Mr Major's speech should help steady the pound in the difficult days ahead.

Daily Express, editorial, 11 September 1992.

The Chancellor won a spectacular victory over the Germans last night – paving the way for a dramatic cut in interest rates.

Daily Mail, 14 September 1992.

When the market opens this morning ... it would not be surprising if the pound also strengthened its position against the mark. Shares should also leap as the prospect of interest rate rises finally recedes.

Daily Mail city editor Tom McGhie, 14 September 1992.

For Britain, last night's package should ensure that sterling holds above its floor in the ERM for the five days remaining until the French vote.

The Times, editorial, 14 September 1992.

Devaluation in Italy ... may encourage the markets to celebrate their victory over the lira by taking a pot shot at the next weakest currency in the ERM, the pound. The evidence of yesterday is that this will not happen and that if the markets did they could be repelled.

Hamish McRae, the *Independent*, 15 September 1992.

Sterling will be an altogether tougher nut to crack, with the reserves newly bolstered.

Daily Telegraph, City Comment, 16 September 1992.

By noon on Wednesday 16 September 1992 the Bank of England base rate was at a peacetime record of 15H% and some £15 billion of reserves had been spent by the Treasury in an effort to stem selling of sterling and keep it at its desired rate within the Exchange Rate Mechanism of the EU. Later that day Britain quit the ERM and allowed sterling to float; it immediately fell by 30% against the mark.

REPOSSESSIONS FALL

Sunday Telegraph headline, 25 July 1993, page 2.

REPOSSESSIONS STILL RISING

Sunday Telegraph headline, 25 July 1993, page 37.

Last Wednesday the Chancellor and the Governor of the Bank of England decided to leave base rates unchanged, almost certainly until November or later.

Gavyn Davies, comparing himself favourably with 'the average newshound', the *Independent*, 12 September 1994. Base rates were raised by 0.5% at 11am the same day.

The growth of post neo-classical endogenous growth theory and the symbiotic relationships between growth and investment.

Gordon Brown MP, Labour shadow Chancellor, speech, 1994. When it was revealed that the speech had been written by his adviser, Ed Balls, the Conservative Michael Heseltine commented: "We thought it was Brown's – but it was Balls'!"

Bank of England governor Eddie George faces the sack if Tony Blair wins power, Labour insiders said last night. He would be the first victim of Gordon Brown's determination to 'purge the establishment' and put his own stamp on economic management. Mr Brown is clearly intent on cutting the power of the governor.

Daily Mail, 1 May 1997. Mr Brown's first act on becoming Chancellor of the Exchequer was to give the Governor of the Bank of England, as chairman of an independent advisory committee, the power to set the base lending rate. All previous chancellors had retained this power for themselves.

The USA

Branch banking ... will mean, I suggest in all humility, the beginning of the end of the capitalist system.

John T. Flynn, 'The Dangers of Branch Banking', *The Forum*, April 1933.

This is the end of Western civilization.

Lewis Douglas, US budget director, on President Roosevelt's decision to take the USA off the gold standard, 18 April 1933.

If we are to begin to try and understand life as it will be in 1960, we must begin by realizing that food, clothing and shelter will cost as little as air.

John Langdon-Davies, *A Short History of the Future*, 1936.

There will be no cars, radios, washing machines or refrigerators after the war ... The post-war world will be so poor that women will have to return to their grand-mother's spinning wheel and men will have to build their own cottages.

Dr Hans Elias of Middlesex University, Waltham, Massachusetts, *New York Herald Tribune*, 2 October 1942.

After the war no American will be allowed to receive more than $25,000 a year.

Quincy Howe, CBS news analyst, 'Twelve Things the War Will Do to America', *Harper's*, November 1942.

During the next four years ... unless drastic steps are taken by Congress, the US will have nearly 8,000,000 unemployed and will stand on the brink of a deep depression.

Henry A. Wallace, US secretary of commerce, November 1945. Between 1945 and 1950 the US economy grew by 50%, while unemployment briefly touched a peak of just under 4 million.

When the US government stops wasting our resources by trying to maintain the price of gold, it will sink to $6 an ounce rather than the current $35 an ounce.

Henry Reuss, chairman of the Joint Economic Committee of Congress, 1967. The US government stopped buying gold in 1971; by 1981 the price had risen to $840 an ounce. In November 1998 it stood at $297.

The World

In all likelihood, world inflation is over.

Per Jacobsson, managing director of the International Monetary Fund, 1959.

See also BUSINESS AND FINANCE, THE GREAT DEPRESSION, POLITICIANS' PROMISES *and* THE WALL STREET CRASH

Education

I do not think ... that the occupiers of land and houses should be taxed in order that all the children in the country should be taught to read and write, especially when it is doubtful whether writing will be of any real use.

Nicholas Vansittart, secretary to the Treasury, 1807.

I do not believe ... it will be possible if desirable, or desirable if possible, to establish a system of compulsory education in this country.

Lord Brougham, 1837.

A system of national compulsory education might do very well for a country in which the government is truly despotic but I do not think that it would do well for such a country like this.

Sir Benjamin Hall MP, 1847.

To give education gratuitously will only degrade the education so given in the estimation of the parents.

Lord Robert Montagu, opposing free education, 1870.

It has been said that children should be kept at school until fourteen years of age; but the amount and importance of the labour which lads between ten and fourteen can perform should not be ignored. Since the present educational system has come into operation, the weeds have very much multiplied in Norfolk which was once regarded as quite the garden of England, weeding being particularly the work of children whose labour is cheap, whose sight is keen, bodies flexible and fingers nimble.

Earl Fortesque, 1880.

To develop resource-based learning as a substitute for, rather than an addition to, traditional teaching and learning strategies.

Part of the 'mission statement' of Mike Fitzgerald, vice-chancellor of Thames

Valley University, 1993, after lecturers had passed a vote of no confidence in him by 181 votes to 12. Following reports that the pass mark had been dropped from 40% to 30% and that external examiners had expressed alarm over the results of 'resource-based learning', the Quality Assurance Agency reported that the university had 'lost sight of basic principles'. Fitzgerald resigned.

Elections

United Kingdom

I intend to see to it that you have a government that is capable of leading the country through the difficult times ahead.

Prime Minister Edward Heath, calling the February 1974 British general election.

Who Governs Britain?

Conservative election slogan, February 1974, following a wave of strike action and the imposition of a three-day week. The electorate chose Labour.

Take Power – Vote Liberal

Liberal election slogan, February 1974. The Liberal Party finished third.

I am not proposing to seek your votes because there is blue sky ahead today.

British Prime Minister James Callaghan, explaining his decision not to call an election in September 1978. The 'Winter of Discontent' followed and Labour lost the election of May 1979.

Labour Isn't Working

Conservative poster slogan, under an image of a very long dole queue, 1979, when unemployment topped one million. Under the Conservative government it topped 3 million in 1982, and stayed there for five years.

The forthcoming general election will be the most open battle in recent political history.

Roy Hattersley MP, Labour spokesman on Home Affairs, March 1983. The general election in June resulted in a Conservative majority of 144, the biggest since 1945. Labour recorded the lowest popular vote ever for a principal party of opposition.

In less than two years there will be a Labour government in Britain. I waste no time in justifying that assertion.

Roy Hattersley, deputy leader of the Labour Party, September 1986. The Conservatives remained in power until 1997.

Lawson helped bring about the second army of unemployed and the failed businesses whose condition now seems likely to drive the Tories disgraced out of power ... Mr Kinnock was magnificent. The party he made, now poised for power tomorrow ... Unless all polls are nonsense, which I don't believe, or my perceptions are worthless, something I humbly doubt ....

Edward Pearce of the *Guardian* forecasts a Labour victory in the British general election of April 1992, which the Conservatives won with a majority of twenty seats.

LABOUR NOSEDIVES IN NEW POLL
Voters' Doubts Begin to Turn Tide for Tories

Headlines, *Sunday Telegraph*, 13 April 1997.

Victory on May Day is by no means in the bag for Tony Blair, and there are no signs of the Labour landslide suggested by the opinion polls .... John Major still has everything to play for.

Anthony Bevins, political editor of the *Independent*, 21 April 1997.

LABOUR'S LEAD IN FREEFALL

Headline, *Daily Express*, 23 April 1997.

At the time of writing, I do not believe that Mr Blair is on course to win the 57 seats he would need for an outright win. There could well be another election within a year.

Bruce Anderson, the *Spectator*, 26 April 1997.

A Labour landslide is quite unlikely. Much more probable is a close result, perhaps even a hung Parliament.

David Carlton, lecturer in politics at Warwick University, *Sunday Telegraph*, 27 April 1997.

I believe that John Major, who has fought brilliantly, is on course for a majority of around 30–40.

Woodrow Wyatt, *The Times*, 29 April 1997.

The opinion polls are measuring dislike of the government, not voting intention, and Labour has failed to enthuse people. There's still a mathematical mountain for them to climb for them to win a majority, and they won't make it. A hung Parliament.

Peter Hitchens, assistant editor of the *Daily Express*, in the London *Evening Standard*, 1 May 1997.

The Labour Party won the British general election of 1 May 1997 with a record landslide majority of 176 seats.

It will be strange if there is a landslide.

William Rees-Mogg, *The Times*, 1 May 1997.

Not a surprise, though a somewhat greater avalanche than I had expected.

William Rees-Mogg, *The Times*, 2 May 1997.

Martin Bell and media interference are resented by the tough Tatton Tories. So the despicable Hamilton will almost certainly win at Tatton. Then, if he's expelled from Parliament, it'll still be a Tory seat.

Woodrow Wyatt, *News of the World*, 20 April 1997. Martin Bell, the Independent candidate in the Tatton constituency, defeated the sitting Conservative MP, Neil Hamilton, with a majority of 11,077.

Michael Portillo is fast emerging as the favourite to succeed John Major if the Tories are defeated today.

Daily Mail, 1 May 1997. Michael Portillo lost his seat on 1 May.

The USA

Mr Lincoln is already beaten. He cannot be re-elected.

Horace Greeley, editor, *New York Tribune*, 14 August 1864. Abraham Lincoln defeated General George B. McClellan by 212 Electoral College votes to 21.

He Kept Us Out Of War!

1916 campaign slogan of President Woodrow Wilson, who took the USA into World War I the following year.

A Chicken for Every Pot
Wages, dividends, progress and prosperity say, "Vote for Hoover"
Hoover and Happiness or Smith and Soup Houses? Which Shall It Be?

Republican campaign advertisements, 1928 – the year before the Wall Street Crash.

In 1932 the chimneys will be smoking, the farmers will be getting good crops that will bring good prices, and so Mr Hoover will be re-elected.

New York Herald Tribune, 18 July 1930.

The re-election of President Hoover with at least 270 votes in the electoral college, four in excess of a majority, is predicted in a statistical study of vote percentages in the several states, based on a poll taken by the Hearst publications.

The *New York Times*, 5 November 1932. Franklin D. Roosevelt defeated Herbert Hoover by 472 Electoral College votes to 59.

FDR will be a one-term president.

Mark Sullivan, *New York Herald Tribune*, 1935.

There was a time when the Republicans were scouring the country for a behemoth to pit against him. Now they begin to grasp the fact that … they can beat him with a Chinaman, or even a Republican.

H. L. Mencken on President Franklin D. Roosevelt, *The American Mercury*, March 1936.

The race will not be close at all. Landon will be overwhelmingly elected and I'll stake my reputation as a prophet on it.

William Randolph Hearst, newspaper publisher, August 1936.

I have never been more certain of anything in my life than the defeat of President Roosevelt. By mid-October people will wonder why they ever had any doubt about it.

Paul Block, newspaper publisher, September 1936.

Landon 1,293,669; Roosevelt 972,897: Final Returns in The Digest Poll of Ten Million Voters.
The most extensive straw ballot in the field – the most experienced in view of its twenty-five years of perfecting – the most unbiased in view of its prestige – a poll that has always previously been correct.

The *Literary Digest*, 31 October 1936. Franklin D. Roosevelt defeated Alf Landon by 523 Electoral College votes to 8, and with a record majority of over 11 million popular votes.

Although the answer to the question, *Does Mr Roosevelt want a third term?* is definitely Yes, to the other question, *If he does, can he get it?* the answer is emphatically No.

Frank R. Kent, historian of the Democratic Party, the *American Mercury*, January 1938.

No Man Is Good Three Times

Republican party slogan, 1940. In November 1940 Roosevelt secured a third term in office by defeating Wendell Wilkie.

Had Enough?

Republican Party slogan, 1944. Americans replied by re-electing Roosevelt for a fourth term.

So: it's to be Thomas Edmund Dewey in the White House on January 20, with Earl Warren as backstop in the event of any accident during years just ahead.

'A Look Ahead', *US News and World Report*, 2 July 1948.

FIFTY POLITICAL EXPERTS UNANIMOUSLY PREDICT A DEWEY VICTORY

Headline, *Newsweek*, 11 October 1948.

Dewey is going to be the next President, and you might as well get used to him.

'TRB', the pseudonym of Richard Stroudt, *New Republic*, 25 October 1948.

DEWEY DEFEATS TRUMAN
G. O. P. Sweep Indicated in States

The early edition of the *Chicago Tribune*, 3 November 1948. President Harry S. Truman held the paper up as he posed for photographers, having defeated Dewey by 303 Electoral College votes to 189.

That boy will back out in the final showdown.

General Douglas MacArthur predicts that Dwight D. Eisenhower will not contest the presidency, 1952. Eisenhower did, and won.

He won't have a chance. I hate to see him and Bobby work themselves to death and lose.

Joseph P. Kennedy predicts failure for his son, and future President John F. Kennedy, 1959.

It will be a Johnson–Humphrey ticket again in '68.

US News and World Report, 13 February 1967.

Lyndon Johnson's long legs are very firmly wrapped around the Donkey, and nothing short of an A-bomb – someone else's A-bomb – could knock him off.

National Review, December 1967.

   After the left-wing senator Eugene McCarthy ran him very close for the New Hampshire primary, Lyndon Johnson withdrew from the 1968 presidential contest.

In spite of his strong performance, it would be wrong to take Senator McGovern seriously.

Richmond News Leader, editorial, 8 March 1972.

If I had to put money on it, I'd say that on January 20, 1973, the guy with his hand on the Bible will be John V. Lindsay.

Jerry Bruno and Jeff Greenfield, *The Advance Man*, 1972.

John V. Lindsay dropped out of the campaign after failing in the early primaries; Senator George McGovern won his party's nomination.

Jimmy Carter's Running for WHAT?

Headline chosen by Reg Murphy, editor, for his column in the *Atlanta Constitution* after the governor of Georgia announced his intention to contest the presidency, 10 July 1974.

You really ought to forget about Iowa. It's not your kind of state.

Tom Whitney, Iowa Democratic state chairman, to Hamilton Jordan, political adviser to Jimmy Carter, 1975.

Is Teddy Running? Are You Kidding … Do Birds Sing in the Morning?

Clay S. Felker, editor and publisher of *New York* magazine, 24 March 1975, on Senator Edward Kennedy, who did not run.

Well, I can tell you who it *won't* be … Jimmy Carter will get a little run for his money, but I can't help but think that to most people he looks more like a kid in a bus station with his name pinned on his sweater on his way to summer camp than a President on his way to the White House.

Dick Tuck, 'The Democratic Handicap: Who'll Be Our Next President? Read It Here First', *Playboy*, March 1976.

Jimmy Carter's victory in Iowa propelled him to convincing victory in the Democratic primaries and convention; he then defeated the incumbent president, Gerald Ford.

The consensus among political professionals here is that Edward Kennedy can have the Democratic Presidential nomination anytime he wants it.

Bruce Morton, political commentator of CBS, 7 September 1979. At the Democratic convention, Senator Edward Kennedy was defeated by President Carter on the first ballot.

I would like to suggest that Ronald Reagan is politically dead.

Tom Pettit, NBC political correspondent, *The Today Show*, 22 January 1980. Reagan defeated President Carter in the 1980 election, and served two terms.

It's no exaggeration to say the undecideds could go one way or another.

Republican candidate George Bush, during the presidential campaign of 1988.

Colin Powell is a black Eisenhower; like Eisenhower in 1951, he will defer announcing his candidature for the Presidency until his chosen moment; like Eisenhower, he will win the Republican nomination, defeating an experienced senator previously regarded as the party leader; like Eisenhower, he will be elected by a large majority in November 1996, defeating a weakened Democratic Administration, and, God willing, will be re-elected by an even larger majority in the year 2000.

William Rees-Mogg, *The Times*, 11 September 1995. Colin Powell did not announce his candidature.

See also POLITICS *and* POLITICIANS' PROMISES

Electricity

When the Paris Exhibition closes electric light will close with it and no more will be heard of it.

Professor Erasmus Wilson of the University of Oxford, 1848.

Sub-division of the electric light is an absolute *ignis fatuus*.

Sir William Preece, engineer in chief at the Post Office, in evidence to a British Parliamentary Committee investigating the applications of Edison's incandescent lamp, 1878.

Good enough for our transatlantic friends ... but unworthy of the attention of practical or scientific men.

The British Parliamentary Committee's opinion of Edison's electric light.

Everyone connected with the subject will recognize it as a conspicuous failure.

US Professor Henry Morton, on Edison's incandescent lamp, 1879.

There is no plea which will justify the use of high-tension and alternating currents, either in a scientific or a commercial sense ... My personal desire would be to prohibit entirely the use of alternating currents. They are as unnecessary as they are dangerous.

Thomas Edison, who had invested heavily in his own direct-current system, on Nikola Tesla's rival alternating-current system, 1889.

TRUST YOU AVOID GIGANTIC MISTAKE OF ADOPTION OF ALTERNATING CURRENT

Telegram from Thomas Edison's friend and partner, the eminent British scientist Lord Kelvin, to the Niagara Falls Electric Company, who ignored it.

It can be predicted with all security that in fifty years light will cost one fiftieth of its present price.

The scientist J. B. S. Haldane, 3 February 1927.

A few decades hence, energy may be free – just like the unmetered air.

John von Neumann, winner of the Fermi Award for Science, 1956.

Elvis

Listen, son, you ain't goin' nowhere. You oughta go back to drivin' a truck.

Jim Denny, manager of the Grand Ole Opry, after Elvis Presley's first performance, 25 September 1954.

This boy is a country rooster crowin' who shouldn't be allowed to sing after the sun comes up in the mornin'.

A black Tennessee radio station DJ rejects 'That's All Right, Mama', 1954.

If I play this they'll run me outa town. I gotta play pure an' simple white country music.

A white Tennessee radio station DJ rejects 'That's All right, Mama', 1954.

This is a weapon of the American psychological war aimed at infecting part of the population with a new philosophical outlook of inhumanity ... in order to prepare for war.

The East German magazine *Young World*, 1956.

I tell you flatly, he can't last.

Jackie Gleeson, 1956.

Nothing in this great, free continent is going to make me put that boy on my programme.

Ed Sullivan, 1956. A week later, Elvis Presley appeared on *The Ed Sullivan Show* for a fee of $17,000.

Singing in any form is foreign to Elvis.

Jack Payne, *Daily Mail*, 1956.

Mr Presley has no discernible singing ability ... His phrasing, if it can be called that, consists of the stereotyped variations that go with a beginner's aria in a bath-tub. For the ear he is an unutterable bore.

Jack Gould, *The New York Times*, 1956.

Who will sing 'Blue Suede Shoes' ten years from now?
D. W. Brogan, *Manchester Guardian*, 1956.

See also POP AND ROCK

The End of the World

The world will end by a giant flood on February 20th 1524.
Johannes Stöffler, Tübingen University. Hundreds of people took to the Rhine
on the appointed day, and were drowned when a storm capsized their boats.

The world will be destroyed by fire on April 3rd 1843.
William Miller of New England originally made this prophecy for 1833, but
decided (when it didn't come true) that he must have been a decade out. The
New York Herald published his 1843 prediction, and when a comet appeared in
March his followers, the 'Millerites', began killing themselves and their families
in order to get to heaven early. On 3 April thousands gathered on a hilltop
overlooking Miller's home. On 4 April Miller decided the date must be 7 July,
and told the faithful to dig their own graves and order coffins. He also sold them
special white shrouds for the occasion. On 8 July he announced the date as
21 March 1844. On 22 March 1844 he decided it was 22 October. The 100,000
Millerites had had enough; they dispersed, and one faction formed the Church
of the Seventh Day Adventists.

The world then to an end will come
In Eighteen Hundred and Eighty-One.
The Life and Prophecies of Ursula Sontheil (Mother Shipton), 1881 edition.

The world then at an end we'll view
In Eighteen Hundred and Eighty-Two.
The Life and Prophecies of Ursula Sontheil (Mother Shipton), 1882 edition.

The world then to an end will come
In Nineteen Hundred and Ninety-One.
The Life and Prophecies of Ursula Sontheil (Mother Shipton), later editions.
The work, allegedly written in 1488, was a hoax perpetrated by Charles Hindley,
a London bookseller and publisher who unmasked himself in *Notes and Queries*
on 26 April 1873. But what he had started, others carried on.

My figures coincide in fixing 1950 as the year when the world must
go smash.
US historian Henry Adams, *Letters*, 22 March 1903.

The deliverance of the saints must take place some time before 1914.

Charles Taze Russell, founder of the Jehovah's Witnesses, *Studies in the Scripture*, vol. 3, 1910 edition.

The deliverance of the saints must take place some time after 1914.

Charles Taze Russell, *Studies in the Scripture*, vol. 3, 1923 edition.

If Christ does not appear to meet his 144,000 faithful shortly after midnight on February 6th or 7th, it means that my calculations, based on the Bible, must be revised.

Margaret Bowen, leader of the Church of Advanced Adventists, who foretold that the Messiah would come to Hollywood in 1925. So far as is known, He didn't.

The Pyramid symbolism, when considered in conjunction with biblical prophecy, indicates that its message is addressed to the present era, and that the final Time of Tribulation, so often prophesied in the Bible, is now upon us.

D. Davidson and H. Aldersmith, in *The Great Pyramid: Its Divine Message*, 1924, calculated that the world would end on 6 September 1936.

A very real problem was, and still is, to ascertain the literal significance and character of the epoch whose crisis date was 6 September 1936.

George F. Riffert, in *Great Pyramid Proof of God*, attempts to explain the failure of the world to end on 6 September 1936; many pyramidologists decided the epochal event must have been the abdication of King Edward VIII.

The 1940 edition of *The Great Pyramid: Its Divine Message* gave 20 August 1953 as the date of the Second Coming.

I think the world is going to blow up in seven years. The public is entitled to a good time during those seven years.

Henry Luce, publisher of *Time*, *Life* and *Fortune*, explains his decision to publish *Sports Illustrated* in 1960. He died in 1967.

Moses made mistakes, Abraham made mistakes, David made mistakes, Elijah made mistakes ...

Herbert W. Armstrong, publisher of *The Plain Truth*, explains why the world did not end in 1972, as he foretold.

A great king of terror will descend from the skies
The year 1999, seventh month,
To resuscitate the great king of Angolmois,
Around this time Mars will reign for the good cause.

Quatrain from the *Centuries* of Nostradamus (Michel de Notredame, physician
to Charles IX of France), 1555–58. If you are reading this, you are probably
in a position to know if it was Regrettable.

The Environment

The Ford engineering staff, although mindful that automobile engines
produce exhaust gases, feels these waste vapours are dissipated
in the atmosphere quickly and do not present an air pollution
problem.

Dan J. Chabek, Ford spokesman, letter to Kenneth Hahn, Los Angeles County
supervisor, who had expressed concern about the health risks of vehicle
exhaust gases, March 1953.

A tree's a tree. How many more do you need to look at?

Ronald Reagan, candidate for the governorship of California, quoted in the
Sacramento *Bee*, 12 March 1966. On 14 September he told the *Bee*, 'I don't
believe a tree is a tree and if you've seen one you've seen them all.'

Approximately 80% of our air pollution stems from hydrocarbons
released by vegetation, so let's not go overboard setting and enforcing
tough emission standards for man-made sources.

Presidential candidate Ronald Reagan, press conference, 10 September 1980.

I know Teddy Kennedy had fun at the Democratic convention when he
said that I said that trees and vegetation cause 80% of the air pollution in
this country. Well, he was a little wrong about what I said. First of all,
I didn't say 80%, I said 92%, 93%, pardon me. And I didn't say air
pollution, I said oxides of nitrogen.

Ronald Reagan, speech, 9 October 1980.
   Trees and other plants absorb carbon dioxide and emit oxygen.

It's exciting to have a real crisis on your hands, when you have spent half
your political life dealing with humdrum things like the environment.

Margaret Thatcher, British Prime Minister, TV interview, 14 May 1982, on
the Falklands conflict.

Their real thrust is not clean air, or clean water, or parks, or wildlife but the fork of government under which America will live … Look what happened to Germany in the 1930s. The dignity of man was subordinated to the powers of Nazism. The dignity of man was subordinated in Russia … Those are the forces this thing can evolve into.

James G. Watt, US secretary of the interior, quoted in *Business Week*, 24 January 1983, on the dangers of environmentalists.

But, Michael, there is no such thing as raw, untreated sewage.

Margaret Thatcher, interviewed by Michael Buerk for BBC TV, 1989.

We've already hunted the grey whale into extinction twice.

TV performer Andrea Arnold, interviewed on ITV in May 1990.

The European Union

We are becoming the United States of Europe under German leadership, a united European continent nobody ever hoped to see.

Kaiser Wilhelm II writes to his sister, 3 November 1940.

The future treaty which you are discussing has no chance of being agreed; if it was agreed, it would have no chance of being ratified; if it was ratified, it would have no chance of being applied. And if it was applied, it would be totally unacceptable to Britain. You speak of agriculture, which we don't like, of power over customs, which we take exception to, and of institutions, which frighten us. *Monsieur le président, messieurs, au revoir et bonne chance!*

Russell Bretherton, an official of the UK Board of Trade who was sent to Messina to attend the inaugural conference of the European Coal and Steel Community, the forerunner of the European Economic Community (itself the ancestor of the European Union), in 1955. Two years later, France, West Germany, Belgium, the Netherlands, Luxembourg, and Italy signed the Treaty of Rome.

There is no question of an erosion of essential national sovereignty.

Edward Heath, British Prime Minister, July 1971, on Britain's entry to the European Community (the immediate forerunner of the European Union).

Of course, those of us who knew were perfectly well aware of it.

Edward Heath, 1995, on the erosion of Britain's sovereignty when she joined the EC.

We'll negotiate a withdrawal from the EEC which has drained our natural resources and destroyed jobs.

Tony Blair, election address to the voters of Sedgefield, 1983.

I have always believed that our country can prosper best within Europe.

Tony Blair, campaigning for the Labour leadership, June 1994.

That is not on the agenda.

Nigel Lawson MP, Chancellor of the Exchequer, dismisses plans for a single European currency on the grounds that it would lead to a United States of Europe, September 1989.

It's a German racket to take over the whole of Europe. You might just as well give it to Hitler.

Nicholas Ridley MP, British Secretary of State for trade and industry, writing in the *Spectator*, 14 July 1990, on monetary union. He resigned that day.

Maastricht is dead. Historians will probably see the Treaty as a bit of a fossil.

Norman Lamont MP, Chancellor of the Exchequer, on the Maastricht Treaty the day before the Prime Minister, John Major, signed it on 14 February 1992. Lamont lost his job the following year.

I hope my fellow heads of government will resist the temptation to recite the mantra of full economic and monetary union as if nothing had changed. If they do recite it, it will have all the quaintness of a rain dance and about as much potency.

John Major, British Prime Minister, *The Economist*, September 1993. Full monetary union – and increasing economic harmonization – began for most EU member countries (but not Britain) with the introduction of the Euro on 1 January 1999.

The French are a nation of collaborators ... Germany's unique contribution to Europe has been to plunge it into two World Wars ... French wine is mostly inferior to that of Australia but in their own rule-twisting way it's probably hard for the French to find that out for themselves ... The purpose of the Government's European policy is to avoid being thrown into some bastardized, federalized, European destiny, actively and fawningly crawling to France and Germany as the lesser countries insult us to the tune of their begging bowls ... I wish I was not in the Community.

Patrick Nicholls MP, vice-chairman of the Conservative Party, writing in the *Western Morning News* of 23 November 1994. He resigned his post that evening.

Evolution

If the book is true, the labours of sober induction are in vain; religion is a lie; human law is a mass of folly, and a base injustice; morality is moonshine, our labours for the black people of Africa were works of madness; and man and woman are better beasts.

Adam Sedgwick, Woodwardian Professor of Geology at the University of Cambridge, on Robert Chambers' *The Vestiges of Creation*, 1844. The almost uniformly hostile reception of Chambers' book, which put forward a version of what was to become the Darwinian theory of evolution, prompted Darwin to delay publication of his own *On the Origin of Species by Means of Natural Selection* for several years.

This year ... has not, indeed, been marked by any of those striking discoveries which at once revolutionize, so to speak, the department of science in which they occur.

Thomas Bell, president of the Linnean Society, sums up its proceedings for 1858. This was the year in which the Linnean Society was presented with Darwin and Wallace's epoch-making papers on evolution by natural selection.

I have read your book with more pain than pleasure. Parts of it I admired greatly, parts I laughed at until my sides were almost sore; other parts I read with absolute sorrow, because I think them utterly false and grievously mischievous. You have deserted ... the true method of induction.

Professor Adam Sedgwick, letter to Charles Darwin following the publication of *On the Origin of Species by Means of Natural Selection*, 1859.

I trust to outlive this mania.

Louis Agassiz, professor of geology at Harvard University: letter written following publication of *On the Origin of Species*, and published posthumously in 1893.

Archaeological remains show no trace of any emergence from barbarism on the part of man, indeed man has gained nothing of moment from the dawn of history. Man's earliest state was his best.

Sir J. W. Dawson, professor of geology and principal of McGill University, *Origin of the World*, 1877.

All the ills from which America suffers can be traced back to the teaching of evolution. It would be better to destroy every other book ever written, and save just the first three verses of Genesis.

William Jennings Bryan, three times Democratic presidential candidate, former US Secretary of State, and a prosecuting attorney in the 'Tennessee Monkey Trial' of John T. Scopes, a teacher prosecuted for instructing his classes in evolution; 1924.

It shall be unlawful for any teacher in any of the universities, normals, and all other public schools of the state which are supported in whole or in part by the public funds of the state, to teach any theory that denies the story of the divine creation of man as taught in the Bible, and to teach instead that man has descended from a lower state of animals.

Statute of the State of Tennessee, 1925. It was not repealed until 1967.

As for camouflage, this is not always easily explicable on neo-Darwinian premises. If polar bears are dominant in the Arctic, then there would seem to have been no need for them to evolve a white-coloured form of camouflage.

Hugh Montefiore, Bishop of Birmingham, in *The Probability of God,* 1985, misses the point about how polar bears came to be dominant in the first place.

See also HOAXES

Executions

Executions are so much a part of British history that it is almost impossible for many excellent people to think of the future without them.

Viscount Templewood (Sir Samuel Hoare), *In the Shadow of the Gallows,* 1951.

If we had the death penalty, [they] would have been forgotten ... We shouldn't have had all those campaigns to get them released.

Lord Denning, former Master of the Rolls, August 1990, on the Birmingham Six, who were jailed for life in 1975 for the IRA Birmingham pub bombings, and released in 1991 after the Court of Appeal declared the verdicts unsafe.

Killer Nick Ingram fried to death at midnight in an American jail's electric chair ... Crowds outside Jackson prison, near Atlanta, Georgia, cheered as the switch was pulled at 7pm local time ... Ingram was pronounced dead by doctors more than twenty minutes later.

John Burke-Davies' graphic eye-witness account in the UK *Daily Sport* of 7 April 1995 betrayed the fact that he was based in Manchester (England) rather than Manchester (Connecticut, Kentucky, New Hampshire, Pennsylvania, Tennessee, or Vermont). Ingram was granted a 24-hour stay of execution, and was electrocuted the following day.

I favour capital punishment. It saves lives.

Nancy Reagan.

Capital punishment is our society's recognition of the sanctity of human life.

Senator Orrin Hatch of Utah, 1988.

F

The Falklands War

Our judgement is that the presence of the Royal Marines garrison ... is sufficient deterrent against any possible aggression.

Margaret Thatcher, Prime Minister, February 1982. Argentina invaded the Falkland Islands six weeks later.

The British won't fight.

General Leopold Galtieri, dictator of Argentina, in discussion with US Secretary of State Alexander Haig in April 1982, a week after his invasion of the Falklands.

The task force involves enormous risks. I say that it will cost this country a far greater humiliation than we have already suffered ... The attempt will fail.

Tony Benn MP on the sailing of the Royal Navy task force to recapture the Falklands, April 1982. Argentinian forces surrendered on 14 June; Galtieri was ejected from office three days later.

Families

By 1975 parents will have ceased to bring up their children in private family units ... Sexual feeling and marriage will have nothing to do with each other.

John Langdon-Davies, *A Short History of the Future*, 1936.

The nuclear family is the cornerstone of women's oppression. It enforces heterosexuality and imposes the prevailing masculine and feminine character structures on the next generation.

Professor Alison Jagger, chairperson of the Committee on the Status of Women in

Philosophy, American Philosophical Association; quoted by John Taylor in *Are You Politically Correct?*, New York, 21 January 1991.

It is in everyone's interests to reduce broken families and the number of single parents; I have seen from my constituency the consequences of marital breakdown.

Conservative MP Tim Yeo, 1994 – shortly before it was revealed that he had had a mistress and had fathered an illegitimate child.

Fascism

Fascism is a religion; the twentieth century will be known as the century of Fascism.

Benito Mussolini, on Hitler's taking power, 1933.

HURRAH FOR THE BLACKSHIRTS!

Headline, *Daily Mail*, 1934, above a report of a rally of Sir Oswald Mosley's British Union of Fascists.

So great a man … so wise a ruler.

Winston Churchill MP on Mussolini, 1935.

Before the organization of the Blackshirt movement free speech did not exist in this country … We shall reach the helm within five years.

Sir Oswald Mosley, leader of the British Union of Fascists, 1938.

I am not, and never have been, a man of the right. My position was on the left and is now in the centre of politics.

Sir Oswald Mosley, former leader of the British Union of Fascists, letter to *The Times*, 1978.

See also DICTATORS, NAZI GERMANY *and* WORLD WAR II

Film

Cinema

My invention can be exploited for a certain time as a scientific curiosity, but apart from that it has no commercial value whatsoever.

Auguste Lumière, co-inventor of the Lumière motion-picture camera, 1895.

It is probable that the fad will die out in the next few years.

The *Independent* (US), 17 March 1910.

The cinema is little more than a fad. It's canned drama. What audiences really want to see is flesh and blood on the stage.

Charlie Chaplin, c. 1916.

Talking Pictures

The talking motion picture will not supplant the regular motion picture ... There is such a tremendous investment to pantomime pictures that it would be absurd to disturb it.

Thomas Edison, quoted in *Munsey's Magazine*, March 1913.

We talk of the worth, the service, the entertaining power, the community value, the recreative force, the educational influence, the civilizing and commercial possibilities of the motion picture. And everyone has, singularly enough, neglected to mention its rarest and subtlest beauty: Silence ... The talking picture will be made practical, but it will never supersede the motion picture without sound.

James R. Quirk, editor and publisher of *Photoplay*, May 1921.

It will never be possible to synchronize the voice with the pictures.

D. W. Griffith, pioneer film-maker, co-founder of United Artists, and director of the silent epics *Birth of a Nation* and *Intolerance*, 1924.

Talking films are a very interesting invention, but I do not believe that they will remain long in fashion. First of all, perfect synchronization between sound and image is absolutely impossible, and, secondly, cinema cannot, and must not, become theatre.

Louis-Jean Lumière, co-inventor of the Lumière motion-picture camera in 1895, quoted in *Films sonores avant*, 1928.

Who the hell wants to hear actors talk?

Harry M. Warner, president of Warner Brothers Pictures, c. 1927.

Films

Breakfast at Tiffany's

Well, I can tell you one thing, Blake: the song has got to go.

Marty Rackin, head of production at Paramount, to director Blake Edwards, on the song *Moon River*.

Gone With the Wind

Forget it, Louis. No Civil War picture ever made a nickel.

Irving Thalberg, MGM production executive, advises Louis B. Mayer not to bid for the film rights of Margaret Mitchell's novel, 1936.

Irving knows what's right.

Louis B. Mayer, co-founder of MGM, taking Thalberg's advice, 1936.

I wouldn't pay fifty thousand bucks for any damn book any damn time.

Jack L. Warner, of Warner Brothers, 1936.

Gone With the Wind is going to be the biggest flop in Hollywood history. I'm just glad it'll be Clark Gable who's falling flat on his face and not Gary Cooper.

Gary Cooper, who turned down the part of Rhett Butler, on Clark Gable, who accepted it, 1938.

I bet it's a pip!

Bette Davis, turning down the part of Scarlett O'Hara, 1938.

Do you think I'm a damn fool, David? This picture is going to be the biggest white elephant of all time.

Director-designate Victor Fleming rejects producer David Selznick's offer of 20% of the profits and insists on a flat fee for his services, 1939.

Heaven's Gate

Why do they want to see the rushes?

Director Michael Cimino reacts to concern among United Artists executives about the $25 million overspend on a film that was then several hours too long, and became the most disastrous flop ever made.

Jesus of Nazareth

Twelve? Who needs twelve? Couldn't we make do with six?

Producer Lew Grade tries to economize on disciples.

One Million Years BC

The characters and incidents portrayed and the names used herein are fictitious and any similarity to the names, characters or history of any person is entirely accidental and unintentional.

Disclaimer at the end of the 1966 cavemen-versus-dinosaurs epic.

The Seashell and the Clergyman

The film is apparently meaningless, but if it has any meaning it is doubtless objectionable.

The British Board of Film Censors bans Cocteau's film, 1956.

Snake Eyes

Brian De Palma's *Snake Eyes* manages to give itself the semblance of a portentous yet popular drama. Don't be fooled, though. It's crap through and through.

Alexander Walker, London *Evening Standard*, 5 November 1998, p. 26.

Snake Eyes: a hugely gripping drama about a cop's on-the-spot investigation of a political assassination.

Alexander Walker, 'Hot Tickets', London *Evening Standard*, 5 November 1998.

Who Framed Roger Rabbit

A deplorable development in the possibilities of animation.

Dilys Powell, film critic, 1988.

The Wizard of Oz

The part's too small.

Ed Wynn turns down the part of the Wizard, 1938.

That rainbow song's no good, it slows the picture right down. Take it out.

Marty Rackin, head of production at Paramount, passes on the suggestion of Louis B. Mayer, who recommended the whole Kansas sequence be cut on the grounds that it was 'boring', after a screening for studio heads.

Film Stars

Fred Astaire

Can't act. Can't sing. Slightly bald. Can dance a little.

Report on a screen test for MGM, 1928.

Lucille Ball

Try another profession. Any other.

The head instructor at the John Murray Anderson Drama School, 1927.

Joan Bennett

Your daughter is sweet, but she'll never photograph.

Walter Wanger of Paramount, to Ms Bennett's mother, 1928. After starring in pictures for Sam Goldwyn, United Artists and Fox, Joan Bennett was signed by Wanger, who then married her.

Dirk Bogarde

Nice of you to come, but your head's too small for the camera, you are too thin, and ... I don't know what it is exactly about your neck ... but it's not right.

Earl St John, of the Rank Organization, after an audition in 1939.

James Cagney

He's just a little runt.

Rejected by Howard Hughes for the lead in *The Front Page*, 1927.

Charlie Chaplin

I'm going to get out of this business. It's too much for me. I'll never catch on. It's too fast. I can't tell what I'm doing or what anybody wants me to do.

c. 1914, quoted by Mack Sennett in 1954.

Maurice Chevalier

URGE CANCEL CHEVALIER DEAL STOP PUBLIC WILL NOT REPEAT NOT ACCEPT ACCENTS STOP EVEN RUTH CHATTERTON TOO ENGLISH FOR AMERICA STOP FRENCH ACCENTS EVEN WORSE STOP

Despite this telegram from Paramount in 1928, Chevalier was signed for his first US hit, *Innocents of Paris*.

Joan Collins

I'm sick of being a movie floozie!

Quoted in 1953, after starring in *The Decameron* and *The Cosh Boys*. She went on to star in *The Bitch* and *The Stud*.

Joan Crawford

Don't get carried away, dear. It says 'six months'.

Advice from her mother after signing a $75 a week 'try-out' contract for MGM in 1924.

Bette Davis

Who *did* this to me?

Sam Goldwyn, after viewing a screen test, 1930.

No one faintly like an actress got off the train.

A studio gofer returns empty-handed after being sent to meet the actress, who was joining the cast of *Bad Sister*, 1931.

I think Joan Blondell will be a big star, Anne Dvorak has definite possibilities, but I don't think Bette Davis will make it.

Director Mervyn LeRoy on the stars of *Three on a Match*, 1932.

Clint Eastwood

You have a chip on your tooth, your Adam's apple sticks out too far, and you talk too slow.

Auditioned by Universal Pictures, 1959.

Clark Gable

It's awful – take it away!

Irving Thalberg of MGM after a screen test, 1920s.

His ears make him look like a taxi-cab with both doors open.

Howard Hughes, after Gable auditioned for *The Front Page*, 1927.

What can you do with a guy with ears like that?

Jack L. Warner turns him down for *Little Caesar*, 1930.
   In 1937 Clark Gable was given the title of 'King of Hollywood', and in 1939 he starred in *Gone With the Wind*.

Cary Grant

You're too bow-legged and your neck is far too thick.

Report on a screen test for Paramount, 1931.

Jean Harlow

My God, she's got a shape like a dustpan!

Screenwriter Joseph March, after a screen test for *Hell's Angels*, 1930.

In my opinion, she's nix.

Howard Hughes, producer of *Hell's Angels*, 1930.

Marilyn Monroe

You'd better learn secretarial work, or else get married.

Emmeline Snively, director of the Blue Book Modelling Agency, 1944.

Mary Pickford

I suppose we'll have to say goodbye to little Mary Pickford. She'll never be heard of again and I feel terribly sorry for her.

Playwright William C. DeMille, brother of Cecil B. DeMille, on the actress' departure in 1911 from Broadway for Hollywood, where she became Charlie Chaplin's leading lady.

Ronald Reagan

Reagan doesn't have the presidential look.

United Artists' report on a screen test for *The Best Man*, 1964.

Robert Redford

He's just another California blond. Throw a stick at Malibu, you'll hit six of them.

The star of *Barefoot in the Park* is rejected – by one casting executive – for *Butch Cassidy and the Sundance Kid*, 1969.

Burt Reynolds

You have no talent.

Auditioned by Universal Pictures, 1959.

Flight

It is entirely impossible for man to rise into the air and float there. For this you would need wings of tremendous dimensions and they would have to be moved at three feet per second. Only a fool would expect such a thing to be realized.

French academician Joseph de Lalande, *Journal de Paris*, 18 May 1782. On 15 October 1783 François Pilâtre de Rozier, did indeed rise into the air and float there, in the Montgolfier brothers' hot-air balloon.

Put these three indisputable facts together:
(1) There is a low limit of weight, certainly not much beyond fifty pounds, beyond which it is impossible for an animal to fly. Nature has reached this limit, and with her utmost efforts has failed to pass it.
(2) The animal machine is far more effective than any we can hope to make; therefore the limit of the weight of a successful flying machine cannot be more than fifty pounds.
(3) The weight of any machine constructed for flying, including fuel and engineer, cannot be less than three or four hundred pounds.
   Is it not demonstrated that a true flying machine, self-raising, self-sustaining, self-propelling, is physically impossible?

Professor Joseph le Conte, Faculty of Natural History, University of California, in *Popular Science Monthly*, November 1888.

It is apparent to me that the possibilities of the aeroplane, which two or three years ago was thought to hold the solution to the problem, have been exhausted, and that we must turn elsewhere.

Thomas Edison, quoted in *New York World*, 17 November 1895.

Heavier than air flying machines are impossible. I have not the smallest molecule of faith in aerial navigation other than ballooning.

Lord Kelvin, president of the Royal Society, 1896.

The demonstration that no possible combination of known substances, known forms of machinery, and known forms of force, can be united in a practical machine by which men shall fly long distances through the air, seems to the writer as complete as it is possible for the demonstration to be.

Simon Newcomb, professor of mathematics and astronomy at Johns Hopkins University, 1900.

Flight by machines heavier than air is unpractical and insignificant, if not utterly impossible.

Simon Newcomb, 1902.

Aerial flight is one of that class of problems with which man will never have to cope.

Simon Newcomb, 1903.

   On 17 December 1903 Orville and Wilbur Wright successfully flew a heavier-than-air machine.

The machine may even carry mail in special cases. But the useful load will be very small. The machines will eventually be fast, they will be used in sport, but they are not to be thought of as commercial carriers.

Octave Chanute, engineer and author of *Progress in Flying Machines*, 1904. One of the first passenger airfields in the USA was named after him.

I do not think that a flight across the Atlantic will be made in our time, and in our time I include the youngest readers.

Charles Stewart Rolls, co-founder of Rolls-Royce Ltd., 1908. Alcock and Brown flew from Newfoundland to Ireland on 14 June 1919, and Charles Lindbergh flew from New York to Paris on 20–21 May 1927.

A popular fallacy is to expect enormous speed to be obtained ... There is no hope of competing for racing speed with either our locomotives or our automobiles.

Harvard astronomer William Pickering, *Aeronautics*, 1908.

See also PLANETS, MOONS AND STARS.

The popular mind often pictures gigantic flying machines speeding across the Atlantic and carrying innumerable passengers in a way analogous to our modern steamships ... It seems safe to say that such ideas are wholly visionary, and even if a machine could get across with one or two passengers the expense would be prohibitive to any but the capitalist who could own his own yacht.

William Pickering, 1910.

With the possible exception of having more pleasing lines to the eye while in flight, the monoplane possesses no material advantages over the biplane.

Glenn H. Curtiss, founder and patron of the Curtiss Award, interviewed in The *New York Times*, 31 December 1911.

Over cities, the aerial sentry or policeman will be found. A thousand aeroplanes flying to the opera must be kept in line and each allowed to alight upon the roof of the auditorium in its proper turn.

Waldemar Kaempfert, managing editor of the *Scientific American*, 28 June 1913.

The first real air-liner, carrying some five or six hundred passengers, will probably appear after or towards the end of the battle between fixed and moving-wing machines. And it will be a flying boat.

Oliver Stewart, *Aeriolus, or the Future of the Flying Machine*, 1927.

People are always asking me to give a name to R101. I hope it will make its reputation with that name.

Lord Thompson of Cardington, 1929. The R101 airship tragically made its name in 1930 when it crashed and exploded, killing all on board.

A very friendly boom, like a pair of gleeful handclaps.

UK government scientific adviser Sir James Lighthill on the noise Concorde would make when passing through the 'sound barrier', 1971. Supersonic flights over land are banned, because of the noise.

The new engines are far quieter than the protypes. People living near the airports will hardly notice the aircraft.

Henry Marking of British Airways on Concorde, June 1975. The engines on the production model were afterwards described officially as 'equivalent to thirty of the noisiest subsonic aircraft all taking off together'.

Russia's TU 144 supersonic airliner, drastically altered in design and now performing extremely well, is likely to win the race to get into airline service before the Concorde.

Air Commodore E. M. Donaldson, air correspondent of the *Daily Telegraph*, 1973. That year, the TU 144 fell out of the sky over the Paris Air Show, killing everyone on board. The project was then abandoned.

See also JET PROPULSION, MILITARY TECHNOLOGY *and* SPACE TRAVEL

Food

Who, for instance, would have conceived that ... sawdust itself is susceptible of conversion into a substance bearing no remote analogy to bread; and though certainly less palatable than that of flour, yet no way disagreeable, and both wholesome and digestible as well as highly nutritive? ... [FOOTNOTE: This discovery, which renders famine next to impossible, deserves a higher degree of celebrity than it has obtained.]

John Herschel, *A Preliminary Discourse on the Study of Natural Philosophy*, 1830.

Such a wasteful food as animal flesh cannot survive: and even apart from the moral necessity which will compel mankind, for its own preservation, to abandon the use of alcohol, the direct and indirect wastefulness of alcohol will make it impossible for beverages containing it to be tolerated. Very likely tobacco will follow it.

T. Baron Russell, *A Hundred Years Hence*, 1905.

See also POLITICIANS' GAFFES

Foreigners

What a po-faced lot these Dutch are.

HRH Prince Philip, during a visit to Amsterdam, 1968.

The price of oil is not determined by the British Parliament. It is determined by some lads riding camels who do not even know how to spell 'national sovereignty'.

Vic Feather, former general secretary of the Trades Union Congress, 1975.

I came to gain a greater appreciation of the similarities and differences between the inscrutable Irish and the insufferable English.

Robin Berrington, cultural affairs and press officer at the US Embassy in Dublin: private observations mistakenly included in a press release in 1981.

Ants ... little yellow men who sit up all night thinking how to screw us.

Edith Cresson, Prime Minister of France, defines the Japanese in 1991.

If any of you have got an A-level, it is because you have worked to get it. Go to any other country and when you have got an A-level, you have bought it.

Michael Portillo, chief secretary to the Treasury, addresses students at Southampton University, 4 February 1994.

They're all the same. They're short, they're fat, they're slimy and they're fundamentally corrupt.

Rod Richards, a junior Conservative Welsh Office minister, on Welsh Labour councillors, December 1994.

Let's be proud of our country and our flag. But let's also have a superb performance off the field, too. Treat our European guests with respect and affection.

The *Sun*, editorial, 8 June 1996, in advance of the European Championship finals.

Get out and clog 'em, lads. GO AND GUT 'EM, GAZZA!

The *Sun*, 11 June 1996, the day of the England v The Netherlands match.

GIVE 'EM A SPAINKING!

The *Sun*, front-page headline, 13 June 1996, the day of the England v Spain match.

LET'S BLITZ FRITZ

The *Sun*, front-page headline, 17 June 1996, previewing the England v Germany match.

The British motor industry is really owned by Nazis.

Jeremy Clarkson, British TV motoring correspondent, quipping at the National Motor Show, reported in the *Daily Telegraph* of 26 October 1998. He also said the South Koreans are 'too busy eating dogs to design a decent car'.

See also IMMIGRATION *and* WORLD WAR I

The Franco-Prussian War

All military men who have seen the Prussian army at its annual reviews of late years will have unequivocally declared that France would walk all over it and get without difficulty to Berlin.

Lord Palmerston, British Prime Minister, 1863.

Prussia is a country without any bottom, and in my opinion could not maintain a war for six weeks.

Benjamin Disraeli, 1864 – the year Prussia beat Denmark. In 1866 Prussia defeated Austria in the Seven Weeks' War.

We are ready, the Prussians are not. We are not lacking so much as a gaiter button.

Marshal Edmond Laboeuf, French minister of war, 4 July 1870.

Prussian forces captured Napoleon III after six weeks' fighting, and two weeks later secured total victory.

The French Revolution

I think it probable that this country will, within two or three years, be in the enjoyment of a tolerably free constitution, and that without it having cost them a drop of blood.

Thomas Jefferson, US plenipotentiary in France, letter to John Jay, 23 May 1788.

Rien.

Louis XVI of France, diary entry, 14 July 1789 – the day the Bastille was stormed.

The French people are incapable of regicide.

Louis XVI of France, 1789. He was guillotined in 1793.

Gas

There is a young madman proposing to light the streets of London – with what, do you suppose? – with smoke!

Sir Walter Scott, misunderstanding the process of extracting gas from coal, 1810.

The Gettysburg Address

The world will little note nor long remember what we say here.

Preamble to one of the best-known speeches in history: US President Abraham Lincoln, 19 November 1863.

I failed; I failed: and that is about all that can be said of it.

Abraham Lincoln's own contemporary assessment of his oratory.

The cheek of every American must tingle with shame as he reads the silly, flat and dishwatery utterances of the man who has to be pointed out to intelligent foreigners as the President of the United States.

The *Chicago Times*, 1863.

Anything more dull and commonplace it would not be easy to reproduce.

The *Times*, 1863.

The Gramophone

It is quite impossible that the noble organs of human speech could be replaced by ignoble senseless metal.

French academician Jean Bouillaud, before inspecting Thomas Edison's phonograph, 30 September 1878.

A crude fake sustained by ventriloquism.
Jean Bouillaud, after inspecting it.

It isn't of any commercial value.
Edison's own evaluation, 1880.

The Great Depression

A severe depression like that of 1920–21 is outside the range of possibility.
The Harvard Economic Society *Weekly Letter*, 16 November 1929.

We believe that the recession in general business will be checked shortly and that improvement will set in during the spring months.
The Harvard Economic Society *Weekly Letter*, 18 January 1930.

There is every prospect that the recovery which we have been expecting will not long be delayed.
The Harvard Economic Society *Weekly Letter*, 30 August 1930.

Recovery will soon be evident.
The Harvard Economic Society *Weekly Letter*, 20 September 1930.

The outlook is for the end of the decline in business during the early part of 1931, and steady revival for the remainder of the year.
The Harvard Economic Society *Weekly Letter*, 15 November 1930.
   In 1931 the Harvard Economic Society *Weekly Letter* ran out of funds and ceased publication.

With the usual increase of out-of-door work in the Northern states as weather conditions moderate, we are likely to find the country as a whole enjoying its wonted state of prosperity.
Robert Patterson Lamont, US secretary of commerce, 3 March 1930.

There has been no significant bank or industrial failure. That danger, too, is safely behind us.
US President Herbert Hoover, 1 May 1930.

Gentlemen, you have come sixty days too late. The depression is over.

Herbert Hoover, receiving a delegation requesting a programme of public works to stimulate the economy, June 1930.

These really are good times, but only a few know it. If this period of convalescence through which we have been passing must be spoken of as a depression, it is far and away the finest depression that we have ever had.

Henry Ford, president of the Ford Motor Co., 1931.

I don't know anything about any depression.

US banker J. P. Morgan Jr, 1931.

See also THE ECONOMY, POLITICIANS' PROMISES *and* THE WALL STREET CRASH

The Great Fire of London

Pish! A woman might piss it out.

The Lord Mayor of London, on being roused from his bed – to which he promptly returned – to view a fire in a bakery in Pudding Lane at 2 am on 13 September 1666.

The Gulf War

Iraqi leaders will not want to undermine the ruling regimes in the Gulf States.

The Royal Institute of International Affairs, press release, April 1990. Iraq invaded Kuwait on 2 August.

They will drown in their own blood.

Saddam Hussein, President and supreme military leader of Iraq, on the assembling of US-led Allied forces in Saudi Arabia, September 1990.

Terrible and wrong as war would be, there is something comforting in the fo-fummery of Mr Bush. A man truly disposed to war, and ready to commit all attendant crimes, does not talk like that.

Edward Pearce, the *Guardian*, 2 January 1991. President Bush ordered the bombing of Baghdad two weeks later, and in February launched a land war.

The mother of battles will be our battle of victory and martyrdom.

Saddam Hussein, 24 February 1991. The land war ended in Iraq's defeat after 100 hours.

Hoaxes

The specimen of lunar vegetation, however, which they had already seen, had decided a question of too exciting an interest ...

Dr Herschel has classified not less than thirty-eight species of forest trees and nearly twice this number of plants ... Of animals, he classified nine species of mammalia, and five of oviparia ...

We were thrilled with astonishment to perceive four successive flocks of large winged creatures, wholly unlike any kind of birds ... We counted three parties of these creatures, of twelve, nine, and fifteen in number, walking towards a small wood ... Certainly they were like human beings, for their wings had now disappeared, and their attitude in walking was both erect and dignified ... They averaged four feet in height, were covered, except on the face, with short and glossy copper-coloured hair ... These creatures were evidently engaged in conversation ... We hence inferred that they were rational beings.

A selection from the *New York Sun*, August 1835, which was hoaxed by one of its own reporters, Robert Locke, who spent his evenings concocting 'reports' from Sir John Herschel's astronomical expedition to the Cape of Good Hope. News of the varied and intelligent life on the moon was retailed by the *New York Times* and the *New Yorker*, and scientific conferences were held to discuss the implications and raise funds for further research. Locke himself exposed the hoax, by publishing a book about it.

Dear Sir,
I am not surprised at your friend's anger but he and you should know that to denounce the murders was the only course open to us. To do that promptly was plainly our best policy.

But you can tell him and all others concerned that though I regret the accident of Lord F. Cavendish's death I cannot refuse to admit that Burke got no more than his deserts.

You are at liberty to show him this and others whom you can trust also, but let not my address be known ...

Yours very truly,

Charles S. Parnell.

The first of the 'Parnell letters', published by *The Times* on 18 April 1887, in which the Irish Nationalist MP Charles Stuart Parnell appeared to condone the 'Phœnix Park Murders' in Dublin, and to support Fenian terrorism. The letters were the work of Richard Pigott, an Irish newspaper proprietor and black-mailer, who subsequently committed suicide, and they cost *The Times* some £200,000 in damages and legal fees.

Our next illustration (Fig. 11) is of a very celebrated person, the Piltdown Man, *Eoanthropus dawsoni*, or Man of the Dawn, so named after his finder, Mr Charles Dawson. We should be very proud of *Eoanthropus*, because he is the first known Englishman ... Since 1912 scientific men all over the world have written articles, indulged in friendly controversy, and found out all kinds of things about the Piltdown Man.

M. & C. H. B. Quennell, *Everyday Life in the Old Stone Age*, 1921. It was not until 1953 that 'scientific men' found out that Piltdown Man was a hoax, most probably perpetrated by Dawson himself, who cobbled 'the first Englishman' together out of odd fragments of human and ape skull.

Neither the beautiful signature nor the pointille on the bread which Christ is blessing, is necessary to convince us that we have here a – I am inclined to say – the masterpiece of Johannes Vermeer of Delft, and, moreover, one of his largest works, quite different from all his other paintings and yet every inch a Vermeer.

Dr Abraham Bredius, former director of the Royal Museum at The Hague, in the *Burlington Magazine*, 1938, on *The Disciples in Emmaus*. The painting was soon discovered to be 'quite different' from other Vermeers in that it was one of the many fakes produced by Hans van Meegeren.

We are absolutely certain of the authenticity of the autobiography, and we wouldn't put McGraw-Hill's and *Life* Magazine's name behind it if we weren't.

Donald M. Wilson, vice-president of corporate and public affairs for Time Inc., 1972, on the 'autobiography' of billionaire recluse Howard Hughes, for which publisher McGraw-Hill paid $750,000 through a 'go-between', Clifford Irving. Hughes himself broke his two decades of public silence to denounce it as a hoax, and Irving pleaded guilty to a charge of fraud and was sent to prison.

MARTIN BORMANN ALIVE

Daily Express, 25 November 1972. He wasn't.

To ask the Home Secretary whether he will review the arrangements for preventing drowning accidents.

Written Parliamentary question tabled by John Stonehouse, Labour MP and former minister, 7 May 1974. Later that year he faked his own death by drowning and escaped to Australia where he lived under an assumed name with his secretary until discovered the following year; afterwards he served a prison sentence for fraud and embezzlement.

See also MARRIAGE

EXPRESS EXCLUSIVE
Engagement next week
Sons will be Protestant, daughters Catholic
CHARLES TO MARRY ASTRID – official
John Warden, *Daily Express*, 17 June 1977. He didn't.

I am 100% convinced that Hitler wrote every single word in those books. It's the journalistic scoop of the post-World War Two period.

Peter Koch, editor of the German magazine *Stern*, 22 April 1983, after its joint acquisition with *The Times* of the rights to exclusive serialization of the 62 volumes of Adolf Hitler's diaries, written between 1932 and 1945.

They all belong to the same archive, and whereas signatures, single documents, or even groups of documents can be skilfully forged, a whole coherent archive covering 35 years is far less easily manufactured. Such a disproportionate and indeed extravagant effort offers too large and vulnerable a flank to the critics who will undoubtedly assail it ... The archive, in fact, is not only a collection of documents which can be individually tested: it coheres as a whole and the diaries are an integral part of it.

This is the internal evidence of authenticity ....

The British historian Hugh Trevor-Roper (Lord Dacre), who had exposed the distinguished Sinologist Sir Edmund Backhouse as a forger of old diaries and who was called in to inspect the 'Hitler Diaries', writing in *The Times* on 24 April 1983.

Doubts were cast on their authenticity the following day, and by the end of May it was clear they were all forged. The 'skilful methods' used involved spilling instant coffee over a set of blank diaries bought from a stationers' in 1982, and walking on them to make them look old.

It [Robert Maxwell's death] was directly linked to fresh allegations which will be made in the next few weeks. Of course there is a link. A story is going to break which would have made his position untenable.

Matthew Evans, chairman of publishers Faber & Faber, November 1991. Author Seymour Hersh had been given 'evidence' proving that the recently deceased publishing tycoon Robert Maxwell had been an agent of Mossad, the Israeli secret service, involved in gun-running and money-laundering. It was a hoax; Maxwell was simply a business crook, and had died of a heart attack brought on by chronic pulmonary œdema whilst urinating over the rail of his yacht.

Heartbroken Princess Di is furious at the Sun for exposing a spy video showing her cavorting half naked with ex-lover James Hewitt.

The *Daily Mirror* of 8 October 1996 – along with nearly every other British newspaper – is hoaxed by remote control by the *Sun*'s story of a videotape, allegedly shot by the Secret Service, of Princess Diana indulging in the preambles to adultery at her husband's Highgrove home. It was in fact shot by one Nick Hedges, using actors who bore a vague and blurry resemblance to the lovers, in Wandsworth.

Over-protective Marcus is more like a lover than a father to Victoria.

Publicity blurb for the Channel Four documentary *Daddy's Girl*, about unnaturally close father–daughter relationships, September 1998. 'Marcus' was in fact Stuart Smith, the boyfriend of would-be model Victoria Greetham, whose father had refused to take part.

Homosexuality

Why should women be included in this Act? It is surely impossible for them.

Queen Victoria, successfully objecting to the inclusion of lesbianism in the Criminal Law (Amendment) Act of 1886, prohibiting 'indecency' between members of the same sex.

The 'homo' is the legitimate child of the 'suffragette'.

Percy Wyndham Lewis, *The Art of Being Ruled*, 1920.

This sort of thing may be tolerated by the French – but we are British, thank God.

Viscount Montgomery of Alamein contributes to a House of Lords debate on a Bill to legalize homosexual acts between consenting adults in private, 1965.

In Anglo-Saxon countries men prefer the company of other men ... In England 25% of men are homosexual.

Edith Cresson, Prime Minister of France (and subsequently an EU Commissioner), 1991.

Horoscopes

TERRY WAITE: In the Year of the Cat we do not expect to see headlines screaming of hostages in plight. As a result, Terry Waite, the Archbishop of Canterbury's special envoy, will have a chance to put his feet up and live more of a normal life.

In the Cat Year I expect Terry to spend more time at home ... But if there is trouble under the Cat's influence it will not last long.

Barry Fantoni's Chinese horoscope for February 1987– February 1988 (the year Terry Waite was kidnapped in Lebanon by Hizbollah and began a record-breaking period of captivity) is included here as a representative of all horoscopes, all the time.

The Hungarian Uprising

The Hungarian people seem to have won their revolution. Soviet troops are now leaving Budapest and apparently are also leaving Hungary.

John MacCormac, *New York Times*, 31 October 1956. By the time the paper went on sale, Soviet forces had surrounded Budapest. Three days later the city was invaded by some 200,000 Soviet troops and 2,500 tanks and armoured vehicles.

The Soviet troops are assisting the Hungarian people to retain their independence from Imperialism.

The British communist paper the *Daily Worker*, 2 November 1956.

See also CZECHOSLOVAKIA

Henrik Ibsen

A Doll's House
Unnatural, immoral.
The *People*, 1889.

Morbid and unwholesome.
The *Observer*, 1889.

Rosmersholm
These Ibsen creatures are neither men nor women, they are ghouls.
Gentlewoman, 1891.

Ghosts
An open drain; a loathsome sore unbandaged.
Daily Telegraph, 1891.

Garbage and offal.
Truth, 1891.

Repulsive and degrading.
Queen, 1891.

Foul and filthy.
Era, 1891.

Hedda Gabler
A bad escape of moral sewer gas.
Pictorial World, 1891.

Photographic studies of vice and morbidity.
Saturday Review, 1891.

The Master Builder
Hopeless and indefensible.
Globe, 1893.

Three acts of gibberish.
Stage, 1893.

Sensuality ... irreverence ... simply blasphemous.
Morning Post, 1893.

The Wild Duck
Commonplace and suburban ... bald and unconvincing.
Daily Telegraph, 1894.

See also PLAYS

Immigration

Two Wongs don't make a white.
Arthur Caldwell, Australia's minister for immigration, outlines his policy in 1947.

Would you like foreigners to come into your house, settle down and help themselves to your fridge?
Jean-Louis Debr, French interior minister, on immigrants, 10 May 1997.

See also RACE

India

I suppose the real difficulty is an utter lack of courage, moral and political, amongst the natives, no individual dares take an independent line of his own, and this really shows how unfit they are for anything like self-government.
King George V, letter to Lord Irwin, 10 March 1928. India gained independence in 1947.

Inventions

The advancement of the arts, from year to year, taxes our credulity and seems to presage the arrival of that period when human improvement must end.

Henry L. Ellsworth, commissioner of the US Office of Patents, annual report for 1843.

Everything than can be invented has been invented.

Charles H. Duell, commissioner of the US Office of Patents, recommends the abolition of his office in 1899. Although this quotation has been cited many times throughout the 20th century, original attribution remains elusive. It may have been a mischievous invention of Henry L. Ellsworth.

Kwiatowski and Stefanski's Improved Water Power Engine is operated by a waterwheel which, via cranks and lazy tongs, pumps water to itself.

British Patent number 5273/1904. One of many attempts to invent a perpetual-motion machine; it assumes 100% conservation of energy – which is, of course, impossible.

See also the various technologies and inventions listed on the contents page.

Iran

Ayatollah Khomeini will one day be viewed as some kind of saint.

Andrew Young, US ambassador to the UN, 1976.

Because of the greatness of the Shah, Iran is an island of stability in the Middle East. This is a great tribute to you, Your Majesty, and to your leadership, and to the respect, admiration and love which your people give to you.

US President Jimmy Carter, 31 December 1977.

Nobody can overthrow me. I have the support of 700,000 troops, all the workers, and most of the people. I have the power.

Mohammed Reza Pahlavi, Shah of Iran, *Washington Post*, 6 March 1978.
He was overthrown within a year.

I should like very much to take a vacation.

Mohammed Reza Pahlavi, Shah of Iran, January 1979, shortly before going into permanent exile.

The threat to US embassy personnel is less now than it was in the spring; presumably it will diminish somewhat further by the end of this year.

Henry Precht, head of the Iran desk at the US State Department: memo to Secretary of State Cyrus Vance on the safety of diplomats in Teheran, 1 August 1979.

It'll be over in a few hours.

Hamilton Jordan, chief-of-staff to US President Jimmy Carter, on the seizure of 63 US embassy staff by 'Islamic students' in Teheran, 4 November 1979. They were held hostage for over a year.

An incomplete success.

US President Jimmy Carter on the failed attempt to rescue the embassy hostages, April 1980. Eight US servicemen died.

Iran–Contra Scandal

We did not – repeat not – trade weapons or anything else for hostages, nor will we.

US President Ronald Reagan, on 13 November 1986, denies allegations that the US sold arms to the Khomeini regime in Iran as part of a deal to release US hostages held by Shi'ites in the Lebanon, and use the profits of the sale to finance the 'Contra' guerillas who were trying to overthrow the left-wing government of Nicaragua. The US Congress had forbidden all aid to the Contras.

My answer therefore and the simple truth is, I don't remember – period.

US President Ronald Reagan, 2 February 1987.

It sort of settled down to trading arms for hostages.

US President Ronald Reagan, 26 March 1987.

I didn't know how that money [to support the Contras] was to be used and I have no knowledge that there was ever any solicitation by our people with these people.

US President Ronald Reagan, 5 May 1987.

As a matter of fact, I was very definitely involved in the decisions about support to the freedom fighters. It was my idea to begin with.

US President Ronald Reagan, 15 May 1987.

J

Jet Propulsion

We follow with interest any work that is being done in other countries on jet propulsion, but scientific investigation into the possibilities has given no indication that this method can be a serious competitor to the air-screw combination engine. We do not consider we should be justified in spending any time or money on it ourselves.

The British Ministry of Supply, replying in 1934 to a letter from the British Interplanetary Association drawing its attention to recent German developments in liquid-fuel rocketry.

In its present state, and even considering the improvements possible ... the gas turbine engine could hardly be considered a feasible application to airframes.

Report of the National Academy of Sciences Committee on Gas Turbines, June 1940. The gas turbine (or 'jet') engine was successfully tested on a Gloster in 1941 and was fitted to the Messerschmitt Me-262 the following year. Sir Frank Whittle, the inventor of the jet engine, who had tried for ten years to get the British authorities to take it seriously, inscribed his copy of this report: *Good thing I was too stupid to know this – F W.*

The Korean War

We are not at war.

US President Harry S. Truman, on sending US forces to assist the United Nations 'police action' in Korea, quoted in *Time*, 10 July 1950.

There is no question whatever about the outcome of this struggle. We shall win.

General Walton Harris Walker, commander of the US Far East Command's 8th Army, quoted in *Time*, 31 July 1950.

Communist Premier Chou En-lai's threat that China 'will not stand aside should the imperialists wantonly invade North Korea' is only propaganda.

Time assesses China's pledge to intervene in the event of US troops crossing the 38th parallel, 9 October 1950 – the day the US First Cavalry did so.

The Chinese have 300,000 men in Manchuria. Of these probably not more than 100–125,000 are distributed along the Yalu River. Only 50–60,000 could be gotten across the Yalu River. They have no air force. Now that we have bases for our Air Force in Korea, if the Chinese tried to get down to Pyongyang there would be the greatest slaughter.

General Douglas MacArthur briefs President Harry S. Truman, 14 October 1950. He was relieved of his command on 11 April 1951.

These cookies are beaten!

Major-General Hobart Gay, commander of the US First Cavalry, quoted in *Time*, 23 October 1950, after UN forces had driven the North Korean army back to the Chinese border and occupied Pyongyang, the North Korean capital.

On 6 November 1950, 300,000 Chinese forces crossed the Yalu River and drove UN troops into full retreat, occupying first Pyongyang and then the South Korean capital, Seoul. The 'police action' ended in stalemate on 27 July 1953, and Korea was partitioned.

L

Last Words

I think I could eat one of Bellamy's veal pies.

William Pitt the Younger, proved wrong in 1806.

Why on earth did I do that?

British army commander Sir William Erskine, who had twice been confined to a lunatic asylum, after throwing himself out of an upper storey window in Lisbon in 1813.

Boys, boys, you wouldn't hang your Sheriff, would you?

Sheriff Henry Plummer, to the citizens of Bannock, Washington, who had finally had enough of being robbed and intimidated by The Innocents, Plummer's gang of 200 vigilantes. They strung him up on 10 January 1864.

Nonsense, man! They couldn't hit an elephant at this dist—.

US General John B. Sedgewick at the Battle of Spotsylvania, 1864.

Hold your horses, boys. There's plenty down there for us all.

Lieutenant-Colonel George Armstrong Custer prepares to lead his 700 men into oblivion at Little Big Horn, 25 June 1876. He had intended to live up to his Cheyenne nickname of 'Squaw-killer' by attacking an Indian settlement. One horse survived.

See also NATIVE AMERICANS

Stop your fooling, fellows!

US brothel-keeper Jim Averell to a mob about to lynch him, 1888.

I feel a little better.

Queen Victoria, 1901.

Put that bloody cigarette out!

H. H. Munro ('Saki'), British novelist and short-story writer, warns a soldier not to provide an easy target for German snipers but takes a fatal bullet himself. Somewhere on the Western Front, 1916.

The bullet hasn't been made that could kill me.

Not quite his last words: Jack 'Legs' Diamond, organizer of the St Valentine's Day Massacre, quoted in 1929. He was gunned down in 1931.

I've never felt better.

Douglas Fairbanks Sr, 1939.

Hey, where are the parachutes?

Bandleader Glenn Miller boards a USAF plane bound for Paris from England on 15 December 1944. Its pilot, Major Norman Basell, replied, "What's the matter, Miller, you wanna live forever?" The plane disappeared without trace.

Well, Mr President, you can't say that the people of Dallas haven't given you a nice welcome!

Mrs John Connally, wife of the governor of Texas, speaks to US President John F. Kennedy as they drive through Dallas on 22 November 1963.

I'm going because I want to avoid all the violence on the streets.

The *Belfast Telegraph* quotes 78-year-old Mrs Elizabeth McClelland, who left Ulster in 1970 for New Zealand. She died in Christchurch, NZ, in February 1972 after being struck on the head by a placard demanding Civil Rights in Ulster.

Bandleaders come and go, but the perennial Duke Ellington, like Tennyson's brook, seems destined to go on for ever.

Bath and West Evening Chronicle, 23 May 1974. Ellington died the following day.

I don't need bodyguards.

Jimmy Hoffa, boss of the US Teamsters' Union, interviewed in *Playboy*, June 1975. On 30 July he disappeared and has not been seen since.

What would they want with an old man like me?

Earl Mountbatten of Burma discounts the possibility that he might be a target of the IRA while on holiday in the Irish Republic, 1978. On 27 August 1979, while on holiday in Ireland, he was killed by an IRA bomb on his boat.

I did not get my Spaghetti-Os, I got spaghetti. I want the press to know this.

Convicted killer Thomas J. Grasso uses his Last Words to send a message to posterity about his Last Meal before being executed in Oklahoma on 20 March 1995.

Letter from America

Whilst I think there is a need for the USA to understand the British, and indeed the European situation, I do not feel that at this stage there is an equivalent need for us to understand the American point of view.

The BBC's assistant director of programme planning responds in 1940 to a suggestion by the British-born and US-resident journalist Alistair Cooke for a series of broadcast 'letters' from the USA. *Letter From America* eventually began as a 13-week experiment in 1946; in November 1998, as Cooke turned 90, it was still running.

M

Marriage

I've found happiness. I know this is safe and true.

Barbara Hutton, the $45 million Woolworth heiress, on marrying her second husband, Count Kurt Heinrich Haughwitz-Hardenberg-Reventlow, in 1933.

I will never marry again.

Barbara Hutton divorces the Count in 1936.

It's sheer heaven.

Barbara Hutton on her 'Cash-and-Cary' marriage to Cary Grant, 1939.

I will never marry again. You cannot go on being a fool forever.

Barbara Hutton divorces Cary Grant in 1942.

It makes me sad to think of all the silly things I've done.

Barbara Hutton on marrying her fifth husband, Porfirio Rubirosa, in December 1952.

Don't call me Mrs Rubirosa.

Barbara Hutton, February 1953.

I ought to have married him eighteen months ago, but at that time I was married. This is positively my final marriage.

Barbara Hutton on Baron Gottfried von Cramm, husband number six, November 1955.

I'm in no hurry to go through all that crazy routine again.

Barbara Hutton, after divorcing Baron Gottfried von Cramm in 1959.

He's a composite of all my previous husbands' best qualities without any of the bad qualities.

Barbara Hutton on her seventh husband, Prince Doan Vinh de Champacak, 1964. In 1966 she wrote her husband a cheque for $1m and left the hotel where they were staying. Afterwards she remained single.

If I don't make this one last, there's something wrong with me.

Hollywood star Mickey Rooney, on marrying his third wife in 1949.

Tell the girls I'm still in the running.

Mickey Rooney, on divorcing his third wife in 1951.

This one is for keeps. We're really in love.

Mickey Rooney marries Elaine Melinken in November 1952.

I guess I'm just an excitable guy.

Mickey Rooney, on his trial separation in 1957. Ms Melinken divorced him the following year.

The perfect end to an imperfect journey.

Mickey Rooney, on his fifth wife, Barbara Thomasson, in 1959. They divorced in 1966.

It's unimportant how many times a person is married. We don't think in chronological numbers. Margie's my wife and we're sure this is a good one.

Mickey Rooney, on marrying for the sixth time in September 1966. In December, Margie Rooney sought a divorce on the grounds of mental cruelty.

I am my own man for the first time.

Mickey Rooney finds Jesus, and his seventh wife, in April 1972. She filed for divorce in October 1974.

At last I've found the real one. Love can conquer anything.

Mickey Rooney marries 25-year-old Jan Chamberlain, 1975.

His previous wives just didn't understand him.

Mrs Rooney VIII, 1975.

There are some marriages that are so ideal and easy looking that you wonder why the rest of us can't manage it too. It's something to do with being each other's match and equal, of keeping together so that half isn't left behind, and maintaining some secret balance and link between the two – hard to define but immediately recognizable when you meet it. Barbara and John Stonehouse have always seemed to me to be married in that way.

Ann Sharpley, *Evening Standard*, January 1971. In 1974 John Stonehouse faked his own death and ran off to Australia with his secretary.

See also HOAXES

Nothing will ever separate us. We'll probably be married another ten years.

Elizabeth Taylor, interviewed in the *Chicago Daily News*, 21 July 1974, on marriage to Richard Burton. They announced their divorce five days later – and later remarried, and redivorced.

Your experience will be a lesson to all of us men to be careful not to marry ladies in very high positions.

President Idi Amin of Uganda, message to Lord Snowdon following his divorce from Princess Margaret, 1976.

I don't think a prostitute is more moral than a wife, but they are doing the same thing.

HRH Prince Philip, Duke of Edinburgh, 6 December 1988.

Marriage is legalized prostitution. It's an insult and women shouldn't touch it.

Jenni Murray, BBC *Women's Hour* presenter, the *Independent*, 20 June 1992.

See also SEX *and* WOMEN

Masturbation

Onanism produces seminal weaknesses, impotence, dysury, tabes dorsalis, pulmonary consumption, dyspepsia, dimness of sight, vertigo, epilepsy, hypochondriasis, loss of memory, manalgia, fatuity, and death.

Dr Benjamin Rush ('The Father of American Psychiatry'), professor of physic and dean of the medical school at the University of Pennsylvania, *Medical Inquiries*, 1812.

Victims of self-abuse have pallid, bloodless countenances, hollow, sunken and half-ghastly eyes, with a red rim about the eyelids, and black-and-blue semicircles around the eyes. Red pimples on the face, with a black spot in their middles, are a sure sign of self-pollution in males, and irregularities in females. Stance is another sign: self-polluters often stand and sit in the posture assumed during masturbation ...

But are not the dangers exaggerated? That would be impossible! Masturbation poisons your body, breaks down your nerves, paralyses your whole system ...

Does it really lead to insanity? This excess causes more insanity than anything else except intemperance. Hundreds have been brought to our lunatic asylums by this single form of vice, and some must be tied down to prevent further destruction.

Oswald Squire Fowler, *Sexual Science*, 1870.

I personally know of a young man sent to the insane asylum as a result of continuous masturbation practices since childhood. At the request of his mother, a fine woman, showing no signs of a degenerative strain, the son was castrated ... Two years later she reported that he was earning a salary of $1,800 a year and had married an unsexed girl.

A happy ending reported in 1880 by Dr Benethia Angelina Owens-Adair, professor at the University of Michigan, and author of the state of Oregon's Human Sterilization Bill.

Masturbation is the producer of ambylopia, retinal haemorrhage, follicular inflammation, catarrh, trachoma, retinal irritation, neuro-retinitis in young ladies, agoraphobia and, in extreme cases, total blindness.

It also causes misprnits. Henry Power, *Relation of Ophthalmic Diseases to Certain Normal and Psychological Conditions of the Sexual Organs*: presidential address to the Ophthalmological Society of the United Kingdom, 1888.

When the habit is discovered, it must in young children be put a stop to by such means as tying the hands, strapping the knees together with a pad between them, or some mechanical plan.

Ada Ballin (editor of *Baby Magazine*), *From Cradle to School: A Book for Mothers*, 1902.

It is called in our schools 'beastliness', and this is about the best name for it ... Should it become a habit it quickly destroys both health and spirits; he becomes feeble in body and mind, and often ends in a lunatic asylum.

Robert (later Lord) Baden-Powell, *Scouting for Boys*, 1908.

It is often said that masturbation is a cause of insanity, epilepsy and hysteria. I believe it to be more likely that the masturbation is the first manifestation of a developing insanity.

Dr Charles Hunter-Dunn, instructor in pædiatrics at Harvard University, *Pædiatrics: The Hygiene and Medical Treatment of Children*, 1920.

At the worst, confinement in poroplastic armour, as for spinal caries, or severe poliomyelitis, may be necessary.

Hector Charles Cameron, in the aptly titled *The Nervous Child*, 1930.

… Cf the long, thin, almost imperceptible black hair growing out of the middle of the palm of the left hand of masturbators.

Rudolf Friedman, Freudian psychiatrist, who wrote this footnote in 1954, must have had some very peculiar patients.

If practised in girlhood, does it affect married life? Yes, those girls who practise it fail to develop as women. They become flat-chested and lose the female glow which draws gentlemen around them. They develop amatory vertigo and become very nervous.

Oswald Squire Fowler, *Sexual Science*, 1870.

No one who has realized the amount of moral evil wrought in girls by medical manipulations can deny that remedy is worse than disease. I have seen young unmarried women, of the middle class of society, reduced by the constant use of the speculum to the mental and moral condition of prostitutes; seeking to give themselves the same indulgence by the practice of solitary vice; and asking every medical practitioner to institute an examination of the sexual organs.

Dr Robert Brudenell Carter, 1900.

See also SEX *and* WOMEN

Robert Maxwell

Quotes by Robert Maxwell

There was a time until recently when the employer changed his machines, his methods or his workforce without asking or consulting anybody. Periodic and quite capricious unemployment was the most dreadful aspect of this situation. Most large employers now consult their workers or their representatives whenever they wish to make major changes.

The very large Robert Maxwell, renowned for his capricious attitude to hiring and firing, writing in *Man Alive*, published by his own Pergamon Press in 1968.

(1) I have no intention of making anyone redundant.
(2) I will never interfere with editorial freedom.
(3) Union recognition will continue.

On acquiring the *Daily Mirror* in July 1984.

Under my management editors in this Group will be free to produce their newspapers without interference with their journalistic skills and judgement.

Chairman's statement to employees of Mirror Group Newspapers, July 1985.
Editorial staff on the *Mirror* often freely chose to run laudatory stories about their employer.

I guarantee unconditionally that the Games will go ahead. I hope you will agree there is nothing more important than that. There will be no deficit at all ... I hope that will put paid to any nonsense ... that I or any of my family will be handing out medals.

On taking over the funding of the Edinburgh Commonwealth Games, 19 June 1986, at which time the organizers were £4 million short of the necessary funds. In due course, decathlete Daley Thompson's gold medal was hung round his neck by Robert Maxwell.

When it comes to elbow-twisting on a major scale I am particularly good at it ... The Games are financially secure. The job is virtually done.

Press conference, 18 July 1986, six days before the opening of the Games. Soon after they ended, Maxwell announced a deficit of £4 million; by refusing to pay some contractors' accounts he reduced it to £3.2 million by October, but by 1988 it had grown, with interest charges, to £3.8 million.

Our guaranteed circulation will be half a million.

Launching his *London Daily News*, 24 February 1987. Circulation on day one was 400,000, after which it fell to 100,000. On 24 July Maxwell scrapped the paper.

It's not an ego trip. I don't go in for ego trips. It's not my style.

On changing the name of the British Printing and Publishing Corporation (BPPC) to Maxwell Communications Corporation (MCC), 25 September 1987. MCC, with Mirror Group Newspapers (MGN) were then spun into a huge and confusing web of private and public companies all controlled, directly or at various removes, by Maxwell himself. In October MCC released an eight-page colour brochure containing nine photographs of its chairman, one of which was captioned 'Robert Maxwell discussing world affairs with Henry Kissinger in Tokyo.'

We must not abandon Gorbachev. Don't you realize that Gorbachev wouldn't do anything without ringing me first?

Persuading Roy Greenslade, editor of the *Mirror*, to drop a story about Soviet troops committing atrocities in Vilnius, Latvia, in February 1990.

My way of running the Labour Party is now very, very successful.

The former Labour MP (1964–70) interviewed in the *Guardian*, March 1990.

Even a one-eyed Albanian can work out there is going to be a premium to the issue price.

Forecasting an oversubscription on the flotation of MGN as a public company, May 1990. Shares quickly fell from their offer price of 125 pence as the underwriters, Salomon Brothers, posted a loss of £5 million on the flotation. Thereafter, Maxwell used the steadily devaluing shares in MCC and MGN as collateral for huge and mounting debts, until eventually the pension funds of his companies became his only 'asset'. At the time of his death in November 1991, Maxwell's companies had amassed debts of over £3 billion.

Robert Maxwell says he'll only allow his sons Ian and Kevin to take over his vast empire if they are capable. 'Money you haven't earned isn't good for you,' he says.

Interviewed in *Woman's Realm*, 8 August 1991.

I am only concerned about needless anxieties which the programme may cause to pensioners in our group.

Telling *Mirror* readers why he issued a gagging writ against the BBC TV *Panorama* programme, preventing it broadcasting a report on his illegal use of pension funds, September 1991.

The truth is our only currency.

A personal statement in the *Mirror*, 29 October 1991. He died a week later.

Quotes about Robert Maxwell

This is obviously the end of Mr Maxwell's dream of being the proprietor of a national newspaper.

Hugh Cudlipp, chairman of IPC (then owners of the *Daily Mirror*) after Rupert Murdoch beat Robert Maxwell for the ownership of the *Sun*, September 1969.

He is a man of great energy, drive and imagination, but unfortunately an apparent fixation as to his own abilities causes him to ignore the views of others if these are not compatible ... The concept of a Board being responsible for policy was alien to him.

We are also convinced that Mr Maxwell regarded his stewardship duties fulfilled by showing the maximum profits which any transaction could be devised to show. Furthermore, in reporting to shareholders and investors he had a reckless and unjustified optimism which enabled him on some occasions to disregard unpalatable facts and on others to state what he must have known to be untrue ...

We regret having to conclude that, notwithstanding Mr Maxwell's acknowledged abilities and energy, he is not in our opinion a person who can be relied on to exercise proper stewardship of a publicly quoted company.

Report of the Department of Trade and Industry into Maxwell's stewardship of Pergamon Publishing, 13 July 1971. Maxwell attempted unsuccessfully to have it overturned in the High Court. What makes it regrettable is that it was ignored during the following two decades.

He is a liar and a crook and I can prove it.

Joe Haines, *Daily Mirror* columnist, addressing a meeting of the newspaper's staff on 12 July 1984. He subsequently changed his mind (twice).

I say to those who are here today and who manage the pension and investment funds that they are unfit to be the managers of those funds if they do not recognize the achievements of Mr Maxwell and invest in the company.

A vote of confidence from Henry Poole, analyst at Alexanders, Laing & Cruikshank, and broker for BPPC, 17 July 1987.

In the work and life of Bob Maxwell we identify not merely one great talent but many; a remarkable innovator in the field of science and technology, an outstanding publisher, an exceptional communicator, manager, and a prominent and broadminded public figure.

The somewhat inappropriate preface to *Progress in Neuro-Psychophormeology and Biological Psychiatry*, by Corneille Radonco-Thomas and Françoise Garcin, published by Pergamon, 1988.

THE MAN WHO SAVED THE *DAILY MIRROR*

Headline in the *Daily Mirror*, 6 November 1991, reporting Maxwell's death the day before.

MAXWELL: £526 MILLION IS MISSING FROM HIS FIRMS

Headline, *Daily Mirror*, 6 December 1991, after confirmation that Maxwell had been stealing from his employees' pension funds.

Robert Maxwell's premature death is a great loss to the world of business and publishing. He was the one man you could rely on in times of trouble.

Lord Stevens of Ludgate, proprietor of the *Daily Express*, 6 November 1991.

I think he had more physical and moral courage than anyone I have ever met.

Former UK ambassador to Washington and ex-Maxwell employee Peter Jay, *Today*, 6 November 1991.

The publisher's final resting place is high on the hillside ... It was from the Mount of Olives, according to Christian belief, that Jesus ascended into heaven after His resurrection.

John Jackson and Harry Arnold, reporting on their employer's funeral in the Maxwell-owned *People*, 10 November 1991.

A man who worked and aspired and achieved dreams unthinkable to the ordinary mortal.

Mary Riddell, *Daily Mirror*, 11 November 1991.

Many of us who started off disliking him ended up captured by his kindness.

Joe Haines, by now author of Maxwell's official biography, *Daily Mirror*, 6 November 1991.

Many of us in the Mirror building despise those who are seeking, within hours of his death, to smear him further ... They will get their come-uppance, one day.

Joe Haines, *Daily Mirror*, 7 November 1991.

From the moment Harold Wilson resigned, rumours, inventions and baseless gossip began, and those whom he hardly knew rushed to claim intimate insights into his life and secrets, with heavy hints of scandal behind both ... As it was with Harold Wilson, so it was and will be with Robert Maxwell ... tosh and falsehood.

Joe Haines, *Daily Mirror*, 11 November 1991.

I think I'll go home and have a good bath.

Joe Haines, *Daily Mirror*, 6 December 1991.

Among the facets of his extraordinary character there was a genuine desire to do good ... He gave splendid birthday parties ... He did not, I think, intend that Mirror Group pensioners should be deprived of their money.

Lord Rees-Mogg, *The Times*, 21 January 1996.

See also HOAXES

McCarthyism

I have here in my hand a list of 205 that were known to the Secretary of State as being members of the Communist Party and who, nevertheless, are still working and shaping policy in the State Department.

Senator Joseph McCarthy, speech, 9 February 1950.

Last night I discussed communists in the State Department. I stated that I had the names of 57 card-carrying members of the Communist Party.

Senator Joseph McCarthy, speech, 10 February 1950.

I frankly feel, in view of the number of cases – there are 81 cases – that it would be a mistake to disclose these names on the floor.

Senator Joseph McCarthy, speech, US Senate, 20 February 1951.

How can we account for our present situation unless we believe that men high in this government are concerting to deliver us to disaster? This must be the product of a great conspiracy, a conspiracy on a scale so immense as to dwarf any previous venture in the history of man. A conspiracy of infamy so black that, when it is finally exposed, its principals shall forever be deserving of the maledictions of all honest men.

Senator Joseph McCarthy, speech, US Senate, 14 June 1951.

I think it is a shoddy, unusual thing to do to use the floor of the Senate to attack your opponent without any proof whatever.

A discredited Senator Joseph McCarthy, speech, US Senate, 1956.

See also CONSPIRACY THEORIES *and* THE USSR

Men

One realizes with horror that the race of men is almost extinct in Europe. Only Christ-like heroes and woman-worshipping Don Juans, and rabid equality-mongrels.

D. H. Lawrence, *Sea and Sardinia*, 1921.

The male is a biological accident; the Y (male) gene is an incomplete X (female) gene, that is, has an incomplete set of chromosomes. In other words, the male is an incomplete female, a walking abortion, aborted at the gene stage.

Valerie Solanas, *Manifesto of the Society for Cutting Up Men*, 1967.

Maleness remains a recessive genetic trait like colour-blindness and hæmophilia, with which it is linked. The suspicion that maleness is abnormal and the Y chromosome is an accidental mutation boding no good for the race is strongly supported by the recent discovery by geneticists that congenital killers and criminals are possessed of not one but two Y chromosomes, bearing a double dose, as it were, of genetically undesirable maleness.

Elizabeth Gould Davis, *The First Sex*, 1971.

Whatever they may be in public life, whatever their relations with men, in their relations with women, all men are rapists, and that's all they are. They rape us with their eyes, their laws, and their codes.

Marilyn French, *The Women's Room*, 1977.

The ethics of all male sexuality are essentially rapist. The idea of the male sex is like the idea of an Aryan race ... It is a political entity that flourishes only through acts of force and sexual terrorism.

John Stollenberg, partner of Andrea Dworkin, *Refusing to Be a Man*.

It serves to perpetuate clubbishness and to exclude women from the club.

Nancy Henley, *Body Politics*, 1977, on the handshake.

Men are dangerous around small children and should be kept as far away from them as possible.

Germaine Greer, the *Independent*, 1981.

The message is that women are incapable. The detachment of the acts from the concrete realities of what women need and do not need is a vehicle for the message that women's actual needs and interests are unimportant or irrelevant ... The message of the false helpfulness of male gallantry is female dependence, the invisibility or insignificance of women, and contempt for women.

Marilyn Frye, *Oppression*, 1988, on men holding doors open for women.

Women must refuse to collaborate in their victimization by silence, and we cannot tolerate images of ourselves being bound and tortured for men's profit and sexual gratification.

Nikki Craft, *New York Times*, on bathing suit tops.

Of the silent comedians, Laurel and Hardy are perhaps the most threatening to women ... They are an æsthetic offence, with their disaster-prone bodies and their exclusive relationship that not only shuts out women but questions their very necessity. They constitute a two-man wrecking team of female – that is, civilized and bourgeois – society.

Molly Haskins, *From Reverence to Rape*, 1987.

See also MARRIAGE, SEX, THE US CONSTITUTION *and* WOMEN

Menstruation

Among the whole range of animated beings, the human female is the only one that has monthly discharge ... On the approach of a woman in this state, milk will become sour, seeds which are touched by her become sterile, grafts wither away, garden plants are parched up, and the fruit will fall from the tree beneath which she sits.

Pliny the Elder, in *Natural History*, c. AD 70.

On contact with this gore, crops do not germinate, wine goes sour, grasses die, trees lose their fruit, iron is corrupted by rust, copper is blackened. Should dogs eat any of it, they go mad. Even bituminous glue, which is dissolved neither by iron nor by waters, polluted by this gore, falls apart by itself.

St Isidore of Seville, *Etymologies, Book XI: Man and His Parts*, c. 610.

The more remote any individual state or society was placed from moral or political habits, and the various causes which are capable of interfering with the actions of nature, the less frequent would be the occurrence of the menstrual phenomenon, and in some instances, it might be wholly unknown or nearly so.

Dr John Power, physician at the Westminster Lying-In Institution, *Essays on the Female Economy*, 1821.

We cannot too emphatically urge the importance of regarding these monthly returns as periods of ill-health, as days when the ordinary occupations are to be suspended ... Long walks, dancing, shopping, riding and parties should be avoided at this time of month invariably and under all circumstances.

Dr W. C. Taylor, *A Physician's Counsels to Women in Health and Disease*, 1871.

See also SEX *and* WOMEN

Meteors

The stone ... is an ordinary one, struck and altered by lightning, and showing nothing unusual in analysis.

Antoine Lavoisier, on behalf of the French Academy of Sciences, fails to identify a meteorite in 1772, despite eyewitness accounts of its falling from the sky.

How sad it is that the entire municipality enters folk tales on an official record, presenting them as something actually seen, while they cannot be explained by physics nor by anything reasonable.

A fine example of 'capital arrogance': French academician Claude Berthollet reacts to an affadavit sworn by the mayor and 300 citizens of Barbotan following a meteorite shower in 1791. Another shower, on the town of L'Aigle in 1803, was correctly identified and described by Jean-Baptiste Biot.

The Middle East

They should settle this problem in a true Christian spirit.

Warren Austin, US delegate to the UN, on the Arab-Israeli war of 1948.

It is far more likely that the Vatican conclave will elect a black Pope than any serious agreement will emerge from it.

Alexander Cockburn and James Ridgeway, the *Village Voice*, 21 August 1978, on the Camp David Summit between US President Jimmy Carter, Israeli Prime Minister Menachem Begin, and Egyptian President Anwar Sadat. It resulted in a treaty on 26 March 1979, and Egyptian recognition of the State of Israel.

See also POLITICIANS' GAFFES

Military Intelligence

We shall always win by reason of pluck ... always the most essential factor.

Major (afterwards Field Marshal and Earl) Douglas Haig, 1896.

Brains! I don't believe in brains. You haven't any, I know, sir.

The Duke of Cambridge, Commander-in-Chief of the British Army, 1854–95.

The only other comparable regiment is the Royal Marines but they are a bit slower. They like to think a bit – and then go and get killed. The Paras just go out and get killed.

Army historian Major Charles Hayman on the Parachute Regiment, *Daily Telegraph*, 29 November 1994.

You can't expect the Rapid Reaction Force to be ready immediately.

Military spokesman, BBC Radio 4 *Today* programme, 1995.

Military Leaders

No doubt he is a little mad at times, but in his lucid intervals he is an uncommonly clever fellow; and I trust that he will have no fit during the campaign, though I must say he looked a little mad as he embarked.

Message from the military secretary in London to the Duke of Wellington concerning Sir William Erskine, who had twice been confined in a lunatic asylum. He was also short-sighted, and often had to have the enemy position pointed out to him. At the Battle of Sabugal in 1811 he sent all his forces in the wrong direction.

See also LAST WORDS

I tell you Wellington is a bad general and the English are bad soldiers; we will settle this matter by lunchtime.

Napoleon briefs his commanders on the eve of the Battle of Waterloo, 18 June 1815.

How very amusing! Actually attacking our camp! Most amusing.

Lieutenant-Colonel Henry Crealock, reacting to the news that Zulu forces had attacked the British camp at Isandhlwana, 22 January 1879. The British were routed.

The French! They're the fellows we shall be fighting next.

Field Marshal Haig on his former allies, 1919.

See also THE BOER WARS, WORLD WAR I *and* WORLD WAR II

Military Technology

I will ignore all ideas for new works and engines of war, the invention of which has reached its limits and for whose improvement I see no further hope.

Julius Frontinus, chief military engineer to the Emperor Vespasian, c. AD 70.

Railways

Transport by railroad car would result in the emasculation of our troops and would deprive them of the great marches which have played such an important rôle in the triumph of our armies.

François Arago, French scientist and politician, 1836; in 1848 he was made minister of war.

Gas

It was a new device in wartime and thoroughly illustrative of the Prussian idea of playing the game.

Sergeant Reginald Grant on the Germans' use of chlorine gas in the Second Battle of Ypres, April 1915. The British and French started using it shortly afterwards.

Guns

Although the needle gun permits rapid fire as long as there is no stoppage, this does not constitute any real advantage, because rapid fire will merely exhaust the ammunition supply.

Austrian Feldzeugmeister Augustin rejects the quick-firing gun, 1851. The Prussians used it to trounce Austrian forces at Könnigrätz in 1866.

Machine guns have not, in my opinion, much future in a campaign against a modern army.

General John Adye, 1894.

It must be accepted as a principle that the rifle, effective as it is, cannot replace the effect produced by the speed of the horse, the magnetism of the charge and the terror of cold steel.

British Cavalry training manual, 1907.

Make no mistake: this weapon will change absolutely nothing.

The director-general of the French infantry on the machine gun, 1910.

Bullets have little stopping-power against the horse.

General Douglas Haig, commander of the 1st Corps of the British Expeditionary Force, 1914.

The machine gun is a much overrated weapon; two per battalion is more than sufficient.

General Douglas Haig, commander of the British First Army, 1915.

Ships and submarines

What, sir, you would make a ship sail against the wind and currents by lighting a bonfire under her decks? I pray you excuse me. I have no time to listen to such nonsense.

Napoleon dismisses the American engineer Robert Fulton, who suggested steam power as a means to combat the Royal Navy, 1803.

My imagination refuses to see any sort of submarine doing anything but suffocate its crew and founder at sea.

H. G. Wells, *Anticipations*, 1902.

The submarine may be the cause of bringing battle to a stoppage altogether, for fleets will become useless, and as other war matériel continues
to improve, war will become impossible.

Jules Verne, 1904.

Most improbable, and more like one of Jules Verne's stories.

Admiral Sir Compton Dombile reads *Danger!*, a short story by Sir Arthur
Conan Doyle about a submarine blockade, 1912.

I reject the notion that territorial waters will be violated, or neutral vessels
sunk. Such will be absolutely prohibited and will only recoil on the heads
of the perpetrators. No nation would permit it, and the officer who
did it would be shot.

Admiral Sir William Hannan Henderson dismisses the dangers of submarine
warfare, c.1913.

Underwater weapons? I call them underhand, unfair and un-English.
They'll never be any use in war and I'll tell you why – I'm going to get
the First Lord [of the Admiralty] to announce that we intend to treat
all submarines as pirate vessels in wartime. We'll hang their crews.

The comptroller of the Admiralty, 1914.

Tanks

A pretty mechanical toy.

Lord Kitchener attends a tank demonstration in 1916.

The idea that cavalry will be replaced by these iron coaches is absurd.
It is little short of treasonous.

General Douglas Haig's aide-de-camp concurs, 1916.

The tank was a freak. The circumstances which called it into existence are
not likely to recur. If they do, they can be dealt with by other means.

Major-General Sir Louis Jackson, 1919.

As for tanks, which are supposed by some to bring a shortening of wars,
their incapacity is striking.

Marshal Henri Pétain, foreword to *Is Invasion Still Possible?* by General
Chauvineau.

The principle and system of Cavalry Training (Mechanized) will be as laid
down in Cavalry Training (Horsed), with certain modifications laid down
in this chapter. Mounted drill (in armoured cars) is based on the same
principles as that of cavalry. The principles of training in field operations

given in Cavalry Training (Horsed) are, in general, applicable to armoured car regiments.

From *Cavalry Training* (1937), which had 23 pages of sword and lance exercises.

The Sheridan Weapons System, with the Shillelagh, will provide the army with a major advancement in tank-like weapons systems and a significant improvement in firepower.

US Colonel Paul A. Simpson, manager of the Sheridan project, 1966. First tests revealed a problem: the shells exploded prematurely and blew the gun turret off.

I really don't know what the Russians have, but I'd like to place a bet for a month's pay that this is better.

Major General Edward H. Burba, senior tank development officer, US Army, introduces a 1967 public demonstration of Sheridan tanks. The demonstration was terminated when a tank filled with smoke and had to be abandoned.

Although the cost of the programme has risen substantially above the original estimates, it is believed that the tank will meet or surpass nearly all of its performance objectives.

US secretary of defense Robert McNamara announces deployment of the Sheridan Weapons System in Vietnam, January 1968. The first 54 tanks logged 446 'failure incidents' including 41 weapon misfires and 25 complete engine replacements. The recoil mechanism of the 152 mm gun was considered 'too unreliable for a combat situation'.

These problems now are solved.

US Army press release as 171 more Sheridans are shipped to Vietnam, 1969. The system was scrapped the following year, at a cost of more than $1 billion.

Aircraft

As a peace machine, its value to the world will be beyond computation. Would a declaration of war between Russia and Japan be made, if within an hour thereafter a swiftly gliding aeroplane might take its flight from St Petersburg and drop half a ton of dynamite above the enemy's war offices? Could any nation afford to war upon any other with such hazards in view?

John Brisbane Walker, *Cosmopolitan*, March 1904.

Another popular fallacy is to suppose that flying machines could be used to drop dynamite on an enemy in time of war.

Astronomer William H. Pickering, *Aeronautics*, 1908.

To affirm that the aeroplane is going to 'revolutionize' naval warfare of the future is to be guilty of the wildest exaggeration.

Scientific American, 16 July 1910.

It is highly unlikely that an airplane, or fleet of them, could ever sink a fleet of Navy vessels under battle conditions.

Franklin D. Roosevelt, 1922.

There is no such thing as the aerial battle. There is only the battle on the ground.

General Maurice Gamelin, 1936.

It is not possible … to concentrate enough military planes with military loads over a modern city to destroy that city.

US colonel John W. Thomason Jr, November 1937.

The position of our enemies will be hopeless. We will be able to put down a vast army, anywhere in the world, within a single week … The whole world will be our back yard. And our enemies will be beaten to their knees.

Shipbuilding engineer Henry J. Kaiser seeks funding for a fleet of giant cargo planes in 1942; he found it from the US Reconstruction Finance Corporation, and millionaire Howard Hughes.

Now, whatever you do, Henry, do not interfere with Howard. He is thorough and he is a genius and do not interfere with him.

Reconstruction Finance Corporation boss Jesse James, to Henry Nelson, head of the War Production Board, who had expressed doubts about the Kaiser/Hughes project after seeing a prototype: it was made of wood, weighed 200 tons, and had a wingspan that exceeded the length of a football pitch. The project was completed in 1947, and produced the 'Spruce Goose', the largest aircraft ever built. It flew for half a mile over Long Beach with Hughes at the helm, and then disappeared into indefinite storage.

The plane is the greatest single step forward in combat aircraft in several decades.

US secretary of defense Robert McNamara on the F-111 'swing wing' fighter-bomber, 15 October 1964.

The F-111 will be superior in its class to any other tactical weapons system in the world.

US Defense Department briefing to Congress, September 1966.

The F-111 in a Nixon administration will be made into one of the foundations of our air supremacy.

Richard M. Nixon, speech, El Paso, Texas, 2 November 1968.

In December 1970 a Senate Committee concluded that the F-111 project had been 'a fiscal blunder of the worst magnitude'; of 500 built, fewer than 100 came 'reasonably close' to performing to specification. Thirteen simply fell out of the sky.

Inter-Continental Ballistic Missiles

There has been a great deal said about a 3,000-mile high-angle rocket. The people who have been writing these things that annoy me, have been talking about a 3,000-mile high-angle rocket shot from one continent to another, carrying an atomic bomb and so directed as to be a precise weapon which would land exactly on a certain target, such as a city.

I say, technically, I don't think anyone in the world knows how to do such a thing, and I feel confident it will not be done for a very long period to come. I think we can leave that out of our thinking. I wish the American public would leave that out of their thinking.

Dr Vannevar Bush, president of the Carnegie Institute of Washingon, DC, December 1945.

See also WAR AND PEACE, WORLD WAR I *and* WORLD WAR II

The Millennium Dome

That damned Dome has disaster written all over it.

The *Sun*, editorial, 12 January 1998, on the £780m Greenwich Millennium Dome.

What a terrible monument to the human ego.

The *Sun*, editorial, 17 February 1998.

The plans for the Millennium Experience are dazzling. If it all comes off, the Prime Minister's prediction will be correct: The Dome will be a great advert for Britain.

The *Sun*, editorial, 25 February 1998, after its proprietor Rupert Murdoch announced a £12 million sponsorship deal for the Greenwich Millennium Dome.

Music and Composers

Johann Sebastian Bach

Deprived of beauty, of harmony, and of clarity of melody.

The German composer and musicologist Johann Scheibe, *Der critische Musikus*, 14 May 1737.

Béla Bartók

Unmeaning bunches of notes, apparently representing the composer promenading the keyboard in his boots. Some can be played better with the elbows, others with the flat of the hand. None requires fingers to perform nor ears to listen to.

Musical Quarterly, July 1915.

Ludwig van Beethoven

Beethoven's Second Symphony is a crude monstrosity, a serpent which continues to move about, refusing to expire, and even when bleeding to death still threshes around angrily and vainly with its tail.

Zeitung für die elegante Welt, review of the first Leipzig performance, 1828.

Seems to lose its way in complete disorder … too much that is harsh and bizarre in it.

Review of the Eroica Symphony in *Allgemaine musikalische Zeitung*, 1805.

An orgy of vulgar noise.

The composer Louis Spohr on the Fifth Symphony, 1823.

Much too long.

The *Harmicon* of London, on the Sixth Symphony, 1823.

If Beethoven's Seventh Symphony is not by some means abridged, it will soon fall into disuse.

Boston critic Philip Hale, 1837.

Eccentric without being amusing.

The *Harmicon* on the Eighth Symphony, 1827.

So ugly, in such bad taste, and in the conception of Schiller's Ode so cheap that I cannot even now understand how such a genius as Beethoven could write it down.

Louis Spohr, in *Selbstbiographie*, 1861, on the Ninth Symphony and the 'Ode To Joy'.

Beethoven always sounds to me like the upsetting of a bag of nails, with here and there an also dropped hammer.

John Ruskin, letter, 6 February 1881.

Hector Berlioz

What a good thing this isn't music.

Gioacchino Rossini, on the *Symphonie Fantastique*, c. 1830.

One ought to wash one's hands after handling one of his scores.

Felix Mendelssohn, 1834.

Berlioz, musically speaking, is a lunatic; a classical composer only in Paris, the great city of quacks. His music is simply and undisguisedly nonsense.

The *Dramatic and Musical Review*, 1843.

He does not know how to write.

The French critic Pierre Scudo, 1852.

It needs no gift of prophecy to predict that Berlioz will be utterly unknown a hundred years hence to everybody but the encyclopædists and the antiquarians.

The *Boston Daily Advertiser*, 1874.

Johannes Brahms

I played over the music of that scoundrel Brahms ... What a giftless bastard! It annoys me that this self-inflated mediocrity is hailed as a genius ... Brahms is chaotic and absolutely dried-up stuff.

Peter Ilych Tchaikovsky, Diary, 9 October 1886.

The real Brahms is nothing more than a sentimental voluptuary, rather tiresomely dressing himself up as Handel or Beethoven and making a prolonged and intolerable noise.

George Bernard Shaw.

Anton Bruckner

The anti-music ravings of a half-wit.

Hans von Bülow, on the symphonies, 1888.

Symphonic boa-constrictors.

Johannes Brahms.

Frederic Chopin

Had he submitted his music to a teacher, the latter, it is to be hoped,

would have torn it up and thrown it at his feet – and this is symbolically
what we wish to do.

Ludwig Rellstab, *Iris im Gebieste der Tonkunst*, 1833.

The entire works of Chopin present a motley surface of ranting hyperbole
and excruciating cacophony ... There is an excuse at present for Chopin's
delinquencies; he is entramelled in the enthralling bonds of that arch-
enchantress, George Sand, celebrated equally for the number and excel-
lence of her romances and her lovers.

Early tabloid criticism: *Musical World*, 28 October 1841.

Claude Debussy

The audience ... expected the ocean, something big, something colossal,
but they were served instead some agitated water in a saucer.

Louis Schneider, in *Gil Blas*, on *La Mer*, 1905.

Edward Elgar

Elgar is one of the Seven Humbugs of Christendom.

George Bernard Shaw, *Music and Letters*, 1920.

Edvard Grieg

Two or three catch-penny phrases served up with plenty of orchestral
sugar.

George Bernard Shaw on *Peer Gynt*, in *The World*, 1892.

Franz Liszt

Liszt is a mere commonplace person, with his hair on end – a snob out of
Bedlam. He writes the ugliest music extant.

A snob being, in those days, 'a vulgar and ostentatious person': the *Dramatic and
Musical Review*, 7 January 1843.

Turn your eyes to any one composition that bears the name of Liszt, if
you are unlucky enough to have such a thing on your pianoforte,
and answer frankly, if it contains one bar of genuine music. Composition
indeed! – decomposition is the proper word for such hateful fungi,
which choke up and poison the fertile plains of harmony, threatening
the world with drought.

Musical World, 30 June 1855.

Gustav Mahler

If that was music, I no longer understand anything about music.

Hans von Bülow on the Second Symphony, c. 1890.

Felix Mendelssohn

Are you overrun in London with 'Champagne Charlie is my Name?'
A brutal Thing; nearly worthless – the Tune, I mean – but yet not quite –
else it would not become so great a Bore. No: I can see, to my Sorrow,
that it has some Go – which Mendelssohn had not.

Edward Fitzgerald, letter to W. F. Pollock, 11 November 1867.

Wolfgang Amadeus Mozart

You ask my opinion about taking the young Salzburg musician into your
service. I do not know where you can place him, since I feel that you
do not require a composer, or other useless people ... It gives one's service
a bad name when such types run about like beggars; besides, he has
a large family.

The Empress Maria Theresa, letter to her son, Joseph II, 1771.

Far too noisy, my dear Mozart. Far too many notes.

The Emperor Joseph II attends the première of *The Marriage of Figaro*,
1 May 1786.

Mozart died too late rather than too soon.

A Bach enthusiast speaks: Glenn Gould, 1984.

Jacques Offenbach

He has written nothing that will live, nothing that will make the world
better. His name as well as his music will soon be forgotten.

Obituary notice in the *Chicago Tribune*, 7 October 1880.

Sergei Prokoviev

Mr Prokoviev might well have loaded up a shotgun with several
thousand notes of various lengths and discharged them against the
side of a blank wall.

Edward Moore reviews *The Love of Three Oranges* for the *Chicago Tribune*,
31 December 1921.

Giacomo Puccini

Puccini represents an evil art – Italian music, to wit – and his success
would have meant the proliferating influence in England of that evil art.
Wherefore, it has been my duty to throw back the score of *Tosca* at him.
Puccini: may you prosper, but in other climes! Continue, my friend, to
sketch in scrappy incidental music to well-known plays. But spare
England: this country has done neither you nor your nation nearly so

much harm as she has done other nations. Disturb not the existing peaceful relations.

J. F. Runciman, *The Saturday Review*, 21 July 1900.

Nikolai Rimsky-Korsakov

What a name! It suggests fierce whiskers stained with vodka!

The *Musical Courier*, 27 October 1897.

Gioacchino Rossini

Rossini would have been a great composer if his teacher had spanked him enough on the backside.

Ludwig van Beethoven.

Camille Saint-Saëns

It is one's duty to hate with all possible fervour the empty and ugly in art; and I hate Saint-Saëns the composer with a hate that is perfect.

J. F. Runciman, *The Saturday Review*, 12 December 1896.

Richard Strauss

An hour of original music in a lunatic asylum.

Claude Debussy on *Till Eugenspiegel*, 1895.

Better to hang oneself than write music like that.

Paul Hindemith on the *Alpensymphonie*, 1917.

Igor Stravinsky

The music of *Le Sacre de Printemps* baffles verbal description. Practically it has no relation to music at all as most of us understand the word.

The *Musical Times*, 1913.

Peter Ilyich Tchaikovsky

Tchaikovsky's First Piano Concerto, like the first pancake, is a flop.

Professor Nicolai Feopemptovich Soloviev of St Petersburg, in *Novoye Vremya*, 13 November 1875.

The violin is no longer played; it is pulled, torn, drubbed ... Tchaikovsky's Violin Concerto gives us for the first time the hideous notion that there can be music that stinks to the ear.

Edouard Hanslick, in the *Neue Freie Press* of Vienna, 5 December 1881.

The finale of the Fourth Symphony of Tchaikovsky pained me by its vulgarity. Nothing can redeem the lack of nobleness, the barbarous side, by which, according to ethnographs and diplomats, even the most polished Russian at times betrays himself.

The *Musical Review* goes in for a bit of racial stereotyping, 26 February 1880.

... in the last movement, the composer's Calmuck blood got the better of him, and slaughter, dire and bloody, swept across the storm-driven score.

The *Musical Courier*, 13 March 1889.

Giuseppe Verdi

Rigoletto lacks melody. This opera has hardly any chance of being kept in the repertoire.

Gazette Musicale de Paris, 22 May 1853.

Richard Wagner

There is no law against composing music when one has no ideas whatsoever. The music of Wagner, therefore, is perfectly legal.

Paris National, 1850.

The latest bore – but it is colossal – is *Tannhäuser*. I think I could compose something like it tomorrow, inspired by my cat scampering over the keys of the piano.

Prosper Mérimée, *Lettres à une inconnue*, 21 March 1861.

Wagner is a man devoid of all talent.

The famously talented composer César Cui, letter to Rimsky-Korsakov, 1863.

Of all the *bête*, clumsy, blundering, boggling, baboon-blooded stuff I ever saw on a human stage, that thing last night beat – as far as the story and acting went – and of all the affected, sapless, soulless, beginningless, endless, topless, bottomless, topsiturviest, tuneless, scrannelpipiest – tongs and boniest – doggerel of sounds I ever endured the deadliness of, that eternity of nothing was the deadliest, so far as its sound went.

Words almost fail John Ruskin, writing to Mrs Burne-Jones about *Die Meistersinger* on 30 June 1882.

Is Wagner a human being at all? Is he not rather a disease? He contaminates everything he touches – he has made music sick.

Friedrich Nietzsche, *Der Fall Wagner*, 1888.

With Wagner amorous excitement assumes the form of mad delirium ... It is a form of Sadism. It is the love of those degenerates who, in sexual transport, become like wild beasts. Wagner suffered from 'erotic madness',

which leads coarse nature to murder and lust, and inspires higher degenerates with works like *Die Walküre, Siegfried*, and *Tristan und Isolde*.
Max Nordau (1849–1923), *Degeneration*.

This revelling in the destruction of all tonal essence, raging satanic fury in the orchestra, this demoniacal, lewd, caterwauling, scandal-mongering, gun-toting music, with an orchestral accompaniment slapping you in the face... the diabolical din of this pig-headed man, stuffed with brass and sawdust, inflated, in an insanity of self-destructive aggrandizement ...
A heavily edited extract from *Geschichte des Dramas*, by J. L. Klein.

Wagner is a madman, a madman from pride. His music of the future is a monstrosity. Sterile by nature like all monsters, Wagner is impotent to reproduce himself.
Henri Prévost, *Etude sur Richard Wagner*.

Musicals

Annie Get Your Gun
Irving Berlin's score is musically not exciting – of all the real songs, only one or two are tuneful.
Lewis Kronenberger, *PM*, 17 May 1946.

Fiddler on the Roof
It seems clear to me that this is no smash hit, no blockbuster.
Variety on the Detroit tryout, 28 July 1964. The show ran for 3,342 performances on Broadway.

Grease
I don't think we can do anything with these reviews. It's a disaster. Close it.
Matthew Serino, head of the advertising agency promoting the show, 14 February 1972. The producers disregarded his advice and transferred it to Broadway, where it broke all records, and was filmed, before closing on 16 April 1980. In 1998 it reopened.

Oklahoma!
No legs, no jokes, no chance.
Broadway impresario Michael Todd, 1943; the show ran for 2,248 performances.

N

Native Americans

The policy of the general government toward the red man is not only liberal, but generous.

US President Andrew Jackson deplores the Native Americans' ungrateful reaction to his policy of clearing them off all their lands east of the Mississippi River, 1830.

The Army is the Indians' best friend.

Lieutenant-General George Armstrong Custer, known to Native Americans as 'Squaw-Killer', 1870.

See also LAST WORDS

I don't go so far as to think that the only good Indians are the dead Indians, but I believe that nine out of every ten are, and I shouldn't inquire too closely into the case of the tenth.

Future US President Theodore Roosevelt continues the liberal and generous policy in *The Winning of the West*, 1889–96.

Nazi Germany

There is no doubt that he has become a much more quiet, more mature and thoughtful individual during his imprisonment than he was before and does not contemplate acting against existing authority.

Otto Leybold, warden of Landsberg Prison, letter to the Bavarian minister of justice about one of his inmates, one A. Hitler, September 1924.

Hitler's influence is now waning so fast that the Government is no longer afraid of the growth of the Nazi movement.

William C. Bullitt, US diplomat, letter to President-elect Franklin D. Roosevelt, 1932.

The day when they were a vital threat is gone ...

It is not unlikely that Hitler will end his career as an old man in some Bavarian village who, in the biergarten in the evening, tells his intimates how he nearly overturned the German Reich. Strange battle cries will struggle to his lips, and he will mention names that trembled at his name. But his neighbours will have heard the tale so often that they will shrug their shoulders and bury their faces deeper in their mugs of Pilsener to hide their smiles. The old man, they will think, is entitled to his pipe dreams. It is comforting to live on the memory of an illusion.

Harold Laski, *Daily Herald*, 21 November 1932.

Herr Hitler is no longer a problem, his movement has ceased to be a political danger and the whole problem is solved. It is a thing of the past.

General Kurt von Schleicher dismisses the threat of National Socialism, 15 January 1933. Schleicher's government collapsed on 28 January, and Hitler was appointed Chancellor two days later.

No danger at all. We've hired him for our act ... Hitler is my prisoner, tied hand and foot by the conditions he has been obliged to accept ... Within two months we will have pushed Hitler so far into the corner that he'll squeak.

Franz von Papen, former Chancellor of Germany, on the appointment of Hitler to the chancellorship by President Hindenberg, 30 January 1933. Within two months Hitler had assumed dictatorial powers and declared the Nazis the only legal party.

Mistreatment of Jews in Germany may be considered virtually eliminated.

Cordell Hull, US Secretary of State, quoted in *Time*, 3 April 1933.

The outer world will do well to accept the evidence of German goodwill and seek by all possible means to meet it and justify it.

Walter Lippmann, US commentator, syndicated column, 18 May 1933.

If I may judge from my personal knowledge of Herr Hitler, peace and justice are the key-words of his policy.

Sir Thomas Moore, Conservative MP, October 1933.

By this revolution the German form of life is definitely settled for the next thousand years.

Adolf Hitler, 1934.

After all, they are only going into their own back garden.

Lord Lothian on Hitler's remilitarization of the Rhineland, March 1936.

Germany has no desire to attack any country in Europe.

David Lloyd George, former British Prime Minister, interview in the *News Chronicle*, 21 September 1936.

See also DICTATORS, FASCISM, POLITICIANS' PROMISES *and* WORLD WAR II

Newspapers

I can tell you how to make money in newspapers – own them!

Press baron Lord Thompson of Fleet, 1961. In 1966 he bought *The Times*; when his son sold the title to Rupert Murdoch in 1981 it was losing £2 million a month.

See also ROBERT MAXWELL

Richard Milhous Nixon

Quotes about Nixon

Sincerity is the quality that comes through on television.

The *Washington Star*, 15 September 1955.

A political has-been at 49.

Newsweek, 19 November 1962.

Nixon is a very much better man today than he was ten years ago ... I do not reject the notion that there is a new Nixon who has outlived and outgrown the ruthless politics of his early days.

Walter Lippmann, the *Washington Post*, 6 October 1968.

Of all the men running, Richard Nixon is the most dangerous to have as President. I would never work for that man. That man is a disaster.

Henry Kissinger in 1968. When Nixon was elected US President, Kissinger went to work for him.

Quotes by Nixon

Mother, I want to be an old-fashioned lawyer, an honest lawyer who can't be bought by crooks.

Speaking to his mother (allegedly) in 1925, aged 12.

We must defend our Constitution against a great wave of indifference to authority, disrespect of its law, and opposition to its basic principles which threatens its basic existence. Shall we of the present generation allow this instrument to be cast into disrepute? Shall we be responsible for its downfall?

Speech, high-school debate, 1928. He won $50 for it.

I'm not a quitter and incidentally Pat's not a quitter. After all her name was Patricia Ryan and she was born on St Patrick's Day.

The 'Checkers speech', defending himself against charges of illegal fund-raising as vice-presidential candidate and courting Irish-American support, 1952. In fact, Patricia Nixon was born on 16 March, the day before St Patrick's Day.

Let's get one thing straight: where our opponents misrepresent and distort the record ... I shall consider it a duty and a privilege to set the record straight.

Speech, 1958.

Wherever any mother or father talks to his child, I hope he can look at the man in the White House and, whatever he may think of his politics, he will say: 'Well, there is a man who maintains the kind of standards personally that I would want my child to follow.'

As Republican candidate for the presidency, in TV debate with John F. Kennedy, 1960.

Just think about how much you're going to be missing. You won't have Nixon to kick around any more because, gentlemen, this is my last press conference.

Press conference after losing to Democrat Pat Brown for the governorship of California, 7 November 1962.

The press are good guys ... I like the press ... The press are very helpful with their questions.

Press conference on re-entering politics, 1965.

Let us begin by committing ourselves to the truth, to see it like it is and tell it like it is; to find the truth, to speak the truth and to live with the truth. That is what we will do.

Speech accepting the Republican nomination as presidential candidate, 8 August 1968.

I won without having to pay the price or make any deals.

Speech acknowledging victory over Hubert Humphrey, November 1968.

This is a great day for France.

At the funeral of President Pompidou, 1974.

I would have made a good Pope.

Interview, 1980.

See also THE VIETNAM WAR *and* WATERGATE

Northern Ireland

For generations, a wide range of shooting in Northern Ireland has provided all sections of the population with a pastime which ... has occupied a good deal of leisure time. Unlike other countries, the outstanding characteristic of the sport has been that it was not confined to any one class.

The Northern Irish Tourist Board seeks to woo new visitors to the province, quoted in the *New Statesman*, 29 August 1969.

BELFAST CHOSEN AS MODEL CITY
The National Society of Christians has selected Belfast as 'The Model City of the World, 1970'.

The Belfast Newsletter, 1970. The Society, which is based in the USA, says that Belfast 'possesses a zealous Christian attitude and participates with active interest in religious functions'.

If it weren't for these troubles, Ireland would be a very happy place.

Lord Brookeborough, Ulster minister of commerce, 1970.

I have never been prouder to be a citizen of Belfast than at this time. Protestant and Catholic, rich and poor, are maintaining a standard of community stability that compares with anything that has ever been recorded in the annals of Europe.

David Bleakley, Northern Ireland minister of community relations, addressing the Ulster Institute for the Deaf in 1972. His speech had to be abandoned when three bombs exploded outside the building.

NOTE: In some of our copies the article *The Power of the Papacy* described the Pope as His Satanic Majesty. This should have read The Roman Antichrist.

The *Protestant Telegraph*, Belfast.

When they plant such bombs, it proves they can scare people, it proves they can kill people, it proves nothing.

Peter Bottomley MP, Northern Ireland minister, on the IRA, 1990.

Thirty injured, nobody dead. At the end of this opera, everybody's dead.

Sir Patrick Mayhew, Secretary of State for Northern Ireland, arriving at a performance of Donizetti's *Lucia di Lammermoor*, on an IRA bomb, 1992.

Prisoners should not be released early until the organisations to which they belong have substantially decommissioned their weapons.

Tony Blair, Prime Minister, on the proposed release of convicted Northern Ireland terrorists, House of Commons, 6 May 1998. By the end of March 1999, 248 prisoners (including 78 murderers) had been released early. A handful of guns – none of them from the IRA – had been 'decommissioned'.

After eight centuries of hatred and conflict, she showed them the path to peace.

US President Bill Clinton, speaking at a fundraising dinner in New York, 14 September 1998, on how his wife Hillary solved the Irish Question.

See also POLITICIANS' GAFFES, POLITICS *and* TERRORISM

Nuclear Physics

On thermodynamical grounds which I can hardly summarize shortly, I do not much believe in the commercial possibilities of induced radio-activity.

Scientist and philosopher J. B. S. Haldane, 1923, on Rutherford's method of releasing the energy of the atom by 'splitting' it.

There is no likelihood man can ever tap the power of the atom. The glib supposition of utilizing atomic energy when our coal has run out is a completely unscientific Utopian dream, a childish bug-a-boo. Nature has introduced a few foolproof devices into the great majority of the elements that constitute the bulk of the world, and they have no energy to give up in the process of disintegration.

The Nobel Prize-winning US physicist Robert Millikan, 1923.

There is by no means the same certainty today as a decade ago that the atoms of an element contain hidden sources of energy.

Lord Rutherford, shortly before 'splitting the atom' and releasing energy in 1923.

The energy produced by the breaking down of the atom is a very poor kind of thing. Anyone who looks for a source of power in the transformation of the atom is talking moonshine.

Lord Rutherford, 1936.

The slow neutron is extraordinarily efficient in causing transmutations with a large evolution of energy, but the neutron itself can only be produced by very inefficient processes, so that there appears to be no chance of gaining more energy from the reaction than has to be supplied.

Lord Rutherford: last lecture before his death in 1937.

That is how the atom is split, but what does it mean? To us who think in terms of practical use, it means – nothing!

Ritchie Calder, educationist and popularizer of science, 1932.

There is not the slightest indication that energy will ever be obtainable. It would mean that the atom would have to be shattered at will.

Albert Einstein, 1932.

Nuclear Power

The basic questions of design, material and shielding, in combining a nuclear reactor with a home boiler and cooling unit, no longer are problems ... The system would heat and cool a home, provide unlimited household hot water, and melt the snow from sidewalks and driveways. All that could be done for six years on a single charge of fissionable material costing about $300.

Robert E. Ferry, general manager of the US Institute of Boiler and Radiator Manufacturers, speech, 1 June 1955.

I do not hesitate to forecast that atomic batteries will be commonplace long before 1980 [and] it can be taken for granted that before 1980 ships, aircraft, locomotives and even automobiles will be atomically fuelled.

General David Sarnoff, chairman of RCA, *The Fabulous Future: America in 1980*, 1955.

Nuclear-powered vacuum cleaners will probably be a reality within ten years.

Vacuum cleaner manufacturer Alex Lewyt, president of Lewyt Corporation, *New York Times*, 10 June 1955.

We have not conducted tests in a way which is hazardous to health.

Dr Willard Libby of the US Atomic Energy Commission, 17 May 1957. In February 1995 it was officially admitted that, throughout the 1940s and 1950s, the USAEC had carried out involuntary radiation tests on over 9,000 US citizens. Prisoners, mental patients, and seriously ill babies had been injected with radioactive isotopes to see what effect they would have.

A nuclear power plant is infinitely safer than eating, because 300 people choke to death on food every year.

Dixy Lee Roy, shortly after vacating the office of chairman of the US Atomic Energy Committee, 1977.

What do you think you get more radiation from, leaning up against an atomic reactor or your wife? I don't want to alarm you, but all human beings have radioactive potassium in their blood – and that includes your wife ... I do not advocate a law forcing couples to sleep in twin beds [but] from the point of view of radiation safety, I must advise you against the practice of sleeping every night with two girls, because then you would get more radiation than from Dresden III.

Dr Edward Teller, 'The Father of the Hydrogen Bomb', at public hearings into the building of the Dresden III reactor in Illinois, 1979.

A normal aberration.

Jack Herbein, vice-president of Consolidated Edison, on reports of a leak at the Three Mile Island nuclear reactor, USA, 28 March 1979.

The coolant leakage is nothing – just a small amount.

Don Curry, press officer for Consolidated Edison, answers reporters' questions on 28 March 1979. A quarter of a million gallons of radioactive coolant had leaked onto the reactor floor.

There have been no recordings of any significant levels of radiation and none are expected outside the plant. The reactor is being cooled according to design by a reactor cooling system, and should be cooled by the end of the day.

Consolidated Edison press statement, 28 March 1979. As it was being issued, the automatic opening of a safety valve released a plume of radioactive gas, which drifted for sixteen miles and caused the whole of Three Mile Island to be evacuated. Inside the plant, atmospheric radiation was measured at 1,000 times normal background level.

This accident is not out of the ordinary for this kind of reactor.

Jack Herbein, president of Consolidated Edison, issues a not terribly reassuring reassurance, April 1979.

I would not call it an accident. I would call it a malfunction.

Edward Teller, interviewed in *Playboy* about the Three Mile Island incident.

The only accident is that this thing leaked out. You could have avoided this whole thing by not saying anything.

Craig Faust, Three Mile Island control room operator, April 1979.

Rapid oxidation; energetic disassembly; abnormal evolution.

Official terminology for 'fire', 'explosion' and 'accident', introduced by the US nuclear power industry for the reporting of incidents after the Three Mile Island accident.

All the waste in a year from a nuclear power plant can be stored under a desk.

Ronald Reagan, quoted in the *Burlington Free Press*, 15 February 1980. The average nuclear reactor generates 30 tons of waste a year.

During over 30 years of civil and commercial nuclear power operations in the UK, there has never been an emergency putting the public at risk.

Dr Robert Hawley, chief executive of Nuclear Electric, addressing the Opportunity 2000 conference in London, 8 September 1995. In 1957 a fire at the Windscale nuclear power station, details of which were suppressed for decades, caused the subsequent deaths of at least twenty members of the public. On 11 September 1995 Dr Hawley's company was fined £250,000 in the High Court for dangerous procedures at its Wylfa nuclear plant.

Nuclear War

Atomic energy might be as good as our present day explosives, but it is unlikely to produce anything very much more dangerous.

Winston Churchill, 1939.

This is the biggest fool thing we have ever done. The bomb will never go off, and I speak as an expert in explosives.

Admiral William Leahy advising President Truman in 1945.

I'm not sure the miserable thing will work, nor that it can be gotten to its target except by oxcart. That we become committed to it as a way to save the country and the peace seems to me to be full of dangers.

Robert Oppenheimer, director of the Manhatten Project, on the eve of Hiroshima, 1945.

The dangers of atomic war are overrated. It would be hard on little, concentrated countries like England. In the United States we have lots of space.

Colonel Robert Rutherford McCormick, 23 February 1950.

Following a nuclear attack on the United States, the US Postal Service plans to distribute Emergency Change of Address Cards. Be sure to carry your credit cards, cash, cheques, stocks, insurance policies, and will. Every effort will be made to clear trans-nuclear attack cheques, including those drawn on destroyed banks. You will be encouraged to buy US Savings Bonds.

US Federal Emergency Management Agency, Executive Order 11490, 1969.

Dig a hole, cover it with a couple of doors and then throw three feet of dirt on top. It's the dirt that does it. You know, dirt is just great stuff. If there are enough shovels to go round, everybody's going to make it.

T. K. Jones, US deputy under-secretary of defense for research, engineering, strategic and theatre nuclear forces, 1981.

Nuclear war could alleviate some of the factors leading to today's ecological disturbances that are due to current high-population concentrations and heavy industrial pollution.

Official at the US Office of Civil Defense, quoted in *The Fate of the Earth* by Jonathan Schell, 1982.

I don't honestly know. I think, again, until someplace – all over the world this is being, research is going on, to try and find the defensive weapon. There has never been a weapon that someone hasn't, come up with a defence. But it could – and the only defence is, well, you shoot yours and we'll shoot ours.

US President Ronald Reagan outlines the doctrine of mutual assured destruction (MAD), quoted verbatim in the *International Herald Tribune*, 1982.

American workers should draw a mushroom cloud and put underneath it: 'Made in America by lazy and illiterate Americans and tested in Japan'.

US senator Ernest Hollings, on the claim by Yoshio Sakurauchi, speaker of the Japanese Parliament, that American workers were lazy and illiterate.

It is not a bomb. It is a device which is exploding.

Jacques le Blanc, French ambassador to New Zealand, on his country's nuclear testing in the Pacific, October 1995.

O

Oil

The standard price of foreign crude by 1980 may well decline and will in any event not experience a substantial increase.

The US Cabinet Task Force on Oil Import Control, whose members included George Shulz (secretary to the Treasury), William Rogers (Secretary of State), Melvyn Laird (secretary of defense), and Walter Hickel (secretary of the interior), *The Oil Import Question: A Report on the Relationship of Oil Imports to the National Security*, 1970. In 1973, Arab members of the Organization of Petroleum Exporting Countries (OPEC) organized an export boycott, followed by a sharp increase in price; in 1980, crude oil cost ten times the 1960 price.

Alaska … has a greater oil reserve than Saudi Arabia.

Ronald Reagan, quoted in the *Washington Post*, 20 February 1980. Official US figures at the time put the proven oil reserves of Alaska at 9.2 billion barrels, with perhaps another 49 billion to be discovered, and of Saudi Arabia at 165.5 billion barrels.

Open University

'University of the Air' … The very term is an illusion in that it holds out hopes it cannot possibly fulfil … To speak of a university of the air is to encourage hopes that the television viewer will be offered the range and depth of courses open to the university student. This would be misleading nonsense.

The Times, 3 April 1965. Britain's university of the air, the Open University, was launched in 1969; it currently offers a full range and depth of university courses to some 80,000 students.

P

Plagiarism

Plagiarists usually defend themselves by insisting that the correspondence between their own work and the complainant's are coincidental. That is, they draw from the same well but not from each other's bucket.

Lawyer Anthony Julius, writing in the *Guardian*, December 1996, and exactly reproducing a metaphor from *Maugham on Copyright* (1828).

Planets, Moons and Stars

Jupiter's moons are invisible to the naked eye and therefore can have no influence on the earth, and therefore would be useless, and therefore do not exist.

Francisco Sizzi, professor of astronomy, dismisses Galileo's discovery in 1610.

The present inhabitation of Mars by a race superior to ours is very probable.

Camille Flammarion, founder of the French Astronomical Society, *La planète Mars et ses conditions d'habitabilité*, 1892.

Irrigation, unscientifically conducted, would not give us such truly wonderful mathematical fitness ... A mind of no mean order would seem to have presided over the system we see – a mind certainly of considerably more comprehensiveness than that which presides over our own public works.

Percival Lowell, founder of the Lowell Observatory, on Martian 'canals', 1908. Using mathematical models, he correctly predicted the existence of the planet Pluto.

MARTIANS BUILD TWO IMMENSE CANALS IN TWO YEARS
Vast Engineering Works Accomplished in an Incredibly Short Time
by Our Planetary Neighbors

Headline, *New York Times*, 27 August 1911, above a report that Lowell's
observatory had spotted two previously unseen straightish lines on the planet.

The final proof of the whole cosmic ice theory will be obtained when the
first landing on the ice-coated surface of the Moon takes place.

The Hörbiger Institute, 1953. Hans Hörbiger's Cosmic Ice Theory – which had been
official Nazi science policy – held that all the planets, except Earth, were coated in
layers of ice several miles thick.

Nothing can be more certain than that the stars have not changed their
declinations or latitudes one degree in the last 71 and three-quarter years.

Captain Woodley RN, with some potentially disastrous navigational advice in 1834.
The positions of the stars, as viewed from Earth, change constantly.

See also HOAXES *and* THE SUN

Plays

Write Me A Murder

This one is going to run and run and run.

Fergus Cashin, in the *Daily Sketch*, on a 1960s thriller that closed within a
month. The phrase has entered British culture, via *Private Eye*, as a by-word
for a hopeless flop.

Samuel Beckett: *Waiting For Godot*

It is pretentious gibberish, without any claim to importance whatsoever.
It is nothing but phoney surrealism with occasional references to Christ
and mankind. It has no form, no basic philosophy and absolutely no
lucidity. It's too conscious to be written off as mad. It's just a waste of
everybody's time and it made me ashamed to think that such balls could
be taken seriously for a moment.

Noël Coward, 1960. Beckett won the Nobel Prize for Literature in 1969.

Erskine Caldwell: *Tobacco Road*

It isn't the sort of entertainment folks buy in the theatre, nor ever have
bought within my memory.

Burns Mantle, *New York Daily News*, 5 December 1933. *Tobacco Road* opened
on 3 December 1933 and ran for 3,182 performances – then one of the five longest
Broadway runs.

Agatha Christie: *The Mousetrap*

Compared to other West End successes this new murder mystery is very weak.

Possibly true when published by the *Sunday Dispatch* in 1952, but *The Mouse-trap* (unlike the *Sunday Dispatch*) is still running, making it the second-longest running production in theatre history. The record is held by Eugène Ionesco's *La Cantatrice Chauve*, which has run continuously in Paris since 11 May 1950.

Arthur Miller: *Death of a Salesman*

Who would want to see a play about an unhappy travelling salesman? Too depressing.

Cheryl Crawford turning down an invitation to stage Miller's most famous and successful play, 1948. It won Miller the Pulitzer Prize the following year.

Eugene O'Neill: *Strange Interlude*

Strange Interlude will probably interest a comparatively small public. It is solid grey in tone, slow-paced and repetitious in performance, and forbidding in length.

Burns Mantle, *New York Daily News*, 31 January 1928. The play was O'Neill's greatest popular success.

John Osborne: *Look Back in Anger*

Mr Osborne will have other plays in him, and perhaps he will settle down, now that he has got this off his mind.

J. C. Trewin, the *Illustrated London News*, May 1956.

Harold Pinter: *The Birthday Party*

If the author can forget Beckett, Ionesco and Simpson he may do much better next time.

The *Manchester Evening News*, May 1958.

George Bernard Shaw: *Mrs Warren's Profession*

Superabundance of foulness ... wholly immoral and degenerate.

New York Herald, 1905.

Offensive ... contemptible ... abominable.

New York Post, 1905.

Decaying and reeking.

New York Times, 1905.

A dramatized stench.

New York Sun, 1905.

Three Plays for Puritans

One might still be hopeful for Mr Shaw's future as a dramatist, despite his present incompetence, if there were any hint in his plays of creative power. But there is no such hint.

Arnold Bennett, in *The Academy*, 9 February 1901, on *Caesar and Cleopatra*, *The Devil's Disciple*, and *Captain Brassbound's Conversion*.

See also IBSEN *and* SHAKESPEARE

The Police

Get this thing straight once and for all. The policeman isn't there to create disorder. The policeman is there to preserve disorder.

Mayor Richard Daley of Chicago, commenting on a police riot at the Democratic National Convention, 1968.

Unfortunately we wear uniforms and the criminals always spot us.

Francisco Luna, police precinct head, explains the rising crime rate in Mexico City; quoted in *Time*, 7 December 1998.

Politicians' Gaffes

United Kingdom

Tony Banks MP

They ain't gaffes. They are ideas.

Tony Banks MP, minister for sport, 4 April 1998, on his habit of perpetrating ideas.

See also POLITICS *and* SPORT

Betty Boothroyd MP

I can have no objection to instruments that merely vibrate.

As speaker of the House of Commons, ruling on MPs' use of pagers, 12 March 1997.

Kenneth Clarke MP

At Consett you have got one of the best steelworks in Europe. It doesn't employ as many people as it used to because it is so modern.

As Chancellor of the Exchequer, interviewed on BBC Radio Newcastle on 3 March 1995. The Consett steelworks had closed twenty years earlier.

Consett … is also one of the major centres in Western Europe for disposable baby nappies.

On 16 March 1995, hoping to make up for his earlier gaffe, the Chancellor praises a factory that closed in 1991.

Edwina Currie MP

People in the North die of ignorance and crisps.

As a newly appointed junior health minister, September 1986.

Most of the egg production in this country is infected with salmonella.

As junior health minister, launching a ruinously expensive health scare with a half-truth, 1988. She resigned a fortnight later.

Sir Norman Fowler MP

We're sending 23 million leaflets to every household in Britain.

As health secretary, on the government's AIDS awareness campaign, 1986.

There's a whole range of things we're doing with condoms.

On AIDS prevention, 1987.

Dame Jill Knight MP

Anyone in his position needs to be whiter than white.

On Nelson Mandela, BBC Radio Ulster, 1990.

Joan Lestor MP

Members exercising their integrity threaten to destroy the whole credibility of the Labour Party.

Addressing her party's National Executive Committee, 1971.

John Major MP

'If' is a very large preposition.

As Chancellor of the Exchequer, on the likelihood of a recession, 1990.

I'm drawing a line under the sand.

As Prime Minister, hoping to end his party's squabbling over the Maastricht Treaty, 1992.

See also CRICKET

Richard Needham MP

I wish that cow would resign.

Speaking to his wife on his car phone, the Northern Ireland minister comments on his leader, Prime Minister Margaret Thatcher, in 1990. The call was recorded by a radio eavesdropper. Mrs Thatcher resigned later that year.

Stephen Norris MP

You have your own company, your own temperature control, your own music and you don't have to put up with dreadful human beings sitting alongside you.

As transport minister, comparing and contrasting public and private transport, 8 February 1995.

The Rev. Ian Paisley MP

We are not going to stand idly by and be murdered in our beds.

On Unionists' response to the IRA, 1970.

See also POLITICS *and* NORTHERN IRELAND

Nicholas Ridley MP

I am leaving port under full steam with my bow doors closed.

British environment secretary, 8 March 1987, two days after the capsize of the car ferry *Herald of Free Enterprise*, in which over 200 passengers drowned. The cause was a failure to close the bow doors. Ridley explained that he was just making a joke.

Jack Straw MP

You can't manufacture children overnight.

As Labour education spokesman, on *Panorama*, BBC TV, 1990.

Baroness Thatcher (formerly Margaret Thatcher MP)

Will this thing jerk me off?

Firing a field gun during a visit to the Falklands, January 1983.

There is no such thing as society. There are individual men and women, and there are families.

Interviewed in *Women's Own*, 31 October 1987.

We have become a grandmother.

Speaking to reporters, 4 March 1989.

See also DOUBLE-ENTENDRES, POLITICIANS' PROMISES *and* POLITICS

Lord Whitelaw (formerly William Whitelaw MP)

He is going round the country stirring up apathy.

On the election strategy of Labour leader Harold Wilson, 1970.

I do not intend to prejudge the past.

On becoming secretary of state for Northern Ireland, 1972.

I have the thermometer in my mouth and I am listening to it all the time.

On party morale during the election campaign of October 1974.

I don't blame anyone, except perhaps all of us.

As Home Secretary, 1980.

We are examining alternative anomalies.

Explaining government policies in the House of Commons, 1981.

I can assure you that I definitely might take action.

As Home Secretary, giving evidence to a House of Commons Select Committee, 1981.

United States of America
George Bush

Boy, they were big on crematoriums, weren't they?

During a visit to Auschwitz, 1987.

I stand for anti-bigotry, anti-semitism and anti-racism.

Campaign speech, 1988.

See also POLITICIANS' PROMISES

Jimmy Carter

I desire the Poles carnally.

A bad translation of 'I have come to learn your opinions and understand your desires for the future' on a visit to Warsaw; reported in the *Daily Mail* of 29 December 1978.

The great president who might have been – Hubert Horatio Hornblower!

Paying a tribute to Democrat elder statesman Hubert Horatio Humphrey at the New York convention of 1980.

See also CONFESSIONS *and* IRAN

Gerald Ford

Mr Nixon was the thirty-seventh President of the United States. He had been preceded by thirty-six others.

Explaining his decision to pardon his predecessor, 1974.

To the great people of the Government of Israel – Egypt, excuse me.

Proposing a toast to Egyptian President Anwar el-Sadat, 28 October 1975.

Whenever I can I watch the Detroit Tigers on radio.

Campaigning in 1976.

I say that if Lincoln was alive today he would turn over in his grave.

Campaigning in 1976.

I don't believe the Poles consider themselves dominated by the Soviet Union ... There is no Soviet domination in Eastern Europe, and there never will be under a Ford administration.

Discussing Poland with his Democrat rival Jimmy Carter in a televised debate, 6 October 1976.

When a man is asked to make a speech, the first thing he has to decide is what to say.

Speech, 1977.

Carter apparently doesn't even know that Michigan is one of the forty-eight States.

Campaigning for Ronald Reagan in 1980. There are 50 States in the USA.

Barry Goldwater

Many Americans don't like the simple things. That's what they have against we conservatives.

The Republican presidential candidate, speaking during the campaign of 1964.

Hubert Horatio Humphrey

There are too many guns in the hands of people who don't know how to use them.

Commenting on the failed attempt by Sarah Jane Moore to assassinate President Gerald Ford, September 1975.

John Fizgerald Kennedy

I take pride in the words, *Ich bin ein Berliner.*

As US President, speaking at the Berlin Wall, June 1963. He meant to say 'I am a Berliner' (*Ich bin Berliner*); what he actually said was, 'I am a sticky bun'. A *berliner* is a sort of central European doughnut.

Alfred Landon

Wherever I have gone in this country, I have found Americans.

The Republican presidential candidate, speaking during the campaign of 1936.

Mike McCurry

Maybe there'll be a simple, innocent explanation. I don't think so, because I think we would have offered that up already ... I don't think it's going to be entirely easy to explain maybe.

The White House media spokesman on the Monica Lewinsky scandal, 16 February 1998; he resigned shortly afterwards.

See also WILLIAM JEFFERSON CLINTON

Ronald Reagan

The United States has much to offer the Third World War.

Speech on Third World development, 1975; he used the phrase nine times.

Who's that?

Reacting to the mention of French President Valéry Giscard d'Estaing on *The Today Show*, 14 November 1979.

I would like to extend a warm welcome to President Mo.

Proposing a toast to President Samuel Doe of Liberia, 1982.

Now would you join me in a toast to President Figueredo, to the people of Bolivia – no, that's where I'm going – to the people of Brazil.

Speech during a visit to Colombia, 1982.

See also THE ENVIRONMENT, THE IRAN-CONTRA SCANDAL, OIL, POLITICIANS' PROMISES, POLITICS *and* THE VIETNAM WAR

Alfred S. Regnery

HAVE YOU SLUGGED YOUR KID TODAY?

Bumper sticker on the car of President Reagan's nominee for the post of director of the Office of Juvenile Justice and Delinquency Prevention, reported in *Newsweek*, 2 May 1983. Under questioning in Congress he was unable to define the word 'delinquency' or 'name a single one of the books he was studying on juvenile crime'.

Edward Stettinius

The United States looks upon Mexico as a good neighbour, a strong upholder of democratic traditions in this hemisphere, and a country we are proud to call our own.

The US Secretary of State greets his hosts at the beginning of an official visit in February 1945. His aides corrected 'own' to 'friend'.

James Watt

I have every kind of mix you can have. I have a black, I have a woman, two Jews and a cripple.

As US secretary for the interior, on the composition of a committee he had just appointed in 1983. He was sacked shortly afterwards.

See also RACE *and* JAMES DANFORTH QUAYLE

Politicians' Promises

Ambition

My decision to remove myself completely from the political scene is definite and positive.

General Dwight D. Eisenhower, 1948. He was US President 1953–61.

I'll never run again. Politics is a filthy business.

Edward Koch (New York City Councillor 1967–68, member of the House of Representatives 1969–74, and mayor of New York 1978–90) after failing to become an assemblyman in 1962.

The thought of being President frightens me. I do not think I want the job.

Ronald Reagan, governor of California, 1973. He was US President 1981–89.

I would prefer trying to grow pineapples in Alaska to being Chancellor.

Bavarian politician Franz-Josef Strauss, 1968.

I hope the German people are never so desperate as to believe they have to elect me as Chancellor.

Franz-Josef Strauss, 1971.

I am not a candidate for Chancellor under present political circumstances.

Franz-Josef Strauss, 1979. In 1980 he stood for chancellor, and lost.

I would not wish to be prime minister, dear. I have not had enough experience for that job. The only full ministerial position I've held is minister for education and science. Before you could even think of being prime minister you'd need to have done a good deal more jobs than that.

Margaret Thatcher, interviewed on children's TV in 1973. With no further ministerial experience, she became Conservative Party leader in 1975, and prime minister in 1979.

BSE (Mad Cow Disease)

Nobody need be worried about BSE in this country or anywhere else in the world.

British agriculture minister John Gummer, House of Commons, 1990.

Coal Industry

The Labour Party is committed to the reintroduction of public ownership of the coal industry.

Martin O'Neill MP, Opposition spokesman on energy, House of Commons, March 1994.

While we envisage a national role for coal in our energy strategy, we do not intend to re-nationalize the industry.

Martin O'Neill MP, Opposition spokesman on energy, speech to the Coal Industry Society, November 1994.

There has been no change in Labour's policy.

Martin O'Neill MP, Opposition spokesman on energy, letter to the *Guardian*, November 1994.

The Economy

Over my dead body. There will be no devaluation.

British Prime Minister Harold Wilson MP, TV interview, October 1967. The pound was devalued on 6 November.

From now on the pound abroad is worth 14 per cent or so less in terms of other currencies. It does not mean, of course, that the pound here in Britain, in your pocket or purse or in your bank, has been devalued.

British Prime Minister Harold Wilson MP, TV and radio broadcast, 19 November 1967. Devaluation naturally caused an immediate rise in the price of imported goods and raw materials.

We thought we could put the economy right in five years. We were wrong. It will probably take ten.

Tony Benn (Anthony Wedgwood Benn) MP, president of the Board of Trade, 1968.

This would, at a stroke, reduce the rise in prices, increase productivity and reduce unemployment.

Conservative Central Office policy briefing during the election campaign of June 1970, afterwards associated with the victorious Conservative leader, Edward Heath. During his period of office productivity fell, unemployment rose, and the annual rate of inflation exceeded 25%.

I am not forecasting a recession over the next twelve months.

Chancellor of the Exchequer Norman Lamont, House of Commons, 4 December 1989. It happened anyway, lasting into 1993.

I am confident the period of low growth will be short-lived.

Chancellor of the Exchequer Norman Lamont, House of Commons,
20 March 1990.

What we are seeing is the return of that vital economic ingredient,
confidence, and green shoots of economic spring are appearing once
again.

Chancellor of the Exchequer Norman Lamont, House of Commons,
9 October 1991.

Membership of the ERM remains at the heart of the Government's
economic policy.

Chancellor of the Exchequer Norman Lamont, shortly before Britain left
the ERM (European Exchange Rate Mechanism) in September 1992.

A drastic reduction in the deficit will take place in the fiscal year '82.

US President Ronald Reagan, 5 March 1981. In 1982 the US deficit rose
to $110.7 billion, breaking the 1976 record of $70 billion.

We've laid a firm foundation for economic recovery in 1982.

US President Ronald Reagan, 18 October 1981. In 1982 US unemployment
rose to 10.4%.

Election Prospects

Go back to your constituencies – and prepare for government!

David Steel MP, leader of the Liberal Party, closing address to delegates at
the 1981 Liberal Party Assembly.

Employment

Our priority is to create jobs. This is not just an economic priority but
also a social and moral one.

Conservative party manifesto, April 1997, page 9.

Governments cannot create jobs.

Conservative party manifesto, April 1997, page 10.

Energy Conservation

I am very glad to support the Energy Conservation Bill. It is long overdue.
I shall urge the government to support it.

Robert Jones, backbench Conservative MP, 1993.

I deplore the Bill ... Frankly we have much more practical things to get on with.

Robert Jones, newly appointed minister for energy conservation, 1994.

Health

We said zero, and I think any statistician will tell you that when you're dealing with very big numbers, zero must mean plus or minus a few.

William Waldegrave MP, health secretary, on hospital waiting lists, 1992.

Adolf Hitler

I have no intention whatever of making that Austrian corporal either Minister of Defence or Chancellor of the Reich.

Paul von Hindenberg, president of Germany, 26 January 1933. He elevated Hitler to the post of chancellor four days later.

Housing

This is not a lightly given pledge. It is a promise. We shall achieve the 500,000 target, and we shall not allow any developments, any circumstances, however adverse, to deflect us from our aim.

British Prime Minister Harold Wilson MP, speech to an election meeting in Bradford, March 1966, on Labour's target for the annual rate of council house building. The following year 400,000 were completed, but in 1968 the housing minister Anthony Greenwood announced that the target had been abandoned because 'there are far too many uncertainties for it to be possible for anyone to say exactly how many will be built in 1970'.

There is no housing shortage in Lincoln today – just a rumour that is put about by people who have nowhere to live.

Councillor Murfin, Lord Mayor of Lincoln.

Industrial Relations

It is certain as the day that a Labour town council, a Socialist or Communist government, would not for a day tolerate strikes in social or other services necessary for the life of the nation.

George Lansbury MP, leader of the British Labour Party, 1934.

My administration will work very closely with you to bring about a spirit of co-operation between the President and air traffic controllers.

US presidential candidate Ronald Reagan, letter to Robert Poli, president of the Air Traffic Controllers' Union, 20 October 1980. When air traffic controllers went on strike in 1981 President Reagan sacked them all.

Libel

If it falls to me to start the fight to cut out the cancer of bent and twisted journalism in our country with the simple sword of truth and the trusty shield of British fair play, so be it.

Jonathan Aitken MP, launching a libel writ against Granada TV and the *Guardian* over their allegations of bribe-taking and dirty dealing in the arms trade, April 1995. In June 1997, the month after he lost his seat at the general election, his case collapsed when it became apparent that his evidence was unreliable. In December 1998 he was committed for trial on charges of perjury and obstruction of justice, to which he pleaded guilty in January 1999. He was sentenced to eighteen months' imprisonment in June 1999.

Loyalty

I am one thousand per cent for Tom Eagleton and have no intention of dropping him from the ticket.

George McGovern, 24 July 1972, after reports that his vice-presidential running mate had undergone electric shock therapy for depression. On 31 July Eagleton was dumped and on 5 August McGovern chose Sargent Shriver, John F. Kennedy's brother-in-law.

Neil Hamilton has my full confidence and support.

British Prime Minister John Major, shortly before sacking him in November 1994.

The Chancellor's position is unassailable.

British Prime Minister Margaret Thatcher, shortly before making Chancellor Nigel Lawson's position untenable in 1989.

Poverty

We shall soon be in sight of the day when poverty will be banished from this nation.

Herbert Hoover, Republican candidate for the US presidency, 1928.

So here is the Great Society. It's the time – and it's going to be soon – when nobody in this country is poor.

US President Lyndon Baines Johnson, 1965.

Quality of Life

Where there is discord, may we bring harmony.

Margaret Thatcher, on election to office in 1979.

My aim is to create a nation at ease with itself.

John Major, on election to office in 1990.

Regional Assemblies

Labour is committed to a regional assembly for Wales and to regional assemblies for England.

Tony Blair, leader of the Labour Party, June 1994.

We are not committed to regional assemblies in England.

Tony Blair, leader of the Labour Party, March 1995.

Taxation

Read my lips: no new taxes.

US vice-president and presidential candidate George Bush, 19 August 1988. New taxes were duly introduced.

We have no plans to widen the scope of VAT.

British Prime Minister John Major, press conference during his successful election campaign of 1992. VAT was subsequently extended to domestic gas, electricity and coal.

See also TAX

Truth

A Nixon–Agnew administration will abolish the credibility gap and re-establish the truth, the whole truth, as its policy.

Spiro T. Agnew, campaign speech as Richard Nixon's running-mate, August 1968.

See also RICHARD NIXON, POLITICS *and* WATERGATE

Politics

Spiro T. Agnew

After all, what does a politician have to lose but his credibility?

Inauguration statement, January 1969.

The charges against me are, if you'll pardon the expression, damned lies. I am innocent of these charges. If indicted I shall not resign.

On allegations of financial corruption, August 1973. He resigned in October.

Tony Banks MP

England should not stage the 2006 World Cup. A South African claim would be superior to that of any European country staging the competition.

Tony Banks MP, Opposition Labour backbencher, January 1997.

The one thing we need to show is that the government is entirely behind the Football Association in its bid [for the 2006 World Cup].

Tony Banks MP, minister for sport, May 1997.

England stands a very good chance of staging the 2006 World Cup, and you can take my word for that because I'm a government minister.

Tony Banks MP, minister for sport, December 1998.

See also POLITICIANS' GAFFES *and* SPORT

Tony Blair MP

This is not the time for soundbites. I feel the hand of history upon our shoulders.

The Prime Minister arrives for talks in Northern Ireland, 7 April 1998.

Stephen Byers MP

I was worried you were going to ask me that. I think it is 54.

As minister of education, asked on 21 January 1998 to solve the sum '8 × 7'.

Alexander Haig

As of now, I am in charge of the White House.

As Secretary of State, following the wounding of President Reagan in an assassination attempt, 1981. As vice-president, George Bush took charge.

Edward Heath MP

Our only problem at the moment is the problem of success.

Speech as Prime Minister, 1973. The next twelve months brought strikes by miners and power workers, fuel and food shortages, electricity rationing, and a three-day working week.

David Hunt MP

John Major will, I predict, turn out to be one of the great political figures of our time.

On the election of John Major as leader of the Conservatives, and Prime Minister, 1990. He was then appointed to Mr Major's cabinet.

Lord Irvine

You are not talking about something from the DIY store which may collapse after a year or two.

The Labour Lord Chancellor, on spending £59,000 of public money on new wallpaper for his official residence in the Palace of Westminster, 3 March 1998.

Neil Kinnock

The sideways shuffles of those who ... call themselves Social Democrats offer no means of progress ... And when the shufflers finally take themselves off to stale centrist pastures in boardrooms, the House of Lords or the European Commission in a sort of moveable *Any Questions?* panel, only the faction watchers in the Lobby and coalition mongers in the City mourn.

As a Labour MP, writing in the *Political Quarterly* of Oct–Dec 1980. After losing the 1992 general election as Labour leader, he opted for a stale centrist pasture as European commissioner for transport.

Helen Liddell MP

Our voters don't tend to have cars.

As deputy leader of the Scottish Labour Party, explaining the victory of the Scottish National Party in a European Parliament by-election for North-East Scotland, 27 November 1998. Labour was beaten into third place by the Conservatives.

Lord MacAlpine

I misjudged. I didn't make a judgement. It was all done third hand.

As chairman of the Conservative Party, after businessman Asil Nadir, who had donated £400,000 to its funds, skipped bail on fraud charges and escaped to North Cyprus in 1993.

John Major MP

Something that I was not aware that happened suddenly turned out not to have happened.

As Prime Minister, giving evidence to the Scott Inquiry, 1994.

The Rev. Ian Paisley MP

I have never made an inflammatory statement in my life.

The Free Presbyterian politician who once described Roman Catholics as 'damnable acolytes of the Antichrist', 1969.

See also NORTHERN IRELAND *and* POLITICIANS' GAFFES

John Prescott MP

The Tories have done many things much damage to here in London, a proud once great city. London beat the racists in Tower Hamlets and the rest of the party proud of you doing it were and we much talk about it outside the rest of London.

Let me leave you with one thought in view of the time which is important to put over a good idea. Why not employ more teachers in

social productivity to challenge the economic productivity only so
shall we show to the Tories where they are. Let us say something to the
unemployed, yes you are after full employment years and we can go back
forward now back to full employment.

As deputy leader of the Labour Party, addressing the London Labour Party
Conference, 26 February 1995.

Ronald Reagan

We were told four years ago that 17 million people went to bed hungry
every night. Well, that was probably true. They were all on a diet.

TV campaign broadcast, 27 October 1964.

I favour the Civil Rights Act of 1964 and it must be enforced at gunpoint
if necessary.

Interview, 1965.

I would have voted against the Civil Rights Act of 1964.

Interview, 1968.

See also THE ENVIRONMENT

Dame Shirley Williams

I am not interested in a 'Third Party'. I do not believe it has any future.

As a Labour MP, 1983, shortly before leaving to found the Social Democratic
Party – which, as things turned out, did not have a future.

Harold Wilson MP

I myself have always deprecated – perhaps rightly, perhaps wrongly –
in crisis after crisis, appeals to the Dunkirk Spirit as an answer to our
problems.

Speech as leader of the Opposition, 22 July 1961.

I believe that the Spirit of Dunkirk will once again carry us through to
success.

Speech as Prime Minister, 12 December 1964.

Tim Yeo MP

I am absolutely confident that I won't have to resign.

As minister for the environment, 4 January 1994, after being revealed as the father
of two illegitimate children. He resigned the next day.

Pop and Rock

Rock'n'Roll

The big question in the music business today is: 'How long will it last?'
It is our guess that it won't.

Cashbox, 1955.

It will be gone by June.

Variety, 1955.

There is no doubt that 'Rock and Roll' music is the most dangerous
thing that has ever happened. It is a monstrous threat. We must oppose
it to the end.

The British musicologist Steve Race, *Melody Maker*, 1956.

Rock'n'Roll is phoney and false and sung, written and played for the
most part by cretinous goons.

Frank Sinatra, 1958.

The teenage vogue for beat music and rock'n'roll is over. Now the demand
is for pop music shows of a broad family appeal.

BBC spokesman, on the axing of *Oh Boy!* and *Dig This* in 1960.

I believe Elvis Presley and the Beatles and the Rolling Stones are going to
answer to God for all the pollution of youth around the world. All this
rock culture is stirring people up to do evil instead of to do good, just as
the people were doing in Noah's day. Just look at their dress and the
glasses they wear. God is going to rain judgement upon the earth – and
this could happen any moment now with all the rock music and illicit sex
and wine, women, and the glasses they wear.

The Rev. Jack Wyrtzen, 1970.

Mariah Carey

I'm inconsolable. I was a very good friend of Jordan. He was probably
the greatest basketball player this country has ever seen. We will never see
his like again.

Singer Mariah Carey, interviewed on CNN, 7 February 1999. On being informed
that it was not Michael Jordan who had died, but King Hussein of Jordan, the singer
was led away by her bodyguards in a state of confusion.

Ian Dury and the Blockheads

I refused to write the music as I didn't really get off on the words. I thought any song that starts off, 'Arseholes, bastards, fucking cunts and pricks,' is not exactly going to be a Number One world hit.

Musician Chas Jankel, 1979. The song, *Plaistow Patricia*, featured on the album *New Boots and Panties*, which was in the British Top Twenty for over a year.

Bob Dylan

Message songs, as everyone knows, are a drag. It's only college newspaper editors and single girls under fourteen that could possibly have time for them.

Interview, 1970.

Buddy Holly

The biggest no-talent I ever worked with.

Paul Cohen of Decca Records, on why he fired him, 1956.

Whitney Houston

I love you, Spain!

The singer greets her fans in Portugal, July 1998.

Cliff Richard

Hardly the kind of performance any parent could wish their child to witness.

Three decades before Sir Cliff entertained Centre Court at Wimbledon: the *Musical Express*, 1958.

The Rolling Stones

The singer'll have to go – the BBC won't like him.

New manager Eric Easton, trying to dump Mick Jagger in 1963.

I give the Stones about another two years. I'm saving for the future. I bank all my song royalties for a start.

Mick Jagger, 1964.

The Spice Girls

I'm as old as you want me to be. I can be a 10-year-old with big tits if you want.

Geri Halliwell, then a member of the group, speaking to a studio manager; reported in the *Daily Telegraph* magazine, 19 April 1998.

Tommy Steele

How long can this Tommy Steele last? Five months?

Mr Justice Harman, trying a contractual lawsuit in 1957.

Led Zeppelin

Four shrieking monkeys are not going to use a privileged family name without permission.

Frau Eva von Zeppelin. They used it anyway.

See also THE BEATLES *and* ELVIS

Population

In all probability the next doubling of the people of England will be in about six hundred years to come, or by the Year of Our Lord 2300, at which time it will have eleven millions of people. The next doubling after that will be, in all probability, in less than twelve or thirteen hundred years, or by the Year of Our Lord 3500 or 3600. At which time the Kingdom will have 22 millions of souls.

Gregory King, *Observations of the State of England*, 1696.

After performing the most exact calculation possible ... I have found that there is scarcely one tenth as many people on earth as in ancient times. What is surprising is that the population of the earth decreases every day, and if this continues, in another ten centuries the earth will be nothing but a desert.

Charles, Baron de Montesquieu, *Lettres persanes*, 1721.

Population is constant in size and will remain so right up to the end of mankind.

L'Encyclopédie, 1756.

When we get piled upon one another in large cities, we shall become as corrupt as in Europe, and go to eating one another as they do there.

Thomas Jefferson, 1787.

It may be safely asserted ... that population, when unchecked, increases in geometrical progression of such a nature as to double itself every twenty-five years.

Thomas Malthus, A *Summary View of the Principle of Population*, 1830. If Malthus had been correct, the UK population of 38 million in 1901 would now have grown to 244 million.

In 1993 there should be a population within the present area of the United States of 580,000,000 ... Lives of 120 years will be as frequent as now are those of 90.

Lawyer Van Buren Denslow, contributing to the programme for the 1893 Chicago

World's Fair. The US population is currently c. 220,000,000. The only person known to have lived to 120 in recent times, a Frenchwoman, died in 1998.

Hardly anyone believes that the birth rate, which has been falling rapidly in recent years, will rise much in the near future, even if it does not fall further still. It is, to say the least, highly probable that in twenty years' time the [UK] population will not exceed 40,000,000.

G. D. H. Cole and Raymond Postgate, *The Common People 1746–1946* (second edition, corrected 1956). In 1966 the UK population was c. 54,000,000; in 1976 it was c. 55,928,000. It is now c. 61,000,000.

Pornography

Public media should not contain explicit or implied descriptions of sex acts. Our society should be purged of the perverts who provide the media with pornographic material while pretending it has some redeeming social value under the public's 'right to know'. Pornography is pornography regardless of the source.

Kenneth Starr, interviewed by Dianne Sawyer for *60 Minutes* in 1987. In 1998, as White House special prosecutor, he published a multi-volume report containing explicit and exhaustive details of acts of frottage, mutual masturbation, fellatio and 'cigar sex' between President Clinton and Monica Lewinsky.

See also WILLIAM JEFFERSON CLINTON

Poultry Rearing

50 years hence ... we shall escape the absurdity of growing a whole chicken in order to eat the breast or wing, by growing those parts separately under a suitable medium.

Winston Churchill MP, in *Popular Mechanics*, 1922.

Prisons

ATTICA PRISON TO BE CONVICTS' PARADISE

Headline, *New York Times*, 2 August 1931. Forty years later, 28 prisoners were killed in a riot sparked by the intolerable conditions in Attica prison.

Uganda has among the best prisons in the world and people from many countries are eager to visit them.

President Idi Amin of Uganda, interviewed in the *Guardian*, January 1976. Among the many enlightened features of Amin's prisons was the requirement for prisoners to execute fellow inmates with sledgehammers.

I find it morally unacceptable for the private sector to undertake the incarceration of those whom the state has decided need to be imprisoned ... Almost all people believe that this is one area where a free market does not exist.

Jack Straw MP, Opposition spokesman on home affairs, addressing the Prison Officers' Association, April 1996.

As a responsible government we have committed ourselves to providing best value and to achieve high performance, efficiency and effectiveness ... The immediate transfer of existing private prisons to the public sector is not affordable and cannot be justified.

Jack Straw MP, Home Secretary, addressing the Prison Officers' Association, 19 May 1998.

Prohibition

There will be no violations to speak of.

Colonel Daniel Porter, supervising revenue agent in charge of enforcing the 18th Amendment to the US Constitution (the Volstead Act), prohibiting the manufacture, transportation and supply of alcoholic beverages, 16 January 1920.

Thirteen states with a population less than that of New York State alone can prevent repeal until Halley's comet returns. One might as well talk about a summer vacation on Mars.

Lawyer Clarence Darrow, January 1921.

In a generation, those who are now children will have lost their taste for alcohol.

John Fuller, *Atlantis: America and the Future*, 1925.

The abolition of the commercialized liquor trade in this country is as final as the abolition of slavery.

Henry Ford, *My Philosophy of Industry*, 1929.

There is as much chance of repealing the 18th Amendment as there is for a humming-bird to fly to the planet Mars with the Washington Monument tied to its tail.

Senator Morris Shepherd of Texas, September 1930.

   The 21st Amendment to the US Constitution, passed in 1933, repealed the Volstead Act.

James Danforth Quayle

In 1988 the question is whether we're going forward to tomorrow or whether we're going to go past to the – to the back!

Campaign speech, 17 August 1988, reported in *Esquire*, August 1992.

I got through a number of things in the area of defense, like showing the importance of cruise missiles and getting them more accurate so that we can have precise precision.

Referring to his legislative accomplishments as a senator; reported in The *New York Times*, 26 August 1988.

The Holocaust was an obscene period in our nation's history – no, not in our nation's history but in World War Two. I mean in this century's history. But we all lived in this century. I didn't live in this century, but in this century's history.

Speech, 15 September 1988, reported in the *New Yorker*, 10 October 1988.

We're going to have the best-educated American people in the world.

Speech, 21 September 1988, reported in *Esquire*, August 1992.

Republicans understand the importance of bondage between a mother and child.

Campaign speech, reported in *US News and World Report*, 10 October 1988.

We expect them to work toward the elimination of human rights in accordance with the pursuit of Justice.

On Salvadorian government officials, 3 February 1989, reported in the *Chicago Tribune*, 4 February 1989.

Space is almost infinite. As a matter of fact, we think it is infinite.
Speech to the Space Council, reported in the *Guardian*, 8 March 1989.

You all look like happy campers to me. Happy campers you are, happy campers you have been, and, as far as I am concerned, happy campers you will always be.
To American Samoans, 25 April 1989, reported in *Esquire*, August 1992.

Hawaii has always been a very pivotal role in the Pacific. It is in the Pacific. It is a part of the United States that is an island that is right here.
Speech, Hawaii, 25 April 1989, reported in *Esquire*, August 1992.

What a waste it is to lose one's mind. Or not to have a mind is being very wasteful. How true that is.
Speech at the United Negro College Fund, whose motto is 'A mind is a terrible thing to waste', 9 May 1989, reported in *Esquire*, August 1992.

I believe we are on an irreversible trend toward more freedom and democracy – but that could change.
Speech, 22 May 1989, reported in *Esquire*, August 1992.

Mars is essentially in the same orbit ... Mars is somewhat the same distance from the Sun, which is very important. We have seen pictures where there are canals, we believe, and water. If there is water, that means there is oxygen. If oxygen, that means we can breathe.
Speech, 11 August 1989, reported in *Esquire*, August 1992.

I stand by all the misstatements that I've made.
To Sam Donaldson, 17 August 1989, reported in *Esquire*, August 1992.

The loss of life will be irreplaceable.
After the San Francisco earthquake, 19 October 1989, reported in *Esquire*, August 1992.

One word sums up probably the responsibility of any vice president, and that one word is 'to be prepared'.
Speech, 6 December 1989, reported in *Esquire*, August 1992.

May our nation continue to be the beakon [sic] of hope to the world.
The Quayles' 1989 Christmas card.

If we do not succeed, then we run the risk of failure.
Speech to the Phoenix Republican Forum, 23 March 1990, reported in *Esquire*, August 1992.

We are ready for any unforeseen event that may or may not occur.

On the Middle East situation, 22 September 1990, reported in *Esquire*, August 1992.

Unfortunately, the people of Louisiana are not racists.

On the election campaign of David Duke, imperial grand wizard of the Ku Klux Klan, 12 October 1990, reported in *Esquire*, August 1992.

My friends, no matter how rough the road may be, we can and we will never, never surrender to what is right.

Speaking to the Christian Coalition about the need for abstinence to avoid AIDS, 15 November 1991, reported in *Esquire*, August 1992.

This president is going to lead us out of this recovery. It will happen.

At a campaign stop at California State University, Fresno, 17 January 1992.

That's fine phonetically, but you're missing just a little bit.

As US vice-president, adding an 'e' to the word 'potato', which had been written on a blackboard by an 11-year-old boy at a school in Trenton, New Jersey, June 1992.

I should have caught the mistake on that spelling bee card. But as Mark Twain once said, 'You should never trust a man who has only one way to spell a word.'

On famously mis-spelling the word 'potato'. He was actually quoting President Andrew Jackson.

I should have remembered that was Andrew Jackson who said that, since he got his nickname 'Stonewall' by vetoing bills passed by Congress.

Confusing Andrew Jackson with Confederate General Thomas J. 'Stonewall' Jackson, who got his nickname at the first Battle of Bull Run.

If you give a person a fish, they'll fish for a day. But if you train a person to fish, they'll fish for a lifetime.

At a job-training centre in Atlanta celebrating the 10th anniversary of the Job Training Partnership Act, which Quayle helped to sponsor while a senator, 13 October 1992, reported in the *New York Times*, 14 October 1992.

It's the best book I've certainly read. And he goes through it; he starts around the turn of the century up through Vietnam. And it's a very good historical book about history.

On Paul Johnson's *Modern Times*, quoted in *Playboy*, January 1993.

R

Race

Races north of the Pyrenees never reach maturity; they are of a great stature and of a white colour. But they lack all sharpness of wit and penetration of intellect.

The Moorish traveller Saïd of Toledo, c. 1100.

I am apt to suspect ... all the other species of man ... to be naturally inferior to the whites. There never was a civilization of any other complexion than white, nor even any individual eminent either in action or speculation.

The philosopher David Hume, 1766.

There is a physical difference between the White and the Black races which I believe will forever forbid the two races living together on terms of social and political equality.

Abraham Lincoln, 1858.

Negro equality? Fudge! How long, in the Government of a God great enough to make and rule the universe, shall there continue knaves to vend, and fools to quip, so low a piece of demagogism as this?

Abraham Lincoln, 1859.

In the skull of the Negro the cranial capacity and the brain itself is much undersized. On the average it will hold thirty-five fluid ounces, as against forty-five for the Caucasian skull.

Robert W. Shufeld, *The Negro as a Menace to American Civilization*, 1907.

The mental constitution of the negro is ... normally good-natured and cheerful, but subject to sudden fits of emotion and passion during which he is capable of performing acts of singular atrocity, impressionable, vain, but often exhibiting in the capacity of a servant a dog-like fidelity which has stood the supreme test ... After puberty sexual matters take first place in the negro's life and thoughts.

Encyclopædia Britannica, 1911.

Most of the attacks on white women of the South are the direct result of the cocaine-crazed Negro brain.

Dr Christopher Koch, member of the Pennsylvania State Pharmacy Board, in evidence to the US Congress, 1914.

Science shows us the infinite superiority of the Teutonic Aryan over all others, and it therefore becomes us to see that his ascendancy shall remain undisputed. Any racial mixture can but lower the result. The Teutonic race, whether in Scandinavia, other parts of the continent, England, or America, is the cream of humanity.

Science fiction writer H. P. Lovecraft, 1916.

The negro is greatly inferior to the white and yellow races, and this has been attributed by some to the early closing of the cranial sutures, by which the normal development of the brain is arrested.

Waverley Encyclopædia, 1930.

They occupy rather a low level in the scale of humanity, and are lacking in those mental and moral qualities which have impressed the stamp of greatness on other races that have distinguished themselves in the history of the world.

The Nuttall Encyclopædia on black people, 1930.

The non-Nordic man takes up an intermediate position between the Nordic man and the ape.

Herman Gauch, *New Elements of Scientific Investigation*, 1934.

The blood particles of a Jew are completely different from those of a Nordic man. Hitherto one has prevented this fact from being proved by microscopic investigation.

Julius Streicher, 1935.

Christ cannot possibly have been a Jew. I don't have to prove that scientifically. It's a fact!

Josef Goebbels, 1940.

Evidently, you did not try to learn anything until you had reached maturity, because you know it is a biological fact that a Negro's skull, where the parts of it are connected by sutures, ossifies by the time a Negro reaches maturity and they become unable to take in information.

Senator Theodore G. Bilbo of Mississippi, letter to a black schoolteacher in Chicago advising her to become a charwoman, 1945.

I ain't going to let no darkies and white folks segregate together in this town.

Eugene Connor, police commissioner for Birmingham, Alabama, 1950.

One employer gave as his reason for not employing a coloured school-leaver: 'Your pigmentation would make you more allergic to frostbite in our frozen food.'

Daily Telegraph, quoted in 'This England', *New Statesman*.

Most of the boarding houses here are not large enough to take coloured and white guests at the same time.

Mrs Dorothy Brookes, Withernsea Landladies' Association, quoted in 'This England', *New Statesman*.

Oh yes, we Tory Councillors have done a lot for race relations. I do think it's very important. After all, but for the Grace of God, we'd be black ourselves, wouldn't we?

Anonymous Conservative councillor, quoted in 'This England', *New Statesman*.

There is no anti-Semitism in Russia. In fact, many of my best friends are Jews.

Alexei Kosygin, Prime Minister of the USSR, 1971.

Coloureds only want three things: first, a tight pussy; second, loose shoes; third, a warm place to shit.

Earl Butz, US secretary for agriculture, reported in *Rolling Stone*; his last recorded public utterance before his resignation in 1976.

Bongo-Bongo-Land.

Alan Clark MP, minister of state for employment, on the origins of a visiting African delegation, 1985.

You'll all end up with slitty eyes if you stay too long.

HRH Prince Philip, Duke of Edinburgh, to British students during a royal visit to China in 1986. A Palace spokesman afterwards explained that His Royal Highness had been concerned that they were spending too long in very bright sunlight.

What is a bloodsucker? When they land on your skin, they suck the life out of you to sustain their life. In the 20s and 30s and 40s, the Jews were the primary merchants in the black community … From our life they drew life and came to strength. They turned it over to the Arabs, the Koreans and others, who are now doing what? Sucking the lifeblood of our own community … You stand out there as if to say this is some of the same garbage they said in Europe. I don't know about no garbage said in Europe.

Louis Farrakhan, president of the Nation of Islam, interviewed in *Time*, 20 February 1994.

I have in front of me photographs of twelve Asian men, all of whom look exactly the same, which I'm sure you'll appreciate.

Judge Alexander Morrison, addressing an all-white jury at Derby Crown Court, 21 February 1995. Afterwards he said he had been 'misinterpreted'.

If we want to play black people we play black people. There is no colour bar.

Jack Walker, owner of Blackburn Rovers, the only all-white English Premier League football team, December 1996.

Radio

Radio has no future.

Lord Kelvin, president of the Royal Society 1890–95, on Marconi's experiments in 1897.

DeForest said in many newspapers and over his signature that it would be possible to transmit the human voice across the Atlantic before many years. Based on these absurd and deliberately misleading statements, the misguided public has been persuaded to purchase stock in his company.

The People vs US radio pioneer Lee DeForest: outline case for the prosecution, 1913.

I am reported to be 'pessimistic' about broadcasting … The truth is that I have anticipated its complete disappearance – confident that the unfortunate people, who must now subdue themselves to 'listening-in', will soon find a better pastime for their leisure.

Science writer, historian and novelist H. G. Wells, *The Way The World Is Going*, 1928.

See also TELEVISION

Railways

What can be more palpably absurd and ridiculous than the prospect held out of locomotives travelling twice as fast as stage-coaches! We should as soon expect the people of Woolwich to suffer themselves to be fired off upon one of Congreve's rockets, as trust themselves to the mercy of such a machine going at such a rate.

The *Quarterly Review*, March 1825. Sir William Congreve had developed some very effective rockets that the Royal Navy used to demolish large parts of Copenhagen in the Napoleonic Wars.

The most absurd scheme that ever entered into the head of a man to conceive ... Every part of the scheme shows that this man has applied himself to a subject of which he has no knowledge, and to which he has no science to apply.

Leading counsel Mr Alderson, in evidence to the Parliamentary Inquiry into George Stephenson's proposal for a railway from Stockton to Darlington, 1825.

I see no reason to suppose that these machines will ever force themselves into general use.

The Duke of Wellington, 1827.

As you well know, Mr President, railroad carriages are pulled at the enormous speed of 15 miles per hour ... The Almighty certainly never intended that people should travel at such breakneck speed.

Martin Van Buren, governor of New York, writing to US President Andrew Jackson, 1829.

Rail travel at high speed is not possible, because passengers, unable to breathe, would die of asphyxia.

Professor Dionysus Lardner, c. 1830.

That any general system of conveying passengers would go at a velocity exceeding ten miles an hour is extremely improbable.

Railway engineer Thomas Tredgold, *Practical Treatise on Railroads and Carriages*, 1835.

I should say no railway ought to exceed 40 miles an hour on the most favourable gradient; but on a curved line the speed ought not to exceed 24 or 25 miles an hour.

George Stephenson, shortly after designing a locomotive capable of 80 mph, 1841.

Railways can be of no advantage to rural areas, since agricultural products are too heavy or too voluminous to be transported by them.

F-J-B Noël, *The Railways Will Be Ruinous For France, And Especially For The Cities Through Which They Go*, 1842.

Trains are not more energy efficient than the average automobile. Both get about 48 passenger miles to the gallon.

US presidential candidate Ronald Reagan, *Chicago Tribune*, 10 May 1980. The average US train, at that time, got about 400 passenger miles per gallon; the average US car got about 43.

It was the wrong kind of snow.

Terry Worrall, spokesman for British Rail, explaining winter disruption on 15 February 1991.

Reincarnation

You and I have been given two hands and legs and half-decent brains. Some people have not been born like that for a reason. The karma is working from another lifetime ... what you sow you have to reap.

Glenn Hoddle, England football manager, interviewed by Matt Dickinson in *The Times*, 30 January 1999, on his belief that people with 'physical deformities' must have 'made mistakes' in another lifetime. He resigned three days later.

See also SPORT

Relativity

I can accept the theory of relativity as little as I can accept the existence of atoms and other such dogma.

Professor Ernst Mach, 1913.

Worthless and misleading.

US Government Observatory director Professor T. J. J. See, addressing the California Academy of Sciences on Einstein's theories, 1924.

We certainly cannot consider Einstein as one who shines as a scientific discoverer in the domain of Physics, but rather as one who in a fuddled sort of way is trying to find some meaning for mathematical formulas which he himself does not believe too strongly, but which he is hoping against hope somehow to establish.

Jeremiah J. Callahan, president of Duquesne University, *Euclid or Einstein*, 1931.

The so-called theories of Einstein are merely the ravings of a mind polluted with liberal, democratic nonsense which is utterly unacceptable to German men of science.

Dr Walter Gross, Hitler's favourite 'Nordic scientist', c. 1936.

The theory of a relativistic universe is the hostile work of the agents of Fascism. It is the revolting propaganda of a moribund, counter-revolutionary ideology.

The Soviet Astronomical Journal, 1930s.

Einstein's theory is unnecessary.

Harold Aspden, *Physics Without Einstein*, 1969.

Rhodesia

Why should white Rhodesians give up everything for some half-baked untried theory of one man, one vote?

John Stokes, Conservative MP, 1965.

The cumulative effects of the economic and financial sanctions might well bring the rebellion to an end within a matter of weeks rather than months.

British Prime Minister Harold Wilson, on bringing the rebel Rhodesian government to its knees in January 1966. It was still there when Wilson finally left office a decade later.

We now have a Rhodesian Constitution and if anybody thinks it can be improved, I would like to know where.

Ian Smith, leader of the whites-only Rhodesian regime, 1971.

We have the happiest Africans in the world.

Ian Smith, 1971.

I am determined to give the blacks a fair crack of the whip.

Ian Smith, 1972.

There are going to be no dramatic changes in Rhodesia.

Ian Smith, 1975.
   In 1980 Rhodesia adopted a multiracial constitution and changed its name to Zimbabwe.

Mugabe is a Marxist terrorist ... an apostle of Satan.

Rhodesian Prime Minister Ian Smith, before Robert Mugabe became Prime Minister of Zimbabwe, 1980.

He's sober and responsible. He's a pragmatist and his government will probably be the best in Africa.

Former Rhodesian Prime Minister Ian Smith, after Mugabe became Prime Minister
of Zimbabwe, 1980.

The Russian Revolutions

I tell you that nothing is going to happen in this forsaken country ...
It's a good time for me to go to the Crimea for a holiday.

Reuters correspondent Guy Beringer, in conversation with Associated Press
correspondent Roger Lewis over a game of billiards in Petrograd, March 1917.
The game was interrupted by an attendant who announced that a revolution
(the 'February Revolution' in the old Russian calendar) had begun.

It can't work – for Lenin and Trotsky are both extremely unpopular ...
Lenin will never be able to dominate the Russian people.

Herman Bernstein, Russian correspondent of the *New York Times*, 9 November
1917, after the 'October Revolution'.

I predict that the present parties now in Russia will last but a matter of
days. They represent but a small, an infinitely small, part of the Socialist
party in Russia, and they must and will fall and Kerensky will come
into his own again.

Meyer London, socialist US congressman, speech reported in the *New York
Times*, 10 November 1917. Kerensky, Prime Minister of the Provisional
Government ousted by the Bolsheviks, fled Russia a few days later.

THINK IMPOSSIBLE FOR SOVIET GOVERNMENT TO LAST LONG

David R. Francis, US ambassador in Moscow, cable to US Secretary of State
Robert Lansing, 7 December 1917.

The Bolshevist government won't last six months more.

Walter Duranty, foreign correspondent of the *New York Times*, 27 May 1920.

There is abundant evidence that the Bolshevik terror is drawing steadily
to its downfall ... Of course the attempt to reverse economic laws and to
ignore the most deeply seated impulses of human nature was certain to fail.
It was only a question of time. Apparently that time is not to be very long.

Former US Secretary of State Elihu Root, *New York Tribune*, 11 November 1921; by
this stage the Bolsheviks had won the civil war that followed the 1917 revolution.

See also COMMUNISM, CONSPIRACY THEORIES, McCARTHYISM
and THE USSR

S

Science

I am tired of this sort of thing called science. We have spent millions in that sort of thing for the last few years, and it is time it should be stopped.

Senator Simon Cameron of Pennsylvania, attempting to cut off funding for the Smithsonian Institution, 1861.

Sex

Erection is chiefly caused by scuraum, eringoes, cresses, crymon, parsnips, artichokes, turnips, asparagus, candied ginger, acorns bruised to powder and drunk in muscatel, scallion, sea shell fish, etc.

Aristotle, *The Masterpiece*, 4th century BC.

Wood pigeoens check and blunt the manly powers; let him not eat the bird who wishes to be amorous.

Martial, *Epigrams*, c. AD 90.

Now concerning the things whereof you wrote unto me: it is good for a man not to touch a woman.

First Epistle of the Apostle Paul to the Corinthians, 7:1

Let no-one say that because we have these parts, that the female body is shaped this way and the male that way, the one to receive, the other to give seed, sexual intercourse is allowed by God. For if this arrangement were allowed by God, to whom we seek to attain, He would not have pronounced the eunuch blessed (Matthew 19:12).

The Gnostic theologian Julius Cassianus, 2nd century.

After the 'change of life' with women, sexual congress, while permissible, should be infrequent, no less for her sake than that of the husband, whose advancing years should warn him of the medical maxim: 'Each time a man delivers himself to this indulgence, he casts a shovelful of earth upon his coffin.'

Nicholas Francis Cooke ('A Physician'), *Satan in Society*, 1876.

See also AIDS, CONCEPTION, CONTRACEPTION, MASTURBATION *and* WOMEN

Shakespeare

There is an upstart crow beautified with our feathers. That with his tyger's heart wrapt in a player's hide, supposes he is as well able to bombast out a blank verse as the best of you, and being an absolute Johannes Factotum, is, in his own conceit, the only Shakescene in a country.

Robert Greene, *Groatsworth of Wit Bought with a Million of Repentance*, 1592.

If Shakespeare's genius had been cultivated, those beauties, which we so justly admire in him, would have been undisgraced by those extravagancies, and that nonsense, with which they are so frequently accompanied.

Earl of Chesterfield, *Letters to his Son*, 1748.

Whaur's yer Wully Shakespeare noo?

Anonymous Scottish theatregoer, hailing the first performance of *Douglas*, by the Rev. John Home, 1756.

One of the greatest geniuses that ever existed, Shakespeare, undoubtedly wanted taste.

Horace Walpole, letter, 1764.

'Was there ever,' cried he, 'such stuff as great part of Shakespeare? Only one must not say so! But what think you – What? – Is there not sad stuff? What? – What?'

George III, quoted in *The Diary of Fanny Burney*, 16 December 1785.

Shakespeare's name, you may depend on it, stands absolutely too high and will go down.

Lord Byron, letter to James Hogg, March 1814.

With the single exception of Homer, there is no eminent writer, not even Sir Walter Scott, whom I can despise so entirely as I despise Shakespeare when I measure my mind against his ... It would positively be a relief to me to dig him up and throw stones at him.

George Bernard Shaw, *Dramatic Opinions and Essays*, Vol 2.

Quite a number of people ... describe the German classical author, Shakespeare, as belonging to English literature, because – quite accidentally born at Stratford-on-Avon – he was forced by the authorities of that country to write in English.

The *Deutscher Weckruf und Beobachter*, a New York National Socialist periodical, July 1941.

I think Shakespeare is shit. Absolute shit! He may have been a genius for his time, but I just can't relate to that stuff. 'Thee' and 'thou' – the guy sounds like a faggot. Captain America is classic because he's more entertaining.

Gene Simmons, of the rock group Kiss.

A play, of itself, the worst that ever I heard in my life.

Samuel Pepys on *Romeo and Juliet*, March 1662.

The most insipid, ridiculous play that ever I saw in my life.

Samuel Pepys on *A Midsummer Night's Dream*, September 1662.

Acted well, though it be but a silly play.

Samuel Pepys on *Twelfth Night*, January 1663.

I saw Hamlet Prince of Denmark played; but now, the old plays begin to disgust this refined age, since his majesty has been so long abroad.

John Evelyn, *Diary*, 26 November 1661.

It is a vulgar and preposterous drama, which would not be tolerated by the vilest populace of France, or Italy ... One would imagine this piece to be the work of a drunken savage.

Voltaire on *Hamlet*, 1748.

A strange, horrible business, but I suppose good enough for Shakespeare's day.

Queen Victoria on *King Lear*.

To anyone capable of reading the play with an open mind as to its merits, it is obvious that Shakespeare plunged through it so impetuously that he had finished it before he had made his mind up as to the character and motives of a single person in it.

George Bernard Shaw on *Othello*, 1897.

Ships

To listen to him you would fancy that with steam you could navigate ships, move carriages; in fact, there's no end to the miracles which, he insists upon it, could be performed.

Cardinal Richelieu, founder of the French Academy in 1634, on the inventor Salomon de Caus; so unimpressed was Richelieu, he had him confined in a lunatic asylum.

Even if the propeller had the power of propelling a vessel, it would be found altogether useless in practice, because the power being applied in the stern it would be absolutely impossible to make the vessel steer.

Naval surveyor Sir William Symonds, 1837.

We have, as an extreme limit of a steamer's practical voyage, without receiving a relay of coals, a run of about 2,000 miles ... Men might as well project a voyage to the moon as attempt to employ steam across the stormy North Atlantic.

Professor Dionysus Lardner, addressing the British Association for the Advancement of Science in 1838 – the year the SS *Great Western* made the first Atlantic crossing by steam power.

There is no greater fallacy than to suppose that ships can be navigated on long voyages without masts and sails.

Lieutenant, afterwards vice-Admiral George Strong Nares, *The Naval Cadet's Guide: or Seaman's Companion*, 1860.

See also THE TITANIC

Smoking

Your 'cigar-ettes' will never become popular.

Cigar makers F. G. Alton turn down an offer of manufacturing rights from Mr John Player, c. 1870.

The power of tobacco to sustain the system, to keep up nutrition, to maintain and increase the weight, to brace against severe exertion, and to replace ordinary food, is a matter of daily and hourly demonstration.

George Black, *The Doctor at Home*, 1898.

20,679 Physicians say "LUCKIES are less irritating."
1930s advertisement for Luckies cigarettes, USA.

More doctors smoke Camels than any other cigarette.
1930s advertisement for Camels, USA.

If excessive smoking actually plays a rôle in the production of lung cancer, it seems to be a minor one.
Dr W. C. Heuper of the US National Cancer Institute, April 1954.

What do these statements have in common?
　Scrofula is cured by the laying on of royal hands;
　A good treatment for tuberculosis is horseback riding;
　Gout is manifestly an affliction of the nervous system.

Answer:
　They were all believed correct by leading members of the medical profession at one time, but were later proved to be false. To this list may be added the statement that cigarette smoking causes lung cancer.
California Medicine, June 1963.

For the majority of people, smoking has a beneficial effect.
Los Angeles surgeon Dr Ian MacDonald, *Newsweek*, 18 November 1963.

See also ADVERTISING

South Africa

We are all satisfied in South Africa now.
General Jan Christian Smuts, past and future prime minister of South Africa, 1926.

Revolution is obviously coming to this country – and will obviously be successful – within the next five years.
Kirkpatrick Sale reports on South Africa for the *Chicago Tribune*, 1961.

This coloured thing, you don't really notice it at all; coloured servants out there don't really mind – they get their food and their board, so why should they mind? Gosh, you get coloured servants all over the world. They don't mind at all.
Cliff Richard, after a tour of South Africa in 1963.

Er ... they shouldn't be killing the rhinos.

Actress and singer Kylie Minogue, on being asked for a comment on 'the situation in South Africa', in *Clio* magazine, 1989.

The chap's got no experience of government. He's hardly made a speech, or held a press conference. Mind you, I suppose it's not entirely his own fault.

South African Foreign Minister Pik Botha, in conversation with British Liberal leader David Steel, 1986, on Nelson Mandela, who had been imprisoned since 1964.

I'm not here to apologize. Apartheid was a policy of good neighbourliness.

P. W. Botha, former President of South Africa, appearing in court to answer charges of refusing to give evidence to the Truth and Reconciliation Commission, 23 January 1998.

Space Travel

Still, to be filled with uneasy wonder and to express it will be enough, for after the rocket quits our air and really starts on its longer journey, its flight would be neither accelerated nor maintained by the explosion of the charges it might then have left. To claim that it would be is to deny a fundamental law of dynamics, and only Dr Einstein and his chosen dozen, so few and fit, are licensed to do that.

That Professor Goddard, with his chair in Clark College and the countenancing of the Smithsonian Institution, does not know the relation of action to reaction, and of the need to have something better than a vacuum against which to react – to say that would be absurd. Of course he only seems to lack the knowledge ladled out daily in high schools.

New York Times, editorial, 1921, on the successful rocketry experiments of Dr Robert Hutchings Goddard, inventor of the bazooka, which he had conducted on his aunt's farm. The 'fundamental law of dynamics' does indeed require something to react against; in the case of rocket fuel fired in the vacuum of space, that 'something' is the rocket itself. Goddard's theory that rockets could be successfully manoeuvred in space was therefore entirely correct. Following the successful launch of Apollo 11 in July 1989 the *New York Times* printed an apology to the late Dr Goddard.

This foolish idea of shooting at the Moon is an example of the absurd length to which vicious specialization will carry scientists working in thought-tight compartments. Let us critically examine the proposal. For a projectile entirely to escape the gravitation of the Earth, it needs a velocity of 7 miles a second. The thermal energy of a gram at this speed is 15,180 calories ... The energy of our most violent explosive – nitroglycerine – is less than 1500 calories per gram. Consequently, even had this explosive nothing to carry, it has only one-tenth of the energy necessary to escape the Earth ... Hence the proposition appears to be basically impossible.

Professor A. W. Bickerton of the University of Christchurch, New Zealand, 1926. Bickerton was wrong for two reasons, both of which were known to him at the time. (1) Liquid fuels, such as the kerosene-liquid oxygen mixture developed by Dr Robert Goddard and others, contain several times more energy than nitroglycerine. (2) A rocket does not need to carry a heavy load of fuel into space, since it burns most of it up whilst getting there. Professor Bickerton was the author of a book called *Perils of the Pioneer*. Writing in the *New Scientist* in 1979, Arthur C. Clarke commented, 'Of the perils that all pioneers must face, few are more disheartening than the Bickertons.'

The whole procedure presents difficulties of so fundamental a nature, that we are forced to dismiss the notion as essentially impractical, in spite of the author's insistent appeal to put aside prejudice and to recollect the supposed impossibility of heavier-than-air flight before it was accomplished. An analogy such as this may be misleading, and we believe it to be so in this case.

Astronomer Richard van der Riet Woolley, reviewing P. E. Cleator's *Rockets in Space* in the 14 March 1936 issue of *Nature*.

The acceleration which must result from the use of rockets ... inevitably would damage the brain beyond repair.

John P. Lockhart-Mummery, MA, BC, FRCS, in *After Us*, 1936.

While it is always dangerous to make a negative prediction, it would appear that the statement that rocket flight to the Moon does not seem so remote as television did less than one hundred years ago is over-optimistic.

Professor J. W. Campbell of the University of Alberta, *Rocket Flight to the Moon*, 1941. Using a mathematical model, Professor Campbell stated that it would take one million tons of fuel to propel one pound of cargo into space; the current actual figure is one ton per pound. Campbell's objections had in fact already been answered by Dr Goddard in *A Method of Reaching Extreme Altitudes*, published by the Smithsonian Institution.

Space travel is utter bilge.

Dr Richard van der Riet Woolley, Astronomer Royal, lecture, London, January 1956. The USSR launched Sputnik 1 the following year.

The USA has lost a battle more important and greater than Pearl Harbor.

Dr Edward Teller, 'father of the hydrogen bomb', interviewed on CBS TV after the successful flight of Sputnik 1, October 1957.

A lump of iron almost anybody could launch.

Rear Admiral Rawson Bennett, interviewed on NBC, on Sputnik 1, October 1957.

No matter what we do now, the Russians will beat us to the Moon ... I would not be surprised if the Russians reached the Moon within a week.

John Rinehart of the Smithsonian Institution, October 1957.

Few predictions seem more certain than this: Russia is going to surpass us in Mathematics and the social sciences ... In short, unless we depart utterly from our present behaviour, it is reasonable to expect that by no later than 1975 the United States will be a member of the Union of Soviet Socialist Republics.

George R. Price, fellow of the American Association for the Advancement of Science and past member of the Manhattan Project, reacting to the Sputnik launch, *Life*, 18 November 1957.

But to place a man in a multi-stage rocket and project him into the controlling gravitational field of the Moon, where the passenger can make scientific observations, perhaps land alive, and return to earth – all that constitutes a wild dream worthy of Jules Verne.

US radio pioneer Lee DeForest, *Reader's Digest*, 1957.

We stand on the threshold of rocket mail.

Arthur E. Summerfield, US postmaster general, 23 January 1959.

The odds are now that the United States will not be able to honour the 1970 manned-lunar-landing date set by Mr Kennedy.

New Scientist, editorial, 30 April 1964.

I'll have my first Zambian astronaut on the Moon by 1965, using my own firing system, derived from the catapult ... I'm getting them acclimatized to space travel by placing them in my space capsule every day. It's a 40-gallon oil drum in which they sit, and then I roll them down a hill. This gives them the feeling of rushing through space. I also make them swing from the end of a long rope. When they reach the highest point, I cut the rope – this produces the feeling of free fall.

Edward Mukaka Nkoloso, director-general of the Zambia National Academy of Space Research, 3 November 1964.

Sport

Women have but one task, that of crowning the winner with garlands.

Baron de Coubertin, founder of the modern Olympic Games, 1902.

See also WOMEN

I make so bold to say I don't believe that in the future history of the world any such feat will be performed by anybody else.

The mayor of Dover salutes Matthew Webb, the first man to swim the English Channel, 1875. Since then over 2,000 people have repeated the feat.

The man who has made the mile record is W. G. George. His time was 4 minutes 12.75 seconds and the probability is that it will never be broken.

Athletics coach Harry Andrews in 1903. Hicham El Guerrouj of Morocco ran the mile in 3 minutes 43.13 seconds in Rome on 7 July 1999.

J'adore ce cricket; c'est tellement anglais [I love cricket; it's so English].

The French actress Sarah Bernhardt reacts to watching a game of football in Manchester, 1905.

The difference between me and other athletes who go to the Olympics is that they go to compete and I go to win.

British athlete David Bedford looks forward to victory in the 10,000 metres at the 1972 Munich Olympic Games. He came sixth.

She's a great player, for a gal. But no woman can beat a male player who knows what he's doing. I'll put Billie Jean and all the other Women's Libbers back where they belong – in the kitchen and in the bedroom.

Bobby Riggs on his 'Battle of the Sexes' challenge match with Billie Jean King, 1973. He lost to King in straight sets.

Here comes Juantorena. Watch him open his legs and show his class.

Ron Pickering, BBC TV athletics, commenting on the 1976 Montreal Olympic Games.

Ah, isn't that nice, the wife of the Cambridge president is kissing the cox of the Oxford crew.

Harry Carpenter sets the scene for the 1977 Oxford–Cambridge boat race for BBC TV.

Lasse Viren, the champion, came in fifth and ran a champion's race.

David Coleman commenting on the 1980 Moscow Olympics for BBC TV.

Zola Budd will become a great British athlete, her heart lies here.

The *Daily Mail* talks up the British credentials of the South African-born middle-distance runner, 1984. Largely as a result of the *Mail*'s campaign, Budd took 'fast track' British nationality and ran for Britain in the 1984 Los Angeles Olympics. In 1988 she revoked her British citizenship and returned to South Africa.

Do my eyes deceive me, or is Senna's Lotus sounding a bit rough?

Murray Walker, BBC TV motor racing.

They are so determined to show up the English that they are going out of their way to be unbelievably polite. They are doing this quite deliberately.

Tony Banks MP, minister for sport, on the dastardly behaviour of Scottish football fans at the World Cup, 24 June 1998.

My biggest mistake was not to include Eileen Drewery in the back-up team for France.

Glenn Hoddle, England team manager, blames his team's exit on the lack of his 'spiritual healer' in his World Cup diary, published in August 1998. England lost to Argentina in a penalty shoot-out.

See also BROADCASTING BOOBS, CRICKET, DOUBLE-ENTENDRES *and* REINCARNATION

Joseph Stalin

We are witnessing the violent and ignominious end of the Caucasian brigand-chief Dzugashvili, known to history as Stalin.

Eugene Lyons, editor-in-chief of the *American Mercury*, 'The End of Joseph Stalin', August 1941. Stalin's end did not come until 1953.

He doesn't want anything but security for his country, and I think that if I give him everything I possibly can and ask nothing from him in return, noblesse oblige, he won't try to annexe anything and will work with me for a world democracy and peace.

US President Franklin D. Roosevelt, assessing Stalin's war aims, 1944.

See also DICTATORS

The Suez Crisis

We are not at war with Egypt. We are in a state of armed conflict.

Anthony Eden, British Prime Minister, on the invasion of the Suez Canal Zone by British and French troops, 1956.

The Sun

The sun ... appears to be nothing else than a very eminent, large and lucid planet, evidently the first, or in strictness of speaking, the only primary one of our system ... Its similarity to other globes of the solar system ... leads us to suppose that it is most probably inhabited ... by beings whose organs are adapted to the peculiar circumstances of that vast globe.

William Herschel – discoverer of Uranus and two of its satellites, and of two satellites of Saturn – in *Philosophical Transactions of the Royal Society*, 1795. In 1801 he described the sun as 'a most magnificent habitable globe', and in 1814 he concluded that the stars were 'so many opaque, habitable, planetary globes'.

Tax

This burden should not be left to rest on the shoulders of the public in time of peace because it should be reserved for the important occasions which, I trust, will not soon recur.

Henry Addington, Prime Minister and Chancellor of the Exchequer, abolishing income tax in 1802. It was reintroduced.

If you ask me if I enjoy being taxed, the answer, of course, is no. But ... I hope that the tax will change the pattern so that merit and hard work are rewarded at the expense of merely having.

Lord Kagan, special adviser to British Prime Minister Harold Wilson on taxation, on the merits of a progressive tax policy, August 1974. In 1980 he received a prison sentence for defrauding the Inland Revenue of money due to them on wealth he 'merely had'.

Rates: this was once a problem for the rich. Because Socialism has improved our way of life, it is now a problem for everybody.

Labour party District Council manifesto, Forest of Dean, 1976.

History shows that when the taxes of a nation approach about 20 per cent of the people's income, there begins to be a lack of respect for government ... When it reaches 25 per cent, there comes an increase in lawlessness.

US presidential candidate Ronald Reagan, *Time*, 14 April 1980. In Britain at that time, income tax was 33% but lawlessness remained well below US levels.

The Community Charge is a courageous, fair and sensible solution.
Far from being a vote loser ... it will be a vote winner.

Michael Portillo, minister for local government, addressing the Conservative
Party Conference, 11 October 1990, on the measure widely known as the
Poll Tax. A month later, Conservative MPs dumped its champion, Prime
Minister Margaret Thatcher; the first action of her successor was to scrap
the Community Charge.

See also POLITICIANS' PROMISES

Telegraphy

I watched his countenance closely, to see if he was not deranged.
I was assured by other Senators after we left the room that there was
no future in it.

Senator Hampton Smith of Indiana, on a demonstration of telegraphy by Samuel
Morse for the US Congress in 1842.

I am not satisfied that under any rate of postage that could be adopted, its
revenues could be made to equal its expenditures.

The US postmaster-general, on rejecting Samuel Morse's offer to sell the rights
of his telegraphic invention for $100,000 in 1845.

Telephone

Well-informed people know it is impossible to transmit the voice over
wires and that were it possible to do so, the thing would be of no
practical value.

The *Boston Post*, 1865 – the year Joshua Coopersmith was charged with fraud for
trying to raise capital to develop a telephone.

Hmph! Only a toy.

Gardiner Greene Hubbard, inspecting the handiwork of his son-in-law, Alexander
Graham Bell, in 1876.

An amazing invention – but who would ever want to use one?

US President Rutherford B. Hayes, after making a telephone call from Washington, DC, to Philadelphia in 1876. In 1877 Western Union turned down Bell's
offer of exclusive rights for $100,000.

Television

For God's sake go down to reception and get rid of a lunatic who's down there. He says he's got a machine for seeing by wireless! Watch him – he may have a razor on him.

The editor of the *Daily Express* sends someone to deal with an inventor called John Logie Baird in 1925. Baird organized a public demonstration instead.

While theoretically and technically television may be feasible, commercially and financially I consider it an impossibility, a development of which we need waste little time dreaming.

US radio pioneer Lee DeForest, interviewed in the *New York Times*, 1926.

Television won't matter in your lifetime or mine.

Rex Lambert, editor of the *Radio Times*, 1936.

Video won't be able to hold on to any market it captures after the first six months. People will soon get tired of staring at a plywood box every night.

Film producer Darryl F. Zanuck, 1946.

See also RADIO

Terrorism

Because Sarin is slightly heavier than air, it hovers close to the ground to cause maximum fatalities.

The *Daily Express*, 21 March 1995, page 4, on a terrorist attack on the Tokyo underground with nerve gas.

Sarin is lighter than air, and would normally disperse quickly in the open air.

The *Daily Express*, 21 March 1995, page 5, on the same incident.

As is inevitable on these occasions, instant theories were advanced on the basis of little or no evidence. One linked the bomb to the deadly raid by Federal agents on David Koresh's Davidian compound in Waco, Texas. Another, even more far-fetched, connected Wednesday morning's explosion with the scheduled execution in Arkansas of a White Supremacist. The more serious speculation was about the involvement of people connected to fundamentalist forces in the Middle East.

The *Economist*, 21 April 1995, on the Oklahoma City bombing. Timothy McVeigh, a right-wing fanatic, was imprisoned for life for carrying out the bombing, which had indeed been intended to commemorate the Waco incident.

IN THE NAME OF ISLAM
Front page headline, *Today*, 21 April 1995, on the Oklahoma City bombing.

See also NORTHERN IRELAND

The Third World

If we had spent £167 million on condoms we wouldn't have had these problems in the first place.
Tory MP Nicholas Fairbairn on sending food aid to drought victims in sub-Saharan Africa, 12 May 1991.

In some countries, genocide is not really important.
François Mitterand, president of France, 1994, on the murder of some 800,000 Tutsis by Hutus in Rwanda.

See also POLITICIANS' GAFFES

Tidal Power

The power of the tides may be made available to produce power on a large scale. If extensively exploited over a long period of time, however, it might result in bringing the Moon too close to earth for safety.
John P. Lockhart-Mummery, MA, BC, FRCS, *After Us*, 1936.

The *Titanic*

I cannot imagine any condition which would cause a ship to founder. Modern shipbuilding has gone beyond that.
Captain Edward J. Smith of the White Star Line, future commander of the *Titanic*, 1906.

The *Titanic* is well able to withstand any exterior damage and could keep afloat indefinitely after being struck.
P. A. S. Franklin, vice-president of the International Mercantile Marine Company, statement issued on the morning of 15 April 1912, by which time the ship, along with most of her passengers and crew, lay at the bottom of the sea. The *Titanic* had, indeed, been designed to withstand iceberg damage and stay afloat, but the rivets used to hold her hull plates together were made of inferior soft steel, and sheared off under the impact.

ALL SAVED FROM TITANIC AFTER COLLISION
RESCUE BY *CARPATHIA* AND *PARISIAN*;
LINER IS BEING TOWED TO HALIFAX
AFTER SMASHING INTO AN ICEBERG

The *New York Evening Sun*, 15 April 1912.

No proof has been found for the widely believed story that the *Aberdeen Press & Journal* ran the report of the *Titanic*'s sinking under the headline NORTH MAN LOST AT SEA.

UFOs

The flights, landings and take-offs of airships called 'flying saucers' and 'flying cigars' of any nationality are forbidden on the territory of the community of Châteauneuf-du-Pape.

Decree issued by the mayor of Châteauneuf-du-Pape in 1954, after the town became known as 'the French Roswell'.

Unemployment

When a great many people are unable to find work, unemployment results.

Former US President Calvin Coolidge, *City Editor*, 1930.

A few years ago everybody was saying we must have much more leisure, everybody is working too much. Now that everybody has got so much leisure – it may be involuntary, but they have got it – they are now complaining they are unemployed. People do not seem to be able to make up their minds, do they?

HRH Prince Philip, Duke of Edinburgh, 60th birthday interview on BBC Radio 2, 1981, as UK unemployment rose to 3 million.

The USA

The vast and unmanageable extent which the accession of Louisiana will give to the United States; the consequent dispersal of our population, and the destruction of that balance which is so important to maintain between the Eastern and Western States, threatens, at no very distant day, the subversion of our Union.

Roger Griswold, Connecticut congressman, contribution to the debate on the Louisiana Purchase, 1803–04.

I have never heard of anything, and I cannot conceive of anything more ridiculous, more absurd, and more affrontive to all sober judgement than the cry that we are profiting by the acquisition of New Mexico and California. I hold that they are not worth a dollar.

US senator Daniel Webber of Massachusetts, speech, 1848. California's gross domestic product is now the fifth highest in the world.

Alaska, with the Aleutian Islands, is an inhospitable, wretched, God-forsaken region, worth nothing, but a positive injury and incumbrance as a colony of the United States.

Orange Ferriss, US congressman of New York, during the debate on the acquisition of Alaska, 1868.

The US Constitution

A shilly-shally thing of milk and water, which could not last.

US statesman Alexander Hamilton on the outcome of the Constitutional Convention, 1787.

Your constitution is all sail and no anchor ... Either some Caesar or Napoleon will seize the reins of government with a strong hand; or your republic will be ... laid waste by barbarians in the twentieth century as the Roman Empire was in the fifth.

British historian Thomas Babington Macaulay, letter to Henry S. Randall, 23 May 1857.

The USSR

Who are the Bolsheviki? They are representatives of the most democratic government in Europe. Let us recognize the truest democracy in Europe, the truest democracy in the world today.

US newspaper publisher William Randolph Hearst, 1918.

In my opinion the attempt to build up a Communist republic on the lines of strongly centralized State Communism, under the iron rule of the dictatorship of the party, is ending in failure.

Russian revolutionary anarchist Prince Kropotkin, 1920.

The labour camps have won high reputations throughout the Soviet Union as places where tens of thousands of men have been reclaimed.

US journalist Anna Louise Strong, *This Soviet World*, 1936.

Only enemies of the Soviet Union can think of the KGB as some kind of secret police.

Yuri Andropov, director of the KGB and future president of the USSR, 1967.

Please let us understand that we are talking about power – Faith, Hope and Power, and the greatest of these is Power. In the Soviet Union, the generals have it and the crowds in the Moscow streets have it not. Nothing else matters.

Edward Pearce, the *Guardian*, 21 August 1991, on the 'hardliners' coup' against President Gorbachev and the siege of the parliament building. The coup failed, and the Soviet Union itself ceased to exist shortly afterwards.

See also COMMUNISM, CZECHOSLOVAKIA, THE HUNGARIAN UPRISING, THE RUSSIAN REVOLUTION *and* STALIN

The Vietnam War

1946–54

We shall never retreat or give up.

Admiral G. Thierry d'Argenlieu, French high commissioner for Indo-China, on France's colonial war against the Vietminh, 24 November 1946.

We will have victory in fifteen months.

General Jean de Lattre de Tassigny, commander-in-chief of French forces in Indo-China, December 1950.

A year ago none of us could see victory. There wasn't a prayer. Now we can see it clearly – like light at the end of the tunnel.

Lieutenant-General Henri-Eugène Navarre, commander-in-chief of French Union forces, 28 September 1953: the first recorded reference to the elusive light at the end of the Vietnam tunnel.

We've taken the place and we shall stay there ... I foresee final victory in the spring of 1956.

General René Cogny, commander, French Union forces, 20 November 1953, on the French occupation of the strategic base of Dien Bien Phu, in northwest Vietnam.

First, the Vietminh won't succeed in getting their artillery through to here. Secondly, if they do get here, we'll smash them. Thirdly, even if they manage to keep on shooting, they will be unable to supply their pieces with enough ammunition to do us any real harm.

Colonel Charles Piroth, deputy commander of French forces at Dien Bien Phu, December 1953.

Victory after six more months of hard fighting.

Lieutenant-General Henri-Eugène Navarre, New Year forecast, 1 January
1954.

If the Communists continue to suffer the losses they have been taking
I don't see how they can stay in the battle.

Paul Ety, French army chief of staff, 20 March 1954.

Dien Bien Phu has fulfilled the mission that was assigned to it by the
High Command.

French army spokesman, 7 May 1954, after the fortress fell to a swift assault by
Vietminh forces.

On 8 May 1954 the French government announced an end to hostilities in
Indo-China. The Geneva Conference left North Vietnam under the rule of the
Communist leader Ho Chi Minh. Elections promised for South Vietnam
never took place.

1954–75

The Vietnamese have ample manpower and even today outnumber
the enemy by 100,000. This matter can be resolved without bringing in
one single American soldier to fight.

General John W. O'Daniel, head of the US Military Mission of Advisers to the
Government of South Vietnam, 7 July 1954.

We have exactly 342 men, the number allowed by the Geneva Armistice
Committee. It would be a breeze if we had more.

General Samuel T. Williams, head of the US Advisory Group, 12 June 1957.

Should I become President I will not risk American lives by permitting
any other nation to drag us into the wrong war at the wrong place
at the wrong time through an unwise commitment that is unwise
militarily, unnecessary to our security, and unsupported by
our allies.

US presidential candidate John F. Kennedy, speech to the Democratic National
Committee, 12 October 1960.

The risks of backing into a major Asian war by way of South Viet Nam
are present but are not impressive. North Viet Nam is extremely vulnerable to conventional bombing, a weakness which should be exploited
in convincing Hanoi to lay off South Viet Nam.

US General Maxwell Taylor, dispatch to President John F. Kennedy, 1 November
1961.

The training, transportation and logistical support we are providing in Vietnam has succeeded in turning the tide against the Vietcong.

General Barksdale Hamlett, US army vice-chief of staff, 10 October 1962.

Victory is in sight.

General Paul D. Harkins, commander of US forces, South Vietnam, 5 March 1963.

It is inconceivable that the Viet Cong could ever defeat the armed forces of South Vietnam.

General William C. Westmoreland, newly appointed commander of US forces in South Vietnam, 25 April 1964.

I didn't just screw Ho Chi Minh. I cut his pecker off.

US President Lyndon B. Johnson on the effect of US bombing of Hanoi, 13 July 1964.

We are not about to send American boys nine or ten thousand miles away from home to do what Asian boys ought to be doing for themselves.

US President Lyndon B. Johnson, election campaign speech, Akron, Ohio, 21 October 1964. Between 1964 and 1968 the number of US troops in Vietnam increased from 20,000 to 500,000.

At last there is light at the end of the tunnel.

US journalist Joseph Alsop, syndicated column, 13 September 1965.

It's silly talking about how many years we will have to spend in the jungles of Vietnam when we could pave the whole country and put parking stripes on it and still be home by Christmas.

Ronald Reagan, candidate for the governorship of California, interviewed in the Fresno *Bee*, 10 October 1965.

We must never forget that if the war in Vietnam is lost ... the right of free speech will be extinguished throughout the world.

Richard M. Nixon, speech, 27 October 1965.

For the first time since we spun into the Vietnam mess, there is hope for the United States ... The credit justly belongs to President Lyndon B. Johnson. He has made the war 'unlosable'.

Sam Castan, senior editor of *Life*, 30 November 1965.

The North Vietnamese cannot take the punishment any more in the South. I think we can bring the war to a conclusion within the next year, possibly within the next six months.

US General S. L. A. Marshall, 12 September 1966.

I believe there is a light at the end of what has been a long and lonely tunnel.

US President Lyndon B. Johnson, speech, 21 September 1966.

From being on the verge of losing its position in South Vietnam lock, stock and barrel, the US has driven the main enemy to the brink of defeat. Never in modern times has there been a smoother, surer, swifter reversal in the tide of a struggle.

Fortune magazine, 'The War We've Won', April 1967.

The troops will be brought home in 18 months.

General Harold K. Johnson, US army chief of staff, 12 August 1967.

The enemy is literally on the verge of starvation.

General William C. Westmoreland, 7 November 1967.

We have reached an important point where the end begins to come into view.

General William C. Westmoreland, 21 November 1967.

Come and see the light at the end of the tunnel.

Official invitation to a New Year's Eve party at the US embassy in Saigon, December 1967. In January 1968 the North Vietnamese and Vietcong launched the Tet Offensive, during which part of the US embassy was briefly occupied by communist troops.

The enemy is about to run out of steam.

General William C. Westmoreland, 2 February 1968.

To save the town it became necessary to destroy it.

Unidentified US army major, on the bombing of Bentre, 7 February 1968.

I do not believe that the enemy can hold up under a long war.

General William C. Westmoreland, 25 February 1968: a view shared by Ho Chi Minh.

We have the enemy licked now. He is beaten. We have the initiative in all areas. The enemy cannot achieve a military victory; he cannot even mount another offensive.

Admiral John S. McCain, commander-in-chief of US Pacific naval forces, February 1969. Later that year the Vietcong mounted 159 simultaneous raids in South Vietnam.

The enemy is reeling from successive disasters. We are, in fact, winning the war.

US journalist William Buckley, syndicated column written in Hong Kong, December 1969.

We take this action not for the purpose of expanding the war into Cambodia, but for the purpose of ending the war in Vietnam and winning the just peace we all desire.

US President Richard M. Nixon, broadcast to the nation, 30 April 1970, on the US invasion and bombing of Cambodia, in violation of its neutrality.

If we just keep up the pressure, these little guys will crack.

US General Earl Wheeler, June 1970.

The Vietnam War has been reduced to what we technicians call a police action.

Major Ted Sioong of the Australian army, 1971.

The enemy is literally beating himself to death.

US journalist Joseph Alsop, syndicated column quoting 'US military sources', 16 June 1972.

If you Americans think you're going to just walk away and leave us, you'll never make it to the airfield.

Colonel Luan, chief of the South Vietnamese police force, April 1975. On 29 April the last US officials left by helicopter from the roof of the US embassy in Saigon. On 1 May the victorious North Vietnamese renamed the former capital Ho Chi Minh City.

Volcanoes

The safety of St Pierre is absolutely assured.

Report of a special commission appointed by Louis Mouttet, governor of Martinique, after Mount Pelée, the dormant volcano near the island's capital, became active, 5 May 1902.

Do not allow yourself to fall victim to groundless panic. Please allow us to advise you to return to your normal occupations.

The mayor of St Pierre, Martinique, public proclamation after a rain of hot cinders fell on the town, 6 May 1902. sOn 8 May 1902 Mt Pelée erupted, destroying the town and killing all but two of its 30,000 inhabitants.

No-one knows more about this mountain than Harry. And it don't dare blow up on him! This goddamned mountain won't blow. Scientists don't know shit from apple butter!

Mountain man Harry Truman, 83, refuses to leave his home on the slopes of the dormant volcano Mount St Helens, Washington, USA, May 1980. On 19 May the volcano erupted, killing Mr Truman, among others.

Votes for Women

Extend now to women suffrage and eligibility; give them the political right to vote and be voted for, render it feasible for them to enter the arena of political strife, and what remains of family union will soon be dissolved.

The *Catholic World*, 1869.

The Queen is most anxious to enlist every one who can speak or write to join us in checking this mad, wicked folly of 'Women's Rights', with all its attendant horrors, on which her poor feeble sex is bent, forgetting every sense of womanly feeling and propriety.

Queen Victoria, letter to Sir Theodore Martin, 28 May 1870.

Women's participation in political life ... would involve the domestic calamity of a deserted home and the loss of the womanly qualities for which refined men adore women and marry them ... Doctors tell us, too, that thousands of children would be harmed or killed before birth by the injurious effect of untimely political excitement on their mothers.

US critic Henry T. Finck, writing in the *Independent*, 30 January 1901.

Sensible and responsible women do not want to vote. The relative positions to be assumed by man and woman in the working out of our civilization were assigned long ago by a higher intelligence than ours.

Former US President Grover Cleveland, 1905.

I see some rats have got in; let them squeal, it doesn't matter.

British Liberal politician David Lloyd-George, on the interruption of an election meeting by Suffragettes, 1910.

See also WOMEN

The Wall Street Crash

Stocks have reached what looks like a permanently high plateau.

Irving Fisher, professor of economics at Yale University, 17 October 1929. On 24 October $6 billion was wiped off stock values on Wall Street.

The worst has passed.

Statement issued by the 35 major Wall Street dealing houses on 24 October 1929.

EXPERTS PREDICT RISING MARKET
Bulls Ready to Back Bankers; Bear Move Touches Bottom
PUBLIC CONFIDENCE IN STOCKS RESTORED
BY MOVE OF 'BIG 4'

The *New York Journal*, 25 October 1929, on the buying-in of stock by the 'Big Four' US banks. On 29 October stocks fell a further $10 billion.

Hysteria has now disappeared from Wall Street.

The Times, 2 November 1929, as prices continued to fall.

The end of the decline of the Stock Market will probably not be long, only a few days at most.

Professor Irving Fisher, 14 November 1929.

For the immediate future at least, the outlook is bright.

Professor Irving Fisher, *The Stock Market Crash – And After, 1930.*
   Stocks fell steadily until December 1932, by which time $50 billion had been wiped off their values.

See also THE GREAT DEPRESSION

War and Peace

Everything announces an age in which that madness of nations, war, will come to an end.

Paul Rabaut Saint-Etienne, *Réflexions politiques sur les circonstances présents*, 1792.

No more hatreds, no more self-interests devouring one another, no more wars, a new life made up of harmony and light prevails.

Victor Hugo, after witnessing manned balloon flight in 1842 – the beginning of the 'Decade of Nationalism'.

My dynamite will sooner lead to peace
Than a thousand world conventions.
As soon as men will find that in one instant
Whole armies can be utterly destroyed,
They will surely abide by golden peace.

Alfred Nobel (1833–96), inventor of dynamite and founder of the Nobel prizes.

To kill a man will be considered as disgusting as we in this day consider it disgusting to eat one.

The US industrialist Andrew Carnegie, forecast for a hundred years hence, 1900.

It seems pretty clear that no civilized people will ever again permit its government to enter into a competitive arms race.

Nicholas Murray Butler, president of Columbia University, 17 October 1914.

Radio will serve to make the concept of Peace on Earth, Good Will Toward Man a reality.

General James J. Harbord, former US staff officer in World War I and chairman of RCA, 1925.

People are becoming too intelligent to have another big war. I believe the last war was too much an educator for there ever to be another on a large scale.

Henry Ford, 1928.

Never in history has mankind been given more reason to look forward to the future with hope. For the blast which blew nineteenth-century nationalism to pieces at Hiroshima may also have cleared the way for a new Renaissance – a new era of co-operation leading up to the twentieth-century Empire of the World.

US military historian Lynn Montross, *War Through the Ages*, 1946.

We now have an opportunity to build a New World Order, based on diplomacy and co-operation.

US President George Bush, 1990.

Watergate

A predictable election-year Mickey Mouse, of course, but surely the Democrats are pushing our sense of humour too far.

Editorial in the *Richmond News*, 22 June 1972, on suggestions that the botched burglary of the Democratic Party's election offices in the Watergate building, Washington, DC, might have been organized, and covered up, by the Republicans.

The illegal we do immediately, the unconstitutional takes a little longer.

National security adviser Henry Kissinger, quipping in the White House, June 1972; quoted in Bill Gulley (with Mary Ellen Reese), *Breaking Cover*, 1980.

All that crap, you're putting it in the paper? It's all been denied. Katie Graham's going to get her tit caught in a big fat wringer if that's published.

John Mitchell, US attorney-general, on the publisher of the *Washington Post*, which broke the story of the Watergate scandal, June 1972. Mitchell, who conducted illegal surveillance and harassment of people on President Nixon's 'enemies list', subsequently served a two-year prison sentence for obstruction of justice.

Within our own staff, under my direction, Counsel to the President Mr Dean has conducted a complete investigation of all leads which might involve any present members of the White House or anybody in Government. I can say categorically that no-one in the White House staff, no-one in this administration, presently employed, was involved in this bizarre incident.

US President Richard M. Nixon, public statement, 29 August 1972. John Dean was himself one of the Watergate conspirators.

I expect the first four years of my sixties to be very interesting.

US President Richard M. Nixon, 60th birthday interview to coincide with his inauguration for a second term, 9 January 1973.

As shameful as Watergate is, the case has a hopeful or reassuring aspect: nothing is being swept under the rug.

Editorial, *Orlando Sentinel*, 13 January 1973.

I can give a show we can sell them, just like we were selling Wheaties.

John Dean, counsel to the President, caught on tape in the Oval Office in discussion with President Nixon, 21 March 1973.

I don't give a shit what happens. I want you all to stonewall it, let them plead the Fifth Amendment, cover-up or anything else, if it'll save it – save the plan. That's the whole point.

US President Richard M. Nixon, in taped discussion with John Dean, John Ehrlichman, Bob Haldeman and John Mitchell in the Oval Office, 22 March 1972.

I have no question that the President will insist on the full disclosure of the facts.

US Secretary of State Henry Kissinger, addressing the American Newspaper Publishers' Association, 23 April 1973.

If the press continues its zealous overkill on this affair, it is not likely to destroy either President Nixon or the Nixon Administration but it will gravely injure something more important – the faith of the people in the freedom of the press.

Editorial in the *Burlington Free Press*, advising the *Washington Post* to exercise responsible self-censorship, 25 April 1973.

Two of the finest public servants it has been my privilege to know.

US President Richard M. Nixon, announcing the sacking of Watergate 'co-conspirators' Bob Haldeman and John Ehrlichman, 30 April 1973.

This office is a sacred trust and I am determined to be worthy of that trust.

US President Richard M. Nixon, broadcast, 30 April 1973.

I reject the cynical view that politics is inevitably, or even usually, a dirty business.

US President Richard M. Nixon, broadcast, 30 April 1973.

There can be no whitewash at the White House.

US President Richard M. Nixon, broadcast, 30 April 1973.

Boys, give me hell every time you think I'm wrong.

US President Richard M. Nixon, to members of the press corps after his broadcast of 30 April 1973.

I was hoping you fellows weren't going to ask me that.

Middle-ranking White House aide Alexander Butterfield, giving evidence to a Senate inquiry into the Watergate affair, responds to a question about a rumour that President Nixon had bugged offices and telephones in the White House, and kept possession of the tapes. It was true. After a lengthy legal battle, Nixon handed some of them over.

Watergate is water under the bridge.

US President Richard M. Nixon, September 1973.

I made a terrible mistake. I pressed the wrong button but Mr Nixon said it didn't matter.

Rose Mary Woods, President Nixon's secretary, tells the Senate inquiry that she accidentally erased eighteen minutes from a crucial 'Watergate tape', 26 November 1973.

I urge the Congress to join me in mounting a major new effort to replace the discredited president ...

US President Richard M. Nixon, State of the Union Address, January 1974.
He had meant to say 'precedent'.

I have no intention of resigning. The President is not going to leave the White House until January 20th 1977.

US President Richard M. Nixon, 24 July 1974, after the vote for the First Article of Impeachment and the Supreme Court ruling that he could not claim 'executive privilege' and must therefore hand over the remaining Watergate tapes. He resigned on 8 August 1974.

This country needs good farmers, good businessmen, good plumbers ...

US President Richard M. Nixon, addressing his staff on the White House lawn, 9 August 1974, after announcing his resignation. The Watergate burglars had been nicknamed 'the plumbers'.

When the President does it, that means it is not illegal.

Former US President Richard M. Nixon, TV interview with David Frost, 20 May 1977.

See also RICHARD MILHOUS NIXON

Weather Forecasting

A woman rang to say she heard there was a hurricane on the way. Well don't worry, there isn't.

Weather forecaster Michael Fish, BBC TV, 15 October 1987. There was.

Westminster City Council

When you have read the documents and after we've had our discussion, it would be helpful if you'd swallow them in good spy fashion otherwise they might self-destruct!

Dame Shirley Porter, leader of Westminster City Council, memo to fellow

Conservative councillors, September 1986. They were discussing a policy to boost the Conservative vote in Westminster by moving out Labour-voting council tenants.

The problem can be quite simply stated: if it is accepted that owner-occupiers are more likely to vote Conservative, then we approach the 1990 election with an enormous handicap ... The short-term objective must be to target the marginal wards and as a matter of utmost urgency redress the balance by encouraging a pattern of tenure which is more likely to translate into Conservative votes.

Councillor Alex Segal, briefing to Conservative councillors, January 1987.

We in Westminster are trying to gentrify the City. We must protect our electoral position which is being seriously eroded by the number of homeless that we have been forced to house. I am afraid that unless something can be done, it will be very difficult for us to keep Westminster Conservative.

Dame Shirley Porter, letter to Prime Minister Margaret Thatcher, January 1987.

On 4 May 1996 the district auditor, John Magill, found that £31.6 million of public money had been used in gerrymandering, and ordered Dame Shirley, the Tesco stores heiress, and five of her former colleagues to pay it back. Dame Shirley, who was ordered to pay £27 million, exiled herself in Tel Aviv. In 1999 the Court of Appeal ruled that, while Dame Shirley's housing policy had worked to the Conservatives' electoral advantage, this was not specifically an offence, and ordered the £27 million surcharge to be quashed.

Westminster sets an example to other authorities. I hope they follow that example.

British Prime Minister John Major, July 1991. Conservative councillors sold three Westminster cemeteries to a property company for five pence each. They then fell into a state of vandalized dereliction.

Women

It is a great glory in a woman to show no more weakness than is natural to her sex, and not to be talked of, either for good or evil, by men.

Thucydides, 5th century BC.

Silence and modesty are the best ornaments of women.

Euripedes, 5th century BC.

Woman may be said to be an inferior man.

Aristotle, 4th century BC.

Women are all, one and, all a set of vultures.

Petronius, 1st century AD.

Unto the woman he said, I will greatly multiply thy sorrow and thy conception; in sorrow shalt thou bring forth children; and thy desire shall be to thy husband, and he shall rule over thee.
Genesis 3:16.

Let the woman learn in silence with all subjection.

But I suffer not a woman to teach, nor to usurp authority over the man, but to be in silence.

For Adam was first formed, then Eve.

And Adam was not deceived, but the woman being deceived was in the transgression.

Notwithstanding she shall be saved in childbearing, if they continue in faith and charity and holiness with sobriety.
First Epistle of Paul the Apostle to Timothy, 2:11–15.

As regards the individual nature, woman is defective and misbegotten.
St Thomas Aquinas (1225–74).

To promote a Woman to bear rule, superiority, dominion or empire, above any Realm, Nation, or City, is repugnant to Nature; contumely to God, a thing most contrarious to his revealed will and approved ordinance, and finally it is the subversion of good Order, of all equity and justice.
John Knox, *First Blast of the Trumpet against the Monstrous Regiment of Women*, 1558.

A woman is a solitary, helpless creature without a man.
Dramatist Thomas Shadwell (c. 1642–92).

Most women have no characters at all.
Alexander Pope, *Moral Essays*, 1732.

Women, then, are only children of a larger growth.
The Earl of Chesterfield, *Letters to His Son*, 5 September 1748.

Women are much more like each other than men; they have, in truth, but two passions, vanity and love; these are their universal characteristics.
The Earl of Chesterfield, *Letters to his Son*, 19 December 1749.

A woman's preaching is like a dog's walking on his hinder legs. It is not done well; but you are surprised to find it done at all.
Samuel Johnson, 1763, quoted in James Boswell's *Life of Johnson*, Vol. I.

Nature intended women to be our slaves. They are our property.
They belong to us, just as a tree that bears fruit belongs to a gardener.
What a mad idea to demand equality for women! Women are nothing
but machines for producing children.

Napoleon Bonaparte (1769–1821).

The fundamental fault of the female character is that it has no sense
of justice ... Since every man needs many women, there could be nothing
more just than that he should be free, indeed obliged, to support many
women. This would also mean the restoration of woman to her rightful
and natural position, the subordinate one.

Arthur Schopenhauer (1788–1860).

Every well-sexed woman invariably throws her shoulders back and
breasts forward as if she would render them conspicuous, and further
signifies sensuality by way of a definite rolling motion of the posterior.

Oswald Squire Fowler, *Sexual Science*, 1870.

There is a large number of women whose brains are closer in size to those
of gorillas than to the most developed male brains. This inferiority is so
obvious that no-one can contest it for a moment; only its degree is worth
discussion ... They are closer to children and savages than to an adult,
civilized man. They excel in fickleness, inconstancy, absence of thought
and logic, and incapacity to reason. Without doubt there exist some
distinguished women ... but they are as exceptional as the birth of any
monstrosity as, for example, a gorilla with two heads; consequently,
we may neglect them entirely.

French anthropologist Gustave Le Bon, essay in *Revue d'Anthropologie*, 1879.

When a woman becomes a scholar there is usually something wrong
with her sex organs.

Friedrich Nietzsche, 1888.

It is the prime duty of a woman of this terrestrial world to look well.

Sir William Osler, professor of medicine at Johns Hopkins University and
physician-in-chief at Johns Hopkins Hospital, 1903.

Direct thought is not an attribute of femininity.

Thomas Edison, 'The Woman of the Future', in *Good Housekeeping*, October
1912.

Brain work will cause her to become bald, while increasing masculinity
and contempt for beauty will induce the growth of hair on the face. In

the future, therefore, women will be bald and will wear long moustaches and patriarchal beards.

Professor Hans Friedenthal of Berlin University, 1914.

The great question ... which I have not been able to answer, despite my thirty years of research into the feminine soul, is, 'What does a woman want?'

Sigmund Freud, 1920, quoted by Charles Rolo in *Psychiatry in American Life*.

There are two kinds of women, goddesses and doormats.

Pablo Picasso, 1930.

The ministrations of a male priesthood do not normally arouse that side of female human nature which should be quiescent during the times of the adoration of almighty God ... It would be impossible for the male members of the average Anglican congregation to be present at a service at which a woman ministered without becoming unduly conscious of her sex.

Report of the Archbishop of Canterbury's commission of enquiry into the ordination of women, revealing hitherto unsuspected reserves of concupiscence in the Anglican male, 1935.

The female sex is in some respects inferior to the male sex, both as regards body and soul.

The Catholic Encyclopædia, 1940.

Women do not find it difficult nowadays to behave like men; but they often find it extremely difficult to behave like gentlemen.

Novelist Compton MacKenzie, 1940.

The woman barrister looks and is ridiculous; and has been so since Portia. Neither should the sex sit on juries; no woman will believe that a witness wearing the wrong hat can be giving the right evidence.

James Agate, *Ego 6*, 1944.

In this play the child rehearses the part he wishes or she wishes to assume in adult life. The girl jumping rope acts out the to-and-fro movement of the man during sexual intercourse. Her own body takes the part of the active man, while the swinging rope imitates her own body adjusting to the movement of the man's. In this game, girl acts both the role of man and of the woman. Thus the girls go through unconscious preparation for their future sexual function as women.

Psychologist Marion Sonnenberg, *Girls Jumping Rope*, 1953.

You treat a car like a woman ... because it is a very highly strung and nervous piece of equipment ... You have to coax it sometimes to get the best out of it, you have to correct it and treat it gently, and at times, maybe on a difficult circuit, you have to give it a really good thrashing, because that is the only way it understands.

Racing driver Jackie Stewart, 1969.

All Berkshire women are very silly. I don't know why women in Berkshire are more silly than anywhere else.

Judge Claude Duveen, Reading County Court, July 1972.

Why should a married woman want a mortgage in her own name? We'll have husbands doing the housework next.

Eric Nash, branch manager of the Magnet and Planet Building Society, 1976.

Biologically and temperamentally, women were made to be concerned first and foremost with child care, husband care, and home care.

Dr Benjamin Spock, 1979.

A society in which women are taught anything at all but the management of a family, the care of men and the creation of the future generation is a society which is on the way out.

L. Ron Hubbard, founder of Scientology, *Questions For Our Time*, 1980.

Every decision a woman makes is right.

Germaine Greer, Danish TV interview, 1981.

Of course we are not patronising women. We are just going to explain to them in words of one syllable what it is all about.

Lady Olga Maitland MP, on the aims of her pro-nuclear weapons campaign 'Women for Peace', 1982.

Women have smaller brains than men.

Ali Akhbar Hashemi Rafsanjani, President of the Islamic Republic of Iran, July 1986.

See also MASTURBATION, MENSTRUATION, MEN, SEX, SPORT *and* VOTES FOR WOMEN

World War I

The bankers will not find the money for such a fight, the industries will not maintain it, the statesmen cannot ... There will be no general war.

Starr Jordan, president of Stanford University, the *Independent*, 27 February 1913.

While it is only natural that one should be stricken with horror at the brutal and shocking assassination of Archduke Francis Ferdinand, it is impossible to deny that his disappearance from the scene is calculated to diminish the tenseness of the situation ... The news of his death is almost calculated to create a feeling of universal relief.

F. Cunliffe-Owen, international affairs correspondent of the New York *Sun*, 29 June 1914.

A great world war would be such an absurdity, such a monstrous out-come from relatively trivial causes ... that any reasonable calculation of probabilities would yield only a slight percentage in favour of such an eventuality.

The *Neue Freie Presse* of Vienna, a few days before Austria's declaration of war on Serbia (28 July 1914).

Happily there seems to be no reason why we should be anything but spectators.

British Prime Minister Herbert Asquith, on the approaching war.

In three months from now the war fever will have spent itself.

The *London Chronicle*, 5 August 1914.

You will be home before the leaves have fallen from the trees.

Kaiser Wilhelm II, message to German troops, August 1914.

My friend, we shall not have time to make them. I shall tear up the Boches within two months.

General Joseph Joffre, rejecting the notion that French troops will need helmets, November 1914; French soldiers went to war without them.

Casualties? What do I care for casualties?

Major-General A. G. Hunter-Weston, nicknamed 'The Butcher of Helles' after he used up three British divisions in successive frontal attacks at Gallipoli, 1915.

The Turk is an enemy who has never shown himself as good a fighter as the white man.

Anonymous staff officer, briefing British and ANZAC troops before the Gallipoli landings, 1915.

With the enthusiasm of ignorance they will tear their way through the German line.

General Douglas Haig, diary entry before the battle of Loos, 26 September 1915, in which there were over 8,000 British casualties. German lines were not breached.

You will be able to go over the top with a walking stick, you will not need rifles. When you get to Thiepval you will find the Germans all dead, not even a rat will have survived.

Anonymous brigadier-general, addressing the Newcastle Commercials on the first morning of the Somme Offensive, 1 July 1916.

The men are in splendid spirits. Several have said that they have never before been so instructed and informed of the nature of the operation before them. The wire has never been so well cut, nor the artillery preparations so thorough.

General Douglas Haig, diary entry, 1 July 1916.

They advanced in line after line, dressed as if on parade, and not a man shirked going through the extremely heavy barrage, or facing the machine-gun fire that finally wiped them out ... I have never seen ... such a magnificent display of gallantry, discipline and determination. Then reports I have had from the very few survivors of this marvellous advance bear out what I saw ... that hardly a man of ours got to the German front line.

Brigadier-General Rees, GOC 94th Infantry Brigade of 31 Division, diary entry on the evening of 1 July 1916. The British artillery barrage was halted before the advance on the orders of Major-General Hunter-Weston. The wire had not been cut in many places, and the Germans concentrated their machine-gun fire in the sectors where it had been. British troops did not carry wire cutters. Some officers advanced across no-man's-land with furled brollies; some soldiers dribbled footballs. Some 21,000 British troops died on the first day of the Somme Offensive, most of these in the first half-hour; by the time it petered out in November there had been over 1,000,000 British, French and German casualties.

The attack on the Somme bore out the conclusions of the British Higher Command, and amply justified the tactical methods employed.

Colonel Boraston, biographer of Field Marshal Earl Haig, 1919.

The experiment has been conclusive. Our method has been tried out. I can assure you that victory is certain. The enemy will learn this to their cost.

French General Robert Nivelle, conceiving the Chemin des Dames offensive in

December 1916, one month after the failure of Haig's 'big push'. When it was launched in April 1917 the Germans, who knew about it in advance, inflicted 120,000 casualties in five days, after which Nivelle was sacked.

This solemn moment of triumph ... is going to lift up humanity to a higher plane of existence for all the ages of the future.

British Prime Minister David Lloyd-George, Armistice Day, 11 November 1918.

See also MILITARY INTELLIGENCE, MILITARY LEADERS *and* MILITARY TECHNOLOGY

World War II

On leaving Montmédy, we come to the Ardennes forests. If certain preparations are made, these are impregnable. This sector is not dangerous.

Marshal Henry Philippe Pétain, March 1934. The German Army smashed through the Ardennes in 1940.

There will be no war in western Europe for the next five years.

John Langdon-Davies, *A Short History of the Future*, 1936.

Britain will not be involved in war. There will be no major war in Europe this year or next year. The Germans will not seize Czechoslovakia. So go about your own business with confidence in the future and fear not.

The *Daily Express*, 23 May 1938.

I believe we are very foolish in this House sometimes, those of us who refuse to believe there is any good in National Socialism, or that there is no unselfishness in men like Hitler and Goering.

A. Beverley Baxter, Conservative MP for Wood Green, House of Commons, 26 July 1938.

It might be worthwhile for the Czechoslovak Government to consider whether they should exclude altogether the project, which has found favour in some quarters, of making Czechoslovakia a more homo-geneous state ... The advantages ... might conceivably outweigh the obvious disadvantages of losing the Sudeten German districts of the borderland.

The *Times* recommends rolling over and saying 'yes' to the Führer's demand for the annexation of the Sudetenland, 7 September 1938.

It is the last territorial claim I have to make in Europe.

Adolf Hitler, on the annexation of the Sudetenland, September 1938.

Whatever the lengths to which others may go, His Majesty's Government will never resort to the deliberate attack on women and children and other civilians for purposes of mere terrorism.

Prime Minister Neville Chamberlain, House of Commons, 14 September 1939.
    Government policy changed some time before the bombing raids on Dresden and Cologne.

[Hitler] would not deliberately deceive a man whom he respected and with whom he had been in negotiation.

Neville Chamberlain, Prime Minister, briefing his Cabinet after negotiations with Hitler at Bad Godesberg, September 1938.

For the second time in our history, a British Prime Minister has returned from Germany bringing peace with honour. I believe it is peace for our time. Go home and get a nice quiet sleep.

British Prime Minister Neville Chamberlain, 30 September 1938, returning from the Munich Conference.

The *Daily Express* Declares That Britain Will Not Be Involved In A European War This Year Or Next Year Either.

Seven-column headline, *Daily Express*, 30 September 1938.

It is my hope, and my belief, that under the new system of guarantees, the new Czechoslovakia will find a greater security than she has ever enjoyed in the past.

Neville Chamberlain, Prime Minister, House of Commons, October 1938.

Thanks to Chamberlain, thousands of young men will live. I shall live.

The middle-aged Lord Castlerosse, writing in *The Spectator* (which nominated the Prime Minister for the Nobel Peace Prize), October 1938.

What has Hitler done of which we can reasonably complain? Let us try to forget his misdeeds of the past, and the methods which, no doubt, we all of us deplore, but which I suggest have been very largely forced upon him.

C. T. Culverwell, Conservative MP for Bristol West, House of Commons, 6 October 1938.

Why can we not make friends with Italy and Germany? There are people saying that Herr Hitler has broken his word. I tell you there is one bargain he has made – that is that the German Navy shall be only one-third of the British Navy – which he has kept, and kept loyally.

R. A. Butler, Conservative MP for Saffron Walden, speech, 15 November 1938.
In December, the German navy began doubling the number of its U-boats.

The chances of Germany making a quick job of overwhelming Poland are not good.

US Major George Fielding Eliot, *Boston Evening Transcript*, 13 May 1939.

The whispered lies to the effect that the Soviet Union will enter into a treaty of understanding with Nazi Germany are nothing but poison spread by the enemies of peace and democracy, the appeasement mongers, the Munichmen of Fascism.

The communist *Daily Worker*, 26 May 1939.

By compelling Germany to sign a non-aggression pact, the Soviet Union has tremendously limited the direction of its war aims.

The *Daily Worker*, 23 August 1939, on the signing of the Nazi–Soviet pact – the principle purpose of which was to agree a carve-up of Poland, in return for a promise by Hitler not to invade the USSR.

The modern German theory of Blitzkrieg (lightning war) is untried and, in the opinion of many experts, unsound.

Time, 12 June 1939.

The French Army is still the strongest all-round fighting machine in Europe.

Time, 12 June 1939.

War today is not only not inevitable, but it is unlikely. The Government have good reason for saying that.

Sir Thomas Inskip MP, minister for co-ordination of defence, August 1939.

No enemy bomber can reach the Ruhr. If one reaches the Ruhr, my name is not Goering. You can call me Meyer.

Reichsmarschall Hermann Goering, addressing the Luftwaffe, September 1939.

Their tanks will be destroyed in the open country behind our lines if they can penetrate that far, which is doubtful.

French General A. L. Georges, 1939.

The aim is to restore peace and order in Poland ... The friendly Soviet Peoples will help the Polish people establish new conditions for its political life.

Pravda, reporting the Red Army's invasion of Poland, 17 September 1939.

The people living in the former Polish State will have a peaceful life in keeping with their national character.

German–Soviet Boundary and Friendship Treaty, 29 September 1939. The USSR annexed 76,000 square miles of Poland, and 13 million people, in the east; the Nazis took the rest. 5,260,000 Polish civilians died during World War II.

Are you aware that it is private property? Why, you will be asking me to bomb Essen next!

Sir Kingsley Wood, British minister for air, rejects an RAF plan to bomb the Black Forest, 30 September 1939.

Germany's Will for Peace – No War Aims against France and England.

Headline in the Nazi Party newspaper, the *Völkischer Beobachter*, 24 October 1939.

We shall only talk of peace when we have won the war. The Jewish-capitalistic world will not survive the twentieth century.

Adolf Hitler, New Year broadcast, 31 December 1939.

One thing is certain: he missed the bus.

British Prime Minister Neville Chamberlain, on Hitler's military strategy, 4 April 1940.

Nothing will happen before 1941.

General Gaston Bilotte, commander of the French north-eastern front, May 1940.

We are not Poles. It could not happen here.

French General Gamelin, May 1940.

There are no urgent measures to be taken for the reinforcement of the Sedan sector.

General Charles Huntziger, commander of the French Second Army, on the 'impregnable' Ardennes defences, 13 May 1940. The Germans smashed through French lines on 14 May; six weeks later, France surrendered. The Maginot Line stopped at the Luxembourg border, as it was thought undiplomatic to continue it along the Luxembourg and Belgian borders, and the French built no defences in the Ardennes sector. The French had expected an attack in this sector, but believed that the Germans would not cross the Meuse until they had brought up their heavy artillery to cover their tanks, thereby giving the French a breathing space of a few days. But the French had reckoned without the Stuka divebombers.

In three weeks England will have her neck wrung like a chicken.

General Maxime Weygand, commander-in-chief of French military forces, 5 June 1940. As Winston Churchill afterwards commented: 'Some chicken, some neck.'

To make a union with Great Britain would be fusion with a corpse.

Marshal Pétain, 16 June 1940, on Churchill's offer of political union between Britain and France.

We hope that Germany will be guided by a spirit that will permit the two great neighbouring peoples to live and work in peace.

French General Charles Huntziger, after signing the French surrender, 22 June 1940.

Like Carthage, England will be destroyed.

Jean Herold-Paquis signs off on Vichy Radio, June 1940.

I have said this before, but I say it again and again: your boys are not going to be sent into any foreign wars.

US President Franklin D. Roosevelt, campaigning for re-election, 30 October 1940.

The United States will not be a threat to us for decades – not in 1945 but at the earliest in 1970 or 1980.

Adolf Hitler, 12 November 1940.

The Americans cannot build aeroplanes. They are very good at refrigerators and razor blades.

Hermann Goering to Adolf Hitler, December 1940.

War between Japan and the United States is not within the realm of reasonable possibility ... A Japanese attack on Pearl Harbor is a strategic impossibility.

US Major George Fielding Eliot, *The Impossible War With Japan*, September 1938.

Japan will never join the Axis.

US General Douglas MacArthur, Manila, September 1940. In Europe, morning papers were announcing that Japan had joined the Axis.

The Hawaiian Islands are over-protected; the entire Japanese fleet and air force could not seriously threaten Oahu.

Captain William T. Pulleston, former chief of US military intelligence, August 1941.

We won't be at war with Japan within forty-eight hours, within forty-eight days, within forty-eight years.

US presidential candidate Wendell Wilkie, speech, 7 December 1941. He was interrupted by the news that Japan had bombed Pearl Harbor.

Well, don't worry about it. It's nothing.
Lieutenant Kermit Tyler, duty officer at the Shafter Information Center, Hawaii,
on radar reports of 50 warplanes approaching Oahu at 180 mph, 7 December
1941.

The British are such clever propagandists, they might well have cooked up
the story.
US congresswoman Jeanette Rankin, casting the only vote against a declaration of
war on Japan on the day following Pearl Harbor, 8 December 1941.

The Russians are finished. They have nothing left to throw against us.
Adolf Hitler, after invading the USSR, July 1941.

I had a good close-up, across the barbed wire, of various sub-human
specimens dressed in dirty grey uniforms, which I was informed were
Japanese soldiers ... I cannot believe they would form an intelligent
fighting force.
Air Chief Marshal Brooke-Popham, who also advised against strengthening
Singapore's air defences, December 1941.

I do hope we're not getting too strong in Malaya, because if so the
Japanese may not attempt a landing.
Anonymous British officer in Singapore, December 1941.

I believe that defences of the sort you want to throw up are bad for the
morale of troops and civilians.
Lieutenant-General Arthur Percival, refusing to countenance landward defences
for Singapore, December 1941. A few months later, Japanese forces poured
down the Malay peninsula and occupied Singapore.

Defeat of Germany means defeat of Japan, probably without firing a shot
or losing a life.
US President Franklin D. Roosevelt, 16 July 1942.

EIGHTH ARMY PUSH BOTTLES UP GERMANS
Headline, *Daily Express*, October 1942, on the desert war.

The duty of the men at Stalingrad is to be dead.
Adolf Hitler, January 1943.

Shut up that Goddam' crying. I won't have brave men here who have
been shot seeing a yellow bastard crying. You're going back to the front
lines and you may get shot and killed, but you're going to fight. If you
don't I'll stand you up against a wall and have a firing squad kill you

on purpose. I ought to shoot you myself, you Goddam' whimpering coward.

US Lieutenant-General George S. Patton Jr at the bedside of a shell-shock victim at the 93rd evacuation hospital, Sicily, 10 August 1943.

MACARTHUR FLIES BACK TO FRONT

Headline, *Daily Express*, on General MacArthur's return to the Philippines, October 1944.

My Führer, I congratulate you! Roosevelt is dead. It is written in the stars that the second half of April will be the turning point for us.

Josef Goebbels, memo to Adolf Hitler, 13 April 1945. By the end of April both men had committed suicide.

X-rays

X-rays will prove to be a hoax.

Lord Kelvin, president of the Royal Society 1890–95, reacting to a newspaper report in 1895; he changed his mind later.

Z

Zaire

The people of Zaire are not thieves. It merely happens that they take more things, or borrow them.

President Mobutu of Zaire (now the Democratic Republic of Congo), 1978.

See also DICTATORS

Index

Roman numerals indicate that the person, publication etc. listed is the *source of the quotation.*
Bold numerals indicate that the person, etc. is the *subject of the quotation.*
See also the alphabetical subject listing in the Contents.